INTERMEDIATE TAGALOG

Learn to Speak Fluent Tagalog/Filipino, the National Language of the Philippines

Joi Barrios, Ph.D.
University of California, Berkeley

TUTTLE Publishing
Tokyo | Rutland, Vermont | Singapore

"Books to Span the East and West"

Tuttle Publishing was founded in 1832 in the small New England town of Rutland, Vermont [USA]. Our core values remain as strong today as they were then—to publish best-in-class books which bring people together one page at a time. In 1948, we established a publishing office in Japan—and Tuttle is now a leader in publishing English-language books about the arts, languages and cultures of Asia. The world has become a much smaller place today and Asia's economic and cultural influence has grown. Yet the need for meaningful dialogue and information about this diverse region has never been greater. Over the past seven decades, Tuttle has published thousands of books on subjects ranging from martial arts and paper crafts to language learning and literature—and our talented authors, illustrators, designers and photographers have won many prestigious awards. We welcome you to explore the wealth of information available on Asia at **www.tuttlepublishing.com**.

Published by Tuttle Publishing, an imprint of Periplus Editions (HK) Ltd.

www.tuttlepublishing.com

LCC Card No. 2014957346
ISBN 978-0-8048-4262-4

First edition
25 24 23 22 8 7 6 5 4
Printed in Malaysia 2201VP

Distributed by
North America, Latin America & Europe
Tuttle Publishing
364 Innovation Drive
North Clarendon, VT 05759-9436 U.S.A
Tel: 1 (802) 773 8930
Fax: 1 (802) 773 6993
info@tuttlepublishing.com
www.tuttlepublishing.com

Japan
Tuttle Publishing
Yaekari Building, 3F
5-4-12 Osaki, Shinagawa-ku
Tokyo 141-0032
Tel: (81) 3 5437-0171
Fax: (81) 3 5437-0755
sales@tuttle.co.jp
www.tuttle.co.jp

Asia-Pacific
Berkeley Books Pte Ltd
3 Kallang Sector #04-01
Singapore 349278
Tel: (65) 6741-2178
Fax: (65) 6741-2179
inquiries@periplus.com.sg
www.tuttlepublishing.com

Nilalaman *Table of Contents*

Acknowledgments

The author would like to thank the following for their help:

Consultant	: Romulo Baquiran Jr.
Book Lead Assistants	: Jan Tristan Gaspi
	Althea Contreras
Research Assistants	: Paulene Rejano
	Abigail Ong
	Raphael Bernabe

Dedication

To my cousin and childhood friend, Deona Enriquez; my husband, Pierre Leblanc; and our son Eli.

A Note to the Learner

The following are online printable PDF documents:

- **Mga Talang Pangkultura** Culture Notes (Lessons 1–19)
- **Pakikinig** Listening (Lessons 1–19)
- Lesson 20
- Grammar Index and Glossary

Introduction

Continuing the Journey towards Speaking, Reading, Listening and Writing Fluently in Tagalog/Filipino

Congratulations, intermediate-level learner!

By using this book, you are now on the next step in your journey towards a better command of Tagalog/Filipino. At this point, you may already know that the name of the national language of the Philippines has been Filipino since the 1987 constitution and that it is based not only on Tagalog (the language of the ethnolinguistic group the Tagalogs) but also on the other languages of the Philippines, as well as English and Spanish. Nevertheless, we also need to recognize that some people still think that the language of the Philippines is either Tagalog, which was designated the basis of the national language by the Surian ng Wikang Pambansa (Institute of National Language) in 1957, or Pilipino, as the language was called in the Department of Education memorandum in 1959.

What is important, I believe, is that you have decided to take your study of the language to the next level. Hopefully, this book will assist you towards this endeavor.

What will you learn through this book?

This textbook is divided into five sections. First, we have review and expansion lessons. Through dialogues and exercises, these lessons will help you remember vocabulary words, phrases and dialogues you have learned either in *Tagalog for Beginners* or whatever introductory textbook you have used in the past. Examples of these are lessons on talking about yourself and your family, asking and giving directions, or shopping.

The next four sections will enable you to develop four skills that you need to know in mastering a language: descriptions (**paglalarawan**) of people, places and feelings; narration (**pagsasalaysay**) of events and stories; explanations (**paglalahad**), such as giving instructions or defining a particular concept; and argumentation (**pangangatuwiran**) or reasoning.

To enhance your learning experience, we have provided a online audio recordings for you. The online audio recordings contains all the learning audios you need for the listening exercises and the following printable pages: listening exercises (Lessons 1–19); culture notes (Lessons 1–19); Grammar Index; Glossary; and Lesson 20.

Hopefully, this book and its accompanying online audio recordings will enable you to test successfully for the Intermediate High or Advanced Low levels of the American Council on the Teaching of Foreign Languages (ACTFL) scale, or Level 2+ (Limited Working Proficiency Plus) to 3 (General Professional Proficiency) of the Interagency Language Roundtable (ILR) scale.

How will you learn?

Each lesson has several components: a dialogue, vocabulary words, sentences, conversation practice; role-plays, listening exercises, translation exercises in selected lessons, culture notes, reading exercises and writing exercises.

Most importantly, this textbook recognizes that there are many kinds of learners. Some of you are heritage learners; some are second-language learners. There are those who will use this book in the classroom; others who will study on their own (individual learners). As you navigate through this book, there will be instructions for the kind of learner that you are.

I am also proud to tell you that I took great care in ensuring that through the culture notes, you will learn a lot about Philippine history and society. Some topics are names given to the "natives" through the 1849 decree through the *Catalogo Alfabetico de Apellidos*, the words **bayan** and **barangay**, traditional medicine, early travel accounts to the Philippines, tattoos and ornaments, Filipino food, historical myths and folk narratives. For many of you using this book in the classroom, your intermediate Filipino/Tagalog class will probably be the last Filipino or Philippine Studies class you will take in college. If you are an individual learner, this book will hopefully encourage you to read more Philippine studies books.

All of the listening exercises and most of the reading exercises in this book are authentic texts. I believe that the use of authentic text is crucial so that learners can better improve their vocabulary and will be better prepared to listen to news programs, and read magazines and newspapers. I have also tried to have a variety of topics, forms and styles: an excerpt of the autobiography of Gregoria de Jesus (Katipunera and wife of Katipunan leader Andres Bonifacio), an essay from "Hospital Diary" of Romulo B. Baquiran, Jr., a letter written by **Makibaka** (women's group) founding chair Lorena Barros, an interview with a woman who was imprisoned in Saudi Arabia, and a poem on *ampalaya* (bitter melon).

What should you remember as a language learner?

First, do not be afraid to make mistakes. Learn grammar but do not be too overly concerned with grammar that it makes you afraid to speak. Remember: even Filipinos make grammatical mistakes.

Second, remember that a language is constantly evolving and there are many varieties and variations of a language. If you are interested in research, it might be useful to know how Tagalog was written in the 19th century. If you are interested in popular culture and social movements, it might be interesting to know colloquial language, slang, even gay and activist words.

Third, be open to the flexibility of meaning. Do not get too confused when **din** and **rin** (meaning "also") have the same meaning. This comes from the letters d and r having the same symbol in the indigenous **baybayin** script.

In *Contracting Colonialism: Translation and Christian Conversion in Tagalog Society Under Early Spanish Rule* (1993), Vicente Rafael quotes the various criticisms of the Spanish friars of the **baybayin**, among them: inadequacy (based on Marcilla's comments that the diacritical marks do not suffice to make the texts readable); ambiguity (the reader needs to "guess" the breaks in each syllable referred to as "suspended consonants" by Lopez) and illegibility (de San Agustin's remarks that two letters can be read eight ways). However, Rafael offers a different view (47):

> This, a **kurlit** (or **kudlit**) marks the boundary where writing is given up to voice, that is, the line that by giving value or stress to a syllable determines the sound of the signifier, thus delimiting the range of signifieds that can be attached to it; as called forth a multiplicity of sounds and consequently other signifiers. Hence, from a Spanish point of view, the "illegibility" and "unreadability" of the script results from the lack of a direct and fixed correspondence between script and sound.

For Rafael, the Spaniards failed to understand that Filipinos related voice and writing in a different way, and were not disturbed by ambiguity. His observations, however, can be affirmed if we look into indigenous Tagalog poetry, with its images and **talinghaga** (metaphor) that suggest a multiplicity of interpretations. These indigenous verses, transmitted as oral literature, contrast sharply with the fixed **aral** or lesson, found at the end of the religious poetry written by Filipinos during the Spanish colonial period.

Thus, while social expediency and practicality may have been valid reasons for the gradual but complete shift to Roman letters, the imposition of a new system of writing also reflected the imposition of the colonizer's worldview.

In other words, do not be bothered when you interchange **din** and **rin** (because you forget that **din** follows words ending in consonants and **rin** follows words that end in vowels). Similarly, do not be make a big deal when in the role-play, you say "**huwag ka nang mag-abala**" (please don't bother) when someone offers you food, even if you actually want to partake of the food.

Remember, the key to culture is language and the best way to learn the Filipino/ Tagalog language is to understand Filipino culture.

Joi Barrios
Berkeley, California

Aralin 1
Lesson

Kilalanan
Getting to Know Each Other

This is a review and expansion lesson. Review what you know and learn new words and phrases that will enable you to talk about yourself, your life history, and your family.

Diyalogo Dialogue**: Isang Panayam** An Interview

Read the following interview. Note the words you know, and the words you are not familiar with. In this interview, Katie, a young Filipina American, is interviewing Rose, a caregiver. Notice how Katie uses the honorifics **po** *and* **opo***, and how Rose does not, indicating that Rose is older than Katie.*

KATIE : **Magandang umaga po. Ako po si Katie.**
Good morning. I am Katie.

ROSE : **Magandang umaga. Maria Rosario ang pangalan ko at Toribio ang apelyido ko. Palayaw ko ang Rose.**
Yes. My name is Maria Rosario and my last name is Toribio. Rose is my nickname.

KATIE : **Kailan at saan po kayo ipinanganak?**
When and where were you born?

ROSE : **Ipinanganak ako noong ika-17 ng Nobyembre 1982 sa Quezon City.**
I was born on the 17th of November 1982 in Quezon City.

KATIE : **May pamilya po ba kayo?**
Do you have a family?

ROSE : **Oo. Nasa Maynila ang asawa ko at dalawang anak.**
Yes, my husband and my two children are in Manila.

KATIE : **Saan po kayo nag-aral, at ano po ang natapos ninyo?**
Where did you study, and what did you finish?

ROSE : **Nag-aral ako ng edukasyon sa Philippine Normal University. Bago ako pumunta sa Amerika, kumuha ako ng kursong Caregiving.**
I studied education at Philippine Normal University. Before coming to America [United States], I took a course on Caregiving.

KATIE : **Ano po ang trabaho ninyo noon?**
What was your job then?

ROSE : **Titser ako noon sa Mababang Paaralan ng Quirino.**
I was a teacher at Quirino Elementary School.

KATIE : **Saan na po kayo nagtatrabaho ngayon?**
Where do you work now?

ROSE : **Nagtatrabaho ako sa Mimosa Family Home.**
I work at Mimosa Family Home.

Bokabularyo Vocabulary

When reviewing old and new Tagalog/Filipino words, it is best to group words together. In this lesson, we shall review words in the following categories: family; days and dates (months, days of the week, numbers); education; jobs or occupation; milestones; and question words.

Try to cover the right column below. Many of the words on the left are familiar to you, having studied the book *Tagalog for Beginners*.

The words we are studying in this lesson are words that are essential for you to talk about yourself and for getting to know a person and a person's life history. After each set of vocabulary words, practice these words by asking and answering questions. This way, you will remember them better.

Here are words you can use when talking about your gender and the family. Note that words used for family are not gendered. For example, the word **asawa** refers to both husband and wife.

Babae *Woman*
Lalaki *Man*
Bakla *Gay man*
Lesbiana *Lesbian*
Transeksuwal *Transexual*
Transgender *Transgender*
Pamilya *Family*
Ina/Nanay *Mother*
Ama/Tatay *Father*
Amain/Inain *Stepfather/Stepmother*
Ama-amahan/Ina-inahan *One who acts like a father or a mother to you*
Magulang *Parent*
Asawa/Kabiyak *Husband or Wife*
Anak *Child*
Anak na Babae *Daughter* (literally, child that is a woman/girl)
Anak na Lalaki *Son* (literally, child that is a man/boy)
Kapatid *Sibling*
Kapatid na babae/lalaki *Sister/Brother*
Lolo/Lola *Grandfather/Grandmother*

Ate/Kuya *Elder Sister/Elder Brother*
Panganay/Panggitna/Bunso *Eldest child/Middle child or children/ Youngest*
Tiya/Tiyahin/Tita *Aunt*
Tiyo/Tiyuhin/Tito *Uncle*
Pamangkin *Nephew/Niece*
Pinsan *Cousin*
Ulila *Orphan*
Apo *Grandchild*
Apo sa tuhod *Great grandchild*
Apo sa talampakan *Great great grandchild*
Kamag-anak *Relative*
Dalaga *Single Woman*
Dalagita *Young single woman* (early teens)
Binata *Single Man*
Binatilyo *Young single man* (early teens)
May asawa *Married person*
Madre *Nun*
Pari/Pastor *Priest/Pastor*
Buhay *Living/Alive*
Patay *Dead/Had passed on*
Mga *Word used to indicate plurality*

Now let us review words we can use when asking questions about families:

Ano *What*
Pangalan *Name*
Ipinagkaloob na Pangalan *Given Name/ First Name*
Apelyido *Last Name/Family Name*
Buong Pangalan *Full Name*
Palayaw *Nickname*
Kaano-ano mo si...? *What is your relation to...?*
Mayroon/May/ Meron *Has/Have*
Oo *Yes*
Hindi *No*
Wala *Don't/Doesn't have*

Mga Pangungusap Sentence Structure

In the book *Tagalog for Beginners*, you studied that in basic Tagalog/Filipino sentences, the predicate precedes the subject. This is especially true in spoken Tagalog/Filipino. In written Tagalog/Filipino, this is sometimes reversed and the word **ay** is inserted. Note that **ay** is an inversion marker. **Ay** can sometimes be used to mean the verb "to be" but it is NOT the verb "to be."

Review of Sentence Construction
Review how sentences are constructed. In some of the sentences below, both the basic form and the inverted form are given. Also shown are the literal meanings of the sentences so that you can review how words come together.

1. **Katie ang pangalan ko.**
   My name is Katie. (literally, Katie MARKER name my.)
   Ang pangalan ko ay Katie. (literally, MARKER name my MARKER Katie.)

2. **Dalaga ako.**
   I am a single woman. (literally, Single woman I.)
   Ako ay dalaga. (literally, I MARKER young woman.)

3. **May asawa ang ate ko.**
   My elder sister is married/has a spouse.
   (Literally, Married/has spouse MARKER elder sister my.)
   Ang ate ko ay may asawa.
   (literally, My elder sister MARKER married/has spouse.)

4. **Mayroon akong kuya.**
   I have an elder brother. (literally, Have 1 elder brother.)

5. **Patay na ang lolo at lola ko.**
   My grandfather and grandmother have passed on.
   (literally, Dead already MARKER grandfather and grandmother my.)
   Ang lolo at lola ko ay patay na.
   (literally, MARKER Grandfather and grandmother MARKER dead already.)

Pagsasanay Practice

Answer the following questions. The first questions should serve as your guide. Study the structure of the sentences. Remember that in conversational Tagalog, the predicate usually precedes the subject.

1. TANONG : **Ano ang buong pangalan mo?**
   What is your full name?
   SAGOT : **Maria Rosario Toribio ang buong pangalan ko.**
   My full name is Maria Rosario Toribio.

2. TANONG : **May kapatid ka bang lalaki?**
   Do you have a brother?
   SAGOT : **Wala akong kapatid na lalaki.**
   I don't have a brother.

3. TANONG : **Ano ang pangalan ng tiya mo?**
   What is your aunt's name?
   SAGOT : **Mila Romero ang pangalan ng tiya ko.**
   My aunt's name is Mila Romero.

4. TANONG : **Kaano-ano mo si Mila Romero?**
   How are you related to Mila Romero?
   SAGOT : **Tiya ko siya.**
   She is my aunt.

5. TANONG : **Ano ang pangalan mo?**
What is your name?
SAGOT : ________________ **ang** __________________ **ko.**

6. TANONG : **Buhay pa ba ang lolo mo?**
Is your grandfather still alive?
SAGOT : ____.

7. TANONG : **Ano ang mga apelyido ng mga lola mo?**
What are your grandmothers' last names?
SAGOT : ___________ **at** ___________ **ang mga** _________________________
_________________________.

8. TANONG : **Ano ang palayaw ng kapatid mo?**
What is your sibling's nickname?
SAGOT : ____.

Now, practice asking questions. Give an appropriate question to the answers provided.

9. TANONG : **Ano** ____?
SAGOT : **Ligaya ang pangalan ng nanay ko.**
My mother's name is Ligaya.

10. TANONG : ____?
SAGOT : **Tiya ko siya.**
She is my aunt.

11. TANONG : ____?
SAGOT : **Oo, babae ang anak ko.**
Yes, my child is a girl.

12. TANONG : ____?
SAGOT : **Wala akong asawa. Binata ako.**
I do not have a wife/husband. I am a bachelor.

Gawain Activity: Family Tree

Make a family tree which includes your family, your grandparents, uncles, and aunts and even your cousins. Classroom learners should share their family trees with the class or in small groups. Individual learners should write at least five sentences about their families.

Bokabularyo Vocabulary at Mga Pangungusap Sentences

To talk about age, birthdays and birthdates, and life milestones, you need to review the numbers 1–10 and months. Please refer to your beginners' book for numbers and months.

Do you remember the following numbers: **isa**, **dalawa**, **tatlo**, **apat**, **lima**, **anim**, **pito**, **walo**, **siyam**, **sampu**?

Do you remember the following months: **Enero**, **Pebrero**, **Marso**, **Abril**, **Mayo**, **Hunyo**, **Hulyo**, **Agosto**, **Setyembre**, **Oktubre**, **Nobyembre**, **Disyembre**?

Here are other useful words to remember/learn:

Edad/Taong gulang *Age*
Ipinanganak *Was born*
Nasyonalidad *Nationality*
Etnisidad *Ethnicity*
Lumaki *Grew up*
Nag-aral *Studied*
Elementarya/Mababang *Elementary*
Paaralan *School*
Mataas na Paaralan *High School*
Kolehiyo *College*
Gradwadong Pag-aaral *Graduate School*
Nagsanay *Trained*
Binigyan ng Libreng Pag-aaral *Was awarded a scholarship*
Nagtrabaho *Worked*
Natanggap *Was accepted*
Bilang Two meanings: "number" and "as a"
Natapos *Finished*
Nagtapos *Graduated*
Sumali/Lumahok *Joined, for example, an organization or a contest*
Naging *Became*
Naging kasapi *Became a member*
Nanalo/Nagwagi *Won (for example, an award)*
Karangalan *Honor; Award*
Pinarangalan *Was honored*
Natalo *Lost*
Nabuntis/Nagdalang-tao *Got pregnant*
Nanganak/nagsilang *Gave Birth*
Nagkaanak *Had a child*
Nagkasakit *Had an illness*
Namatay/Yumao *Died/Passed away*
Dekada *Decade*
Siglo *Century*
Noong panahon ng giyera *During war time*
Noong panahon ng kolonyalismong Espanyol *During the Spanish colonial period*
Noong panahon ng kolonyalismong Amerikano *During the American colonial period*
Noong panahon ng pananakop ng mga Hapon *During the Japanese / Occupation*
Noong Batas Militar *During Martial Law (1972–1986)*[1]

Study the following sentences using the words above.Try to practice using compound or complex sentences. Note the use of connecting words you have learned in *Tagalog for Beginners*, such as **at** (and), **pero** (but), **dahil** (because), and **pagkatapos** (after). Please practice these words.

Ipinanganak ako sa Maynila pero lumaki ako sa Mindanao.
I was born in Manila but I grew up in Mindanao.

Pagkatapos ng mataas na paaralan, nag-aral siya sa Unibersidad ng San Francisco. *After high school, he/she studied at the University of San Francisco.*

Dahil sa kanyang mahusay na trabaho, pinarangalan siya bilang "Pinakamahusay na Empleyado."
Because of his/her excellent work, he/she was honored as "Best Employee."

Naging gerilya siya noong panahon ng pananakop ng mga Hapon.
He/she became a guerilla during the Japanese Occupation.

---

[1] Martial Law in the Philippines was declared on September 21, 1972 by then President Ferdinand Marcos. It was technically lifted in 1981. However, many believe that the "real end" of Martial Law was in February 1986, after the "people's power revolution."

Pagbabalik-Aral sa Gramatika Grammar Review

To prepare for questions and answers, let us first review some of the grammar notes you have studied in *Tagalog for Beginners*.

"May/Mayroon/Meron"

In *Tagalog for Beginners*, you studied the difference between **may**, **mayroon**, and **meron**, all of which mean "has/have." Remember that the word order is different for **may** and **mayroon**. However, **mayroon** and **meron** are exactly the same except for the spelling—the word **meron** only comes from the way the word is pronounced. For example:

TANONG : **May anak ka ba?**
Do you have a child? (literally, Have child/son/daughter/**ba**?)
SAGOT : **May anak ako.**
I have a child.

TANONG : **Mayroon ka bang anak?**
Do you have a child? (literally, Have you **ba** LINKER **na** child?)
SAGOT : **Mayroon akong anak.**
I have a child. (literally, Have I LINKER **na** child.)

TANONG : **Meron ka bang anak?**
Do you have a child? (literally, Have you **ba** LINKER **na** child?)
SAGOT : **Meron akong anak.**
I have a child. (literally, Have I LINKER **na** child.)

Using "Hindi" (no) and "Wala" (not have)

Remember in Tagalog/Filipino, we use **hindi** for "no," and **wala** to say "don't/doesn't have." For example:

TANONG : **Ipinanganak ka ba sa Maynila?**
Were you born in Manila?
SAGOT : **Hindi. Ipinangangak ako sa Cebu.**
No, I was born in Cebu.

TANONG : **Mayroon ka bang kapatid na lalaki?**
Do you have a brother?
SAGOT : **Wala akong kapatid na lalaki.**
I don't have a brother.

Contracting the Linker "Na"

The word **na** has many uses, among them, its function as a linker between adjectives and nouns. When contracted, it becomes **ng**. For example:

Buo na pangalan *Full name*
Buong pangalan *Full name*

"Ng" and "Nang"

We use **ng** as a marker for objects. For example:

Nag-aral ako ng medisina. *I studied medicine.*
Nagsilang ako ng babae. *I gave birth to a girl.*

We use **nang** for the following: before adverbs; to mean "when" (**noong**); to mean "for/so that" (**upang**; **para**); as a ligature for repeated action.

Nagtrabaho ako sa Manila Printing Company nang matagal na panahon.
I worked for Manila Printing Company for a long time.

Nang nag-aaral ako sa unibersidad, nakatira ako sa dormitoryo.
When I was studying at the university, I stayed in a dormitory.

Mag-ensayo siya palagi nang maging mahusay kang gitarista.
Always practice so that you can be a good guitarist.

Mag-ensayo ka nang mag-ensayo.
Practice and practice.

Pagsasanay Practice

Let us review words and phrases we studied earlier so that we can use them to talk about life events. Study the brief life histories of three people below. Then create/write a dialogue between the interviewer and the person. Classroom learners should work in pairs while individual learners should write dialogues to practice asking and answering questions. The first one has clues which can help you.

Person 1: Rene Asuncion

Rene was born in 1921 in Manila but he grew up in Pampanga. He studied college at the University of the Philippines and became an elementary school teacher after graduation. During the Japanese Occupation of the Philippines, he became a member of the Hukbalahap (**Hukbo ng Bayan Laban sa Hapon** [People's Army Against the Japanese]). After the war, he took his master's degree in education and became a school principal. He had four children. In 1970, he received the "**Natatanging Guro** (Outstanding/Most Special Teacher)" award. He passed away in 1981.

TANONG : **Kailan at saan ipinanganak si Rene?**
SAGOT : **Ipinanganak ___________ sa _____________ sa _________.**

TANONG : ____?
SAGOT : **Lumaki siya sa Pampanga.**

TANONG : **Saan siya nag-aral ng kolehiyo?**
SAGOT : _____________ **siya sa** _______________________________.

TANONG : **Sa anong organisasyon siya sumapi noong panahon ng pananakop ng mga Hapon?**
SAGOT : ____.

TANONG : **Ano ang ginawa niya pagkatapos ng giyera?**
SAGOT : ____.

TANONG : ____?
SAGOT : **Apat ang anak niya.**

TANONG : **Anong karangalan ang ibinigay sa kanya?**
SAGOT : ____.

TANONG : ____?
SAGOT : **Yumao siya noong 1981.**

PERSON 2: Courtney Macdonald
Courtney was born in 1992 to a Filipina mother and an American father of Irish-German descent. She grew up in Texas but in high school got accepted to the Missouri Academy of Math and Sciences. After high school, she became a biology student at UC Berkeley. She wants to be a doctor. In 2011, Courtney received the "Outstanding Student" award from the Office of the Chancellor.

TANONG : ____?
SAGOT : ____.

TANONG : ____?
SAGOT : ____.

TANONG : ____?
SAGOT : ____.

TANONG : ____?
SAGOT : ____.

Tanong : ____?
Sagot : ____.

Person 3: Clark Beringer
Clark was born in New York in 1975. He studied at the La Guardia High School of Music & Art and Performing Arts, and trained to be a concert pianist. He was awarded a scholarship at the Julliard School. In 2005, he won second prize in the International Chopin Piano Competition in Warsaw, Poland. In 2007, he married Donna Biglang-awa, a Filipina. They have two children, a boy, and a girl.

Tanong : ____?
Sagot : ____.

Tanong : ____?
Sagot : ____.

Tanong : ____?
Sagot : ____.

Tanong : ____?
Sagot : ____.

Tanong : ____?
Sagot : ____.

Online PDF

Mga Talang Pangkultura Culture Notes
Pagbibigay-Pangalan sa mga Katutubo Naming the Natives

Talakayan/Gawain/Pagsusulat Discussion/Task/Writing

Based on the culture notes, classroom learners can form small groups and respond to the following discussion questions/tasks.

1. What is your father's name? What is your mother's name? Where are they from? **Ano ang apelyido ng tatay mo? Ano ang apelyido ng nanay mo? Taga-saan sila?**
2. List the names of people you know that seem to be indigenous, for example, **Tala** (star), **Sining** (art), **Silay** (ray), or **Ligaya** (happiness). If you don't know the meaning of the names of your friends or acquaintances, look them up.
3. If you were to choose your name, what indigenous Tagalog name would you like? **Kung ikaw ang pipili ng pangalan mo, aling pangalan ang gusto mo?**

If you are an individual learner, choose one of the questions above and answer it.

Pakikinig Listening
Artista ng Bayan People's Artist

Pagbabasa Reading
Talambuhay ni Gregoria De Jesus
Biography of Gregoria De Jesus

The following text is an excerpt from the autobiography "**Mga Tala ng Aking Buhay at Mga Ulat ng Katipunan**" (*Notes from my Life and Reports on the Katipunan*) by Gregoria de Jesus, published in 1932 by Limbagang Fajardo (Fajardo Publishing) in Manila. De Jesus was a member of the Katipunan, the secret organization that launched the revolution that ended Spanish colonial rule in the Philippines (1565–1898). She was also the widow of Andres Bonifacio, founder of the Katipunan.

Before reading the autobiography, study/review the following vocabulary words: **bayan** (town/country/people); **lalawigan** (province); **pinagbaunan** (place where something was buried); **sandata** (weapon); **himagsikan** (revolution); **kasunduan** (agreement); **tiniente** (lieutenant); **paaralang bayan** (municipal school); **kura** (parish priest); **ipinagkaroon** (reason for obtaining); **lasong asul** (blue ribbon)

Here is the first part of the autobiography.[2] Note how de Jesus frames her life through the 1896 revolution against the Spanish colonizers:

Ako'y si Gregoria de Jesus, taong tunay dito sa bayang Kalookan, lalawigan ng Rizal. Isinilang ako ng araw ng Martes, ika-9 ng Mayo ng taong 1875, sa pook na pinagbaunan ng libo-libong sandatang ginamit sa himagsikan at pinagdausan din naman ng kasunduan ng mga punong naghimagsik bago lumabas ng bayan, lugar na tinatawag na Daang Baltazar noong araw at ngayo'y P. Zamora, blg. 13. Ang ama ko'y si Nicolas de Jesus, taong tunay din sa bayang ito na ang hanapbuhay ay Maestro de Obra ng Cantero Carpentero at isa sa naghawak ng ilang tungkulin noong panahon ng Kastila, naging teniente segundo, teniente mayor at gobernadorsilyo. Ang ina ko ay si Baltazara Alvarez Francisco na taga-bayang Nobeleta, lalawigan ng Kabite, pamangkin ni Heneral Mariano Alvarez ng Magdiwang sa Kabite, na siyang unang gumalaw ng himagsikan sa nasabing lalawigan.

Ako'y nag-aral sa Paaralang Bayan at natapos ko ang mga unang baitang ng karunungan na katimbang ng Intermedya kung itutulad sa panahong ito. Naaalala ko pa na minsan akong nagwagi sa eksameng ibinigay ng Gobernador Heneral at ng Kura sa bayan, na ipinagkaroon ko ng gantimpalang medalyang pilak na may lasong asul bilang pagkilala sa kaunti kong nalalaman.

[2] Note that I have standardized the spelling of the words in this excerpt.

1. Where and when was Gregoria de Jesus born? What would be the significance of this place later during the revolution?
2. What was the former name of the place now known as P. Zamora?
3. What are the names of Gregoria's parents?
4. Where did Gregoria study?
5. What grade did she finish?
6. What kind of award did she get?

Pagsusulat Writing

Please write 4–5 sentences on any of the following:

1. A brief autobiography;
2. A biography of a person you have interviewed. This can be a member of your family, a classmate, or a friend.
3. A biography of a fictitious person.

Paglalagom Summing Up

In this lesson, we have:

- Studied/reviewed words that enable us to talk about life histories;
- Reviewed the construction of sentences;
- Practiced connecting words that enable us to write complex sentences;
- Practiced skills in reading, listening, and writing biographies.

This lesson enabled you to test what you know and do not know at this point, and thus have a better grasp of your "learning needs." Feel free to review this lesson again, until you feel comfortable that you can talk/write about yourself and your life history with confidence.

CONGRATULATIONS!

Aralin
Lesson

2

Pagbibigay ng mga Direksiyon

Giving Directions

Like Lesson 1, Lesson 2 is a review and expansion lesson. Practice how to ask and give directions as well as the names of places which you may find in your community.

Diyalogo Dialogue: Paano Ako Pupunta sa Palengke?

How Will I Go to the Market?

In this dialogue, Katie is on her way to the market.

KATIE : **Puwede ho bang magtanong?**
Can I ask a question?[1]

PULIS : **Oho.**
Yes.

KATIE : **Paano ho ako pupunta sa palengke?**[2]
How do I go to the market?

---

[1] In English, when we want to ask a question, we say "Excuse me," the equivalent of which is the formal "**Mawalang-galang na ho**" (literally, without respect). However, what is more common when asking for directions is to say, "**Puwede ho bang magtanong**?"

[2] This refers to a "wet market" which sells both produce—fish, meat, vegetables, fruits, rice, and other items—housewares, clothes, etc. It is called "wet" because the fish and seafood vendors are constantly cleaning their stalls and thus, the floor is wet in their area of the market.

Pulis : **Dumiretso ka sa kalyeng ito. Kumanan ka sa Kalye Masayahin. Kumaliwa ka sa ikatlong kanto. Ang palengke ay nasa kanan.**
Go straight on this street. Turn right on Masayahin Street. Turn left on the third corner. The market is on your right.

Katie : **Hindi po ba banda roon ang simbahan?**
Isn't the church around there?

Pulis : **Oo, iyong malaking simbahan ang palatandaan na malapit na ang palengke. Lampasan mo ang simbahan, tapos dumiretso ka lang.**
Yes, the church is the landmark that the market is nearby. Go past the church, then just go straight ahead.

Katie : **Malalakad ho ba?**
Can I walk [going to the market]?

Pulis : **Puwede. Pero puwede ka ring sumakay ng traysikel dito. Bumaba ka sa kanto ng Maginhawa at Mapayapa.**
You can. But you can also take a tricycle here. Get off at the corner of Maginhawa and Mapayapa [streets].

Katie : **Gaano katagal po ba papuntang palengke?**
How long will it take to go to the market?

Pulis : **Kung sasakay ka ng traysikel, mga limang minuto lang. Kung maglalakad ka, makakarating ka roon sa loob ng labinlimang minuto.**
If you take a tricycle, around five minutes. If you walk, you will arrive there in about fifteen minutes.

Katie : **Salamat ho.**
Thank you.

Bokabularyo Vocabulary

Review/Study the following words that you can use when talking about the community, and asking and giving directions. Many of these words should be familiar to you because they have been introduced in *Tagalog for Beginners* and are just listed here for review.

LANDMARKS: palengke (market); **simbahan** (church); **aklatan** (library), **munisipyo** (municipal hall); **estasyon ng pulis** (police station); **ospital** (hospital), **sinehan** (movie theater); **botika** (drugstore); **tindahan ng bulaklak** (flower shop); **restawran** (restaurant); **eskuwelahan** (school); **museo** (museum); **post office** (post office); **estatwa** (statue)

MEANS OF TRANSPORTATION/WORDS RELATED TO TRANSPORTATION: **traysikel** (tricycle); **dyipni** (jeepney); **bus** (bus); **tren** (train); **kotse** (car); **bisikleta** (bicycle); **kalesa** (horse-drawn carriage); **paradahan** (parking lot; terminal); **sakayan ng dyipni/bus** (jeepney/ bus stop); **terminal ng tren** (train terminal)

WORDS THAT DESCRIBE LOCATION: **harap** (in front of); **tabi** (beside); **tapat** (across from); **likod** (at the back); **ibabaw** (above); **ilalim** (below); **itaas** (up); **ibaba** (down); **kanto** (corner; also used when referring to blocks)

WORDS FOR STREETS AND PLACES: **kalye** (street); **abenida** (avenue); **eskinita** (alley), **kabisera** (town center)

ADJECTIVES: **tall** (mataas); **maliit** (small); **malapit** (near); **malayo** (far); **malalakad** (can be reached by walking)

VERBS: **kumanan** (turn right); **kumaliwa** (turn left); **dumiretso** (go straight); **lumampas** (go past); **sumakay** (ride); **bumaba** (get off); **malalakad** (will be able to walk); **makakarating** (will be able to arrive)

OTHER WORDS AND EXPRESSIONS: **puwede** (can/may); **palatandaan** (landmark); **gaano katagal** (how long); **gaano kalayo** (how far); **gaano kahaba** (how long); **biyahe** (trip)

Mga Pangungusap Sentences

Review/Practice constructing sentences using the imperative or command form. For example:

1. **Kumanan ka!**	*Turn right!*
2. **Kumaliwa ka!**	*Turn left!*
3. **Dumiretso ka**	*Go straight!*
4. **Lampasan mo ang Kalye Roces.**	*Go past Roces Street.*
OR **Lumampas ka sa Kalye Roces.**	

Review/Practice the use of the conditional word **kung** (if). For example:

1. **Kung sasakay ka ng dyipni, limang minuto ang biyahe.**
   If you were to ride/take a jeepney, the trip will take five minutes.
2. **Kung maglalakad ka, baka abutin ka ng labinlimang minuto.**
   If you were to walk, perhaps it will take you fifteen minutes.

Review/Practice questions using **gaano**.

1. **Gaano kalayo ang istasyon ng tren?**
   How far is the train station?
2. **Gaano kahaba ang biyahe?**
   How long is the trip?
3. **Gaano katagal ako maghihintay sa bus?**
   How long will I wait for the bus?

Pagsasanay Practice

Practice asking and giving directions. Study the map below of the University of the Philippines Diliman. The university is like a small village because aside from its classroom buildings, offices and libraries, it also has its own shopping center, two churches, a hospital, a hotel, and recreational facilities. Note the four jeepney routes: Katipunan Avenue; Pantranco Avenue; Ikot (literally, to go around or clockwise); and Toki (a pun—literally the scrambled letters of Ikot; meaning "counterclockwise".)

In each of the dialogues, make sure you talk about a landmark, and an alternative way to reach the destination. Clues are provided in the first dialogue.

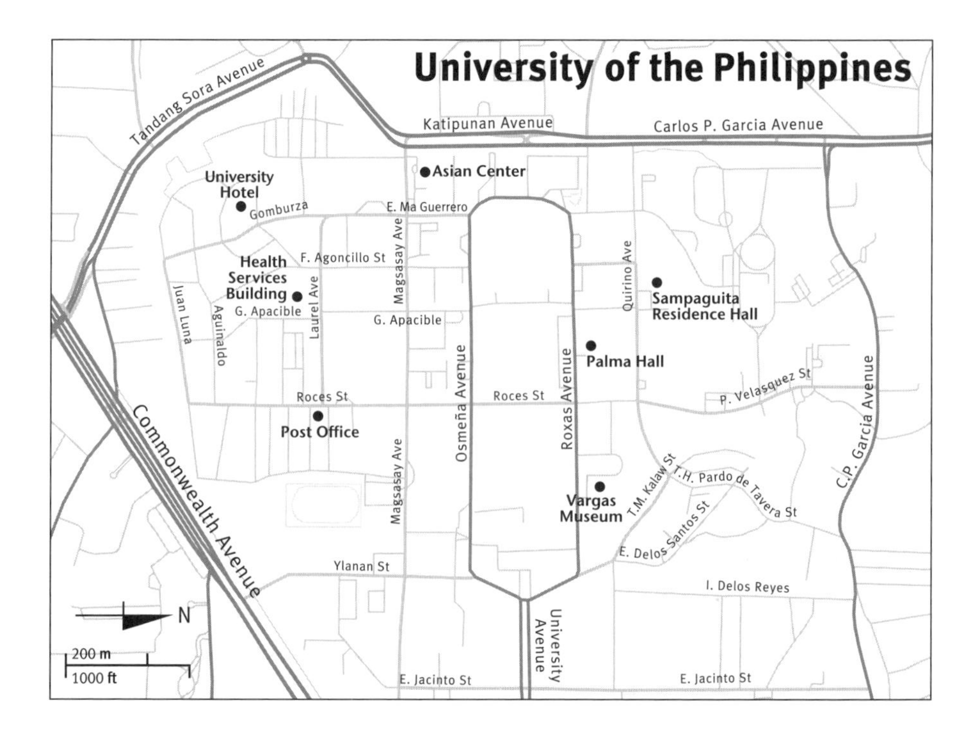

SITUATION 1: You are at the University Hotel. Your conference is in Palma Hall. If you walk, it will take you fifteen minutes, but if you take the Katipunan jeepney at the Asian Center, it will only take five minutes.

YOU : **Paano ho ako pupunta sa Palma Hall?**
HOTEL CLERK : **Lumabas ka ng hotel at maglakad ka sa Kalye Guerrero. Lumampas ka sa Sunken Garden. __________ ka sa Kalye Roxas. Nasa ___________ mo ang Palma Hall.**

YOU : **Puwede ba akong sumakay ng dyipni?**
HOTEL CLERK : **Oo. ____________________________ sa Asian Center.**

YOU : **Gaano katagal ho kung maglalakad ako?**
HOTEL CLERK : **Kung maglalakad ka, __________________ ang biyahe.**

YOU : **Gaano katagal ho kung sasakay ako ng dyipni?**

SITUATION 2: You are at the Vargas Museum on Roxas Street. You want to go to the Health Services Building. Your classmate thinks you should take the jeepney but you want to walk.

YOU : **Paano** ____?
YOUR CLASSMATE : **Puwede kang sumakay ng** ____________________________.
Kung sasakay ka ng ________________________________,
____.

YOU : **Gusto kong** ____________________________________.
YOUR CLASSMATE : **Kung maglalakad ka,** ___________________________.
____.

SITUATION 3: You are a new resident at Sampaguita Residence Hall. You want to go to the Post Office. You ask your friend at the dormitory how to get to the post office. You want to take the jeepney because it is too hot to walk.

YOU : ____?
YOUR FRIEND : ____.

YOU : ____?
YOUR FRIEND : ____.

YOU : ____?
YOUR FRIEND : ____.

Gramatika at Pagsasanay Verb Affixes

In this lesson, we are reviewing six verb affixes, which you have learned in *Tagalog for Beginners*: the more common **um** and **mag**, used when the focus is on the actor or the doer of the action; **in-**, used when the focus is on the object; the combination **in-an**, for locative focus or focus on the location of the action; and the affixes **na** (object focus) and **naka** (actor focus) which show "ability" or which are relatively equivalent to the words "can" or "was able to" in English. We call the **na-** and **naka-** affixes "abilitative" affixes.

Let us review three verbs and how they can be conjugated. Review the following formulas you have studied in *Tagalog for Beginners*:

Mag- affix – completed, **nag** + root word = **naglakad**; incompleted, first two syllables of completed aspect + root word = **naglalakad**; contemplated, change **n** to **m** of the incompleted version = **maglalakad**.

Um- affix – completed, **um** + root word (before the first vowel) = **sumakay**; incompleted, first two syllables of completed aspect + root word = **sumasakay**; contemplated, first syllable of root word + root word = **sasakay**.

In- affix – completed, **ni** + root word = **nilakad**; incompleted, **ni** + first syllable of root word + root word = **nilalakad**; contemplated, first syllable of root word + root word + **-in**, then change **d** to **r** for ease of speaking = **lalakarin**.

In-an affixes – completed, **in** (before the first vowel) + root word + **an** = **sinakyan**; incompleted, first two syllables of completed aspect **+ -an** = **sinasakyan**; contemplated, first syllable of root word + root word + **an** = **sasakyan**.

Naka- affix – completed, **naka** + root word = **nakalakad**; incompleted, **naka** + first syllable of root word + root word = **nakalalakad**; contemplated, change **n** to **m** of the incompleted version = **makalalakad**.

Na- affix – completed, **na** + root word = **nalakad**; incompleted, **na** + first syllable of root word + root word = **nalalakad**; contemplated, change **n** to **m** of the incompleted version = **malalakad**.

In some instances, you will read/hear **makakalakad** or **makakasakay** instead of **makalalakad** or **makasasakay**. Is this correct? Grammarians will argue, that this is grammatically wrong because it is the first syllable of the root word that should be doubled and not **ka**. However, it is common in spoken Filipino.

Affix	Focus	Root	Completed	Incompleted	Contemplated
mag	actor	lakad	naglakad	naglalakad	maglalakad
um	actor	sakay	sumakay	sumasakay	sasakay
um	actor	baba	bumaba	bumababa	bababa
-in-	object	lakad	nilakad	nilalakad	lalakarin
-in-an	locative	sakay	sinakyan	sinasakyan	sasakyan
in-an	locative	baba	binabaan	binababaan	bababaan
naka	actor	lakad	nakalakad	nakalalakad	makalalakad
na	object	lakad	nalakad	nalalakad	malalakad
naka	actor	sakay	nakasakay	nakasasakay	makasasakay
na-an	object	sakay	nasakyan	nasasakyan	masasakyan
naka	actor	baba	nakababa	nakabababa	makabababa

Study the following groups of sentences. Note that the focus (either the actor or the object) is underlined. The first two sentences per set are in the completed aspect while the last two are in the contemplated aspect.

1. **Lakad** (*To walk*)

   Naglakad <u>ako</u> sa University Avenue papunta sa Amphitheater. *I walked along University Avenue going to the Amphitheater.* (actor focus)

   Nilakad ko ang <u>University Avenue</u> papunta sa Ampthitheater. *I walked along University Avenue going to the Amphitheater.* (object focus)

   Makalalakad <u>ka</u> mula University Avenue papunta sa Amphitheater. *You will be able to walk from University Avenue going to the Amphitheater.* (actor focus)

   Malalakad mo ang <u>University Avenue</u> papunta sa Amphitheater. *You will be able to walk from University Avenue going to the Amphitheater.*

2. **Sakay** (*To ride*)

   Sumakay <u>ako</u> ng dyipni na may karatulang Ikot papunta sa ospital. *I took a jeepney with an "Ikot" sign going to the hospital.* (actor focus)

   <u>Dyipni na may karatulang "ikot"</u> ang sinakyan ko papunta sa ospital. *I took a jeepney with an "Ikot" sign going to the hospital.* (locative focus)

   Makasasakay <u>ka</u> rito sa sakayang ito ng dyipni na papuntang ospital. *You will be able to ride a jeepney going to the hospital at this jeepney stop.* (actor focus)

   <u>Dyipni na papuntang ospital</u> ang masasakyan mo rito sa sakayang ito ng dyipni. *You will be able to ride a jeepney going to the hospital at this jeepney stop.* (object focus)

3. **Baba** (*get off*)

   Bumaba <u>ako</u> sa estasyon ng tren sa Cubao. *I got off at the Cubao train station.* (actor focus)

   <u>Estasyon ng tren sa Cubao</u> ang binabaan ko. *I got off at the Cubao train station.* (locative focus)

   Hindi <u>ka</u> makababababa sa tapat ng munisipyo dahil bawal. *You cannot get off across from the town hall because it is forbidden.*

   Hindi mo mababababaan ang tapat ng munisipyo dahil bawal. *You cannot get off across from the town hall because it is forbidden.*

Practice using these verbs (**lakad**, **sakay**, **baba**) by asking and answering questions. The questions are grouped into situations.

Situation 1: You went to a museum. To get to the museum, you took bus 25 at the corner of Sampaguita and Rosal Streets. Then, you got off in front of the library. You then walked two blocks to get to the museum.

Tanong : **Saan ka pumunta?**
Sagot : **Pumunta ako sa** ______________________.

Tanong : **Paano ka pumunta sa** ______________________ **?**
Sagot : ______________________ **ako ng bus.**

Tanong : **Aling bus ang sinakyan mo?**
Sagot : **Bus** ______________ **ang** ______________ **ko.**

Tanong : **Saan ka sumakay ng bus?**
Sagot : ______________ **ako ng bus sa** ______________________.

Tanong : **Saan ka bumaba ng bus?**
Sagot : ______________________________________.

Tanong : **Gaano kalayo ang nilakad mo papunta sa museo?**
Sagot : ______________________ **kanto ang nilakad ko papunta sa museo.**

Situation 2: You are in a hotel and you want to go to Tribu Restaurant. You asked the hotel clerk if you could walk. He said that the restaurant is 8 blocks away and suggested you take a jeepney. You can get off in front of the restaurant.

Tanong : ______________________ **ko po ba papunta sa restawrang Tribu?**
Sagot : **Oo,** ______________________ **mo papunta sa restawrang Tribu.**

TANONG : **Gaano kalayo ho?**
SAGOT : ______________________ **kanto ang layo ng restawran mula sa hotel.**

TANONG : **Ano ho ang masasakyan ko?**
SAGOT : **Puwede kang** ______________________________________ **ng dyipni.**

TANONG : **Saan ho ako bababa?**
SAGOT : ____ .

SITUATION 3: You want to drop by your friend's house after your class. Your friend tells you that you cannot walk to his/her house because it is too far, but you can also take a short Light Rail Transit (LRT) train ride going to Monumento. He/She tells you to get off at the Cubao train station and then to walk one block.

TANONG : ____ **ba ang bahay mo?**
SAGOT : **Hindi,** __________________. **Pero puwede kang** _________ **ng** _____ .

TANONG : **Aling tren ang** ____ **ko?**
SAGOT : _________________________ **ka ng** __________________________ .

TANONG : **Saan ako** ____ ?
SAGOT : **Bumaba ka sa** ___________________________________. **Pagkatapos,**
____ .

Mga Talang Pangkultura People and Places
Barangay and Bayan, Part I[3]

Online PDF

Talakayan/Gawain/Pagsusulat Discussion/Task/Writing

Based on the dialogue you have read earlier and the culture notes, classroom learners can form small groups and respond to one or all of the following discussion questions/tasks.

1. How do you go to work/school? How long does it take? How much does it cost? Where do you get on/get off the bus/train/jeepney?
Ano ang sinasakyan mo papuntang trabaho/eskuwelahan? Gaano katagal? Magkano ang pamasahe mo? Saan ka sumasakay at bumababa?
2. Where do you go on weekends: shopping mall, movie theater, park, friend's house? How do you go there?
Saan ka pumupunta tuwing Sabado at Linggo? Paano pumunta roon?

[3] Part II of this culture notes can be found in Lesson 9.

3. If you have lived in or have visited the Philippines, do you know of any **Barangay** name? Why did you live there?
   Saang barangay ka tumira? Bakit ka tumira roon?

If you are an individual learner, choose one or more of the questions above and answer it/these.

Pakikinig Excerpt from "Cheche Lazaro Presents EDSA at ang Pinoy" **EDSA and the Filipino**

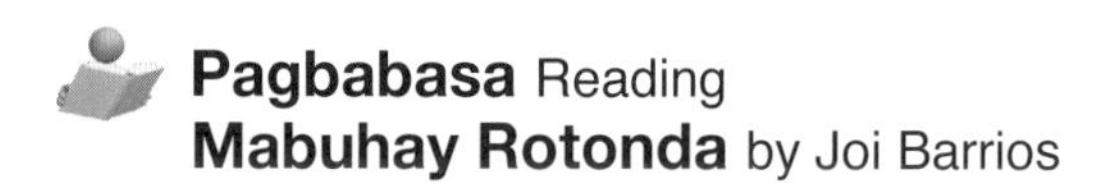

Pagbabasa Reading **Mabuhay Rotonda** by Joi Barrios

Read the following creative non-fiction piece on an incident that occurred in Welcome Rotonda, the boundary between Quezon City and Manila.

Before reading, study the following vocabulary words: **mabuhay** (long live); **daloy** (flow); **Batas Militar** (Martial Law); **pamahalaan** (government); **kabit-bisig** (linked arms); **putok ng baril** (gunfire)

These words are derived from English and/or Spanish; can you guess their meanings? Remember only the spelling of these words have been changed: **rali**; **umatake**; **kritikal**; **kondisyon**; **detalye**, **aktibista**.

After reading the short piece, answer the comprehension questions that follow.

Mabuhay!

Mabuhay Rotonda ang bagong pangalan ng palatandaan na naghihiwalay sa Lungsod ng Quezon at Maynila. Umiikot ang mga kotse at dyipni sa Rotonda, at dahil dito, mas mabilis ang daloy ng trapiko.

Pero hindi trapiko ang naaalala ko sa Welcome Rotonda. Ika-27 ng Setyembre 1984. Dalawampu't dalawang taong gulang ako. Batas Militar sa Pilipinas, at may rali laban sa pamahalaang Marcos. Nasa likod ako ng rali; hindi ko alam na sa harapan, umatake na ng tear gas at water cannons ang mga pulis.

May sumigaw, "Kapitbisig, takbo, takbo!" Tumakbo kami, mabilis kahit kapit-bisig, walang lumalabas sa linya. May narinig kaming mga putok ng baril. Takbo, Takbo! Mula sa Kalye Mayon, kaliwa sa Kalye P. Florentino, lampas sa maraming kanto, dire-diretso hanggang sa makarating kami sa National Press Club malapit sa Manila Post Office.

Noong araw na iyon, nabaril si Fidel Nemenzo[4], isang kaibigan. Dinala siya sa ospital at sa loob ng maraming oras, kritikal ang kondisyon niya.

Hindi ko sigurado kung tama ang alaala ko. Sa Kanlaon Avenue ba kami nagsimula tumakbo? Dumaan ba kami sa Blumentritt? Ang totoo, hindi ko naaalala ang mga kalye. Hindi ko tiningnan ang pangalan ng mga kalye nang tumatakbo kami. Limampung taong gulang na ako ngayon, at marami nang hindi matandaang detalye.

Pero ito ang alam ko. Tama ang bagong pangalan ng Welcome Rotonda. Mabuhay ka, Fidel, at mabuhay ang lahat ng aktibistang hindi natakot sa teargas, sa water cannon, at sa baril.

1. What is the new name of Welcome Rotonda?
2. How did the author and the other rallyists go to the National Press Club from Mayon Street?
3. What government building is near the National Press Club?
4. Who got shot?
5. What can the author not recall exactly?
6. What is the age of the author today?

Pagsusulat Writing
Mga Direksiyon

Using the vocabulary words you have learned in this lesson, write about one or more of the following:

1. The route you take to your favorite restaurant;
2. The route you take to a nearby town/city you go to;
3. A recent incident where you got lost;
4. Directions to a tourist attraction in your town or city.

Paglalagom Summing Up

In this lesson we have:

- Reviewed words related to transportation and giving directions;
- Studied abilitative affixes **na-** and **naka-**;
- Practiced giving directions.

---

[4] Dr. Fidel Nemenzo is currently Professor of Mathematics at the University of the Philippines. He is married to Professor Marivic Raquiza, and they have a son, Anton.

Aralin 3
Lesson

Pamimili sa Palengke
Shopping at a Market

This is our third review and expansion lesson. Review words and phrases for money, buying and selling, items which can be bought at a market, and cooking terms.

Diyalogo Dialogue
Nagbago ang Isip Ko! I Changed My Mind!

*Katie, is a regular customer (***suki***) of Mang Jose, who sells pork and beef at a popular market. To address Jose, Katie uses the word* **Mang***, a term used to address older men. Review and practice the use of particles such as* **naman** *and* **lang** *in natural speech.*

KATIE : **Magandang hapon po, Mang Jose.**
Good afternoon, Mang Jose.

MANG JOSE : **Ikaw pala, Katie! Magandang hapon naman.**
It's you Katie! Good afternoon too.

KATIE : **Pabili ho ng isang kilong baboy.**
Please let me buy a kilo of pork.

MANG JOSE : **Anong hiwa ng baboy?**
What kind of cut of pork?

KATIE : **Iyon hong pansinigang. Magkano ho ang isang kilo?**
[The cut] that's for sinigang *[sour soup]. How much is a kilo?*

MANG JOSE : **Siyento otsenta lang.**
Just a hundred and eighty pesos.

KATIE : **Napakamahal naman. Wala na ho bang tawad? Suki niyo naman ako.**
It is too expensive! Is there no discount? I am your regular customer.

MANG JOSE : **Pinakamababa na sa palengkeng ito dito sa puwesto ko. Sige, siyento sitenta, para sa iyo.**
[The price] I am giving you is the cheapest—the cheapest in the market, here in my meat stall. Okay, just one hundred and seventy for you.

KATIE : **Nagbago ho ang isip ko. Sa halip, bakang pambulalo na lang. Magkano ho?**
I changed my mind. Instead, just beef used for soup. How much?

MANG JOSE : **Dos siyentos, tapat na ho iyon.**
Two hundred, final price [literally, "frankly"].

KATIE : **Gusto ko hong bumili ng dalawang kilo. At saka bibilhan ko na rin ho ng bakang pangkare-kare ang kapitbahay ko.**
Also, I will buy a kilo of [beef] for making kare-kare *for my neighbor.*

MANG JOSE : **Magkasingpresyo lang ho iyong pambulalo at pangkare-kare. Anim na raan ho lahat.**
The [beef] for bulalo *and* kare-kare *have the same price. Six hundred total.*

KATIE : **Heto ho ang bayad ko.**
Here is my payment.

MANG JOSE : **Heto ang sukli mo.**
Here is your change.

Bokabularyo Vocabulary

Many of the words used in the dialogue are familiar to you from *Tagalog for Beginners* lessons on shopping, numbers, and food. Review these words and expand your knowledge by studying the following: new words, enclitic particles used in everyday conversations, adjectives, and adjectival affixes.

WORDS USED IN BUYING AND SELLING IN A MARKET: **bumibili** (buying); **nagtitinda/ nagbebenta** (selling); **tindahan** (store); **palengke** (market); **mahal** (expensive); **mura** (cheap/inexpensive); **suki** (regular customer); **tawad** (discount; also means "forgiveness"); **tapat** (frank; also, "faithful, sincere;" used in the dialogue to mean "final price"); **puwesto** (stall in a market; also means "position"); **hiwa** (cut); **hiwa ng baboy** (cut of pork); **pinamili** (items bought)

WORDS USED IN MEASUREMENTS AND COUNTING: **kilo** (kilogram); **dos siyentos** (two hundred); **tres siyentos** (three hundred); **kuwatro siyentos** (four hundred); **kinyentos** (five hundred); etc. Note that Filipinos tend to shift between using indigenous words in counting, for example, **sandaan** (one hundred) and **sanlibo** (one thousand) to **dos siyentos** (two hundred). It is more common to hear **sandaan** than **siyento**, although it is more common to hear **siyento singkuwenta** (one hundred and fifty) rather than **sandaan at limampung piso**. Thus, note that whatever you use is not grammatically incorrect, there are just more common ways of using numbers for money

WORDS FOR FOOD: **baboy** (pork/pig), sometimes used with the word **karne**, thus **karneng baboy** to refer only to pork; **baka** (beef/cow), sometimes used with the word **karne**, thus **karneng baka**, to refer only to beef; **karne** (meat); **manok** (chicken); **isda** (fish); **hipon** (shrimp); **tahong** (mussels); **talaba** (oyster); **alimango** (crab); **gulay** (vegetables); **prutas** (fruits); **bigas** (uncooked rice); **sahog**, **sangkap** (ingredient); **karneng pansahog**, refers to meat used to flavor what is generally a vegetable dish, for example, such as "chicken chopseuy"

POPULAR DISHES/WAYS OF COOKING: **bulalo** (beef soup made with beef bones and bone marrow); **kare-kare** (oxtail and/or tripe with peanut soup); **sinigang** (sour soup); **adobo** (chicken and/or pork cooked in vinegar and salt/soy sauce); **gisado** (sauteed dish); **inihaw** (grilled dish); **prito** (fry); **gisa** (saute); for example, **pritong isda** (fried fish)

OTHER ADJECTIVES: **sariwa/presko** (fresh); **bilasa** (putrescent/decaying/not fresh, usually used to describe fish); **malansa** (fishy); **bago** (new); **bagong huli** (freshly caught; usually used when referring to fish); **luma** (old); **mabango** (fragrant); **mabaho** (foul-smelling); **magaan** (light); **mabigat** (heavy)

ADJECTIVAL AFFIXES: **magkasing-** (same) or **magka-**, for example, **magkasing-presyo** or **magka-presyo** (of the same price), **magkasing-timbang** (of the same weight); **napaka-** (very), for example, **napakamahal** (very expensive); **napakasariwa** (very fresh)

ADJECTIVAL AFFIXES: **pang-** (used for) with variations **pam-** (before labial consonant such as **p**, **b**, **m**, **w**) and **pan-** (used for dental consonants such as **t**, **d**, **n**, **l**, **r**, and **s**), for example, **pambulalo** (used for **bulalo**); **pansinigang** (used for **sinigang**); and **pangkare-kare** (used for **kare-kare**). **Pang-** is used for all other consonants such as **k**, **g**, **h**, **ng**, **y**. For vowels, **pang-** is used, for example, **pang-adobo** (used for **adobo**)

ENCLITIC PARTICLES USED IN EVERYDAY CONVERSATIONS: **lang** (just); **naman** (so; likewise)

OTHER WORDS: **nagbago** (changed); **isip** (mind); **kaya** (and so, therefore); **sa halip** (instead)

Mga Pangungusap Sentences

Review/Practice using the completed aspect while talking about a shopping experience. Note the use of the linker **na** (introduced in *Tagalog for Beginners* as well as in Lesson 1) when pairing adjectives with nouns.

1. **Gusto ni Katie na bumili ng baboy na pansinigang pero nagbago ang isip niya.**
   Katie wanted to buy pork for sinigang *but she changed her mind.*
2. **Sa halip, bumili si Katie ng bakang pambulalo sa puwesto ni Mang Jose.**
   Instead, Katie bought beef used for bulalo *from Mang Jose's stall.*
3. **Suki si Katie ni Mang Jose kaya nakatawad siya.**
   Katie is Mang Jose's regular customer so she was able to get a discount.
4. **Nagpabli ng bakang pangkare-kare ang kapitbahay ni Katie.**
   Katie's neighbor asked her to buy beef for the kare-kare *dish.*
5. **Kuwatro siyentos ang halaga ng lahat ng pinamili ni Katie.**
   All the items that Katie bought cost four hundred [pesos].

Review/Practice the following questions one can ask/be asked when shopping at a market.

1. **Aling hiwa ng baboy ang gusto mo?**
   What kind of cut of pork would you like?
2. **Magkano ho ang isang kilo ng bakang pambulalo?**
   How much is the beef used for bulalo?
3. **Mayroon ho bang tawad?**
   Is there a discount?
4. **Wala ho bang tawad?**
   Is there no discount?

Gramatika at Pagsasanay

Practice the shopping dialogue through the following situations. Before this exercise, review, and practice adjectives using affixes and the word **mas** (more).

First, let us practice the affixes **napaka-**, **pinaka-** and **magkasing-**, as well as the word **mas**.

1. **mura** (inexpensive) – **napakamura** (very inexpensive); **mas mura** (more inexpensive); **pinakamura** (most inexpensive); and **magkasingmura** (of the same inexpensive price)

2. **mahal** – __________ (very expensive); _________ (more expensive); __________ (most expensive); ___________ (of the same expensive price)

3. **sariwa** (fresh) – __________ (very fresh); ___________ (fresher); __________ (freshest); _________________ (of the same quality of freshness)

4. **malansa** (fishy, not fresh, usually used for fish but can also describe meat that is no longer fresh) – ____________ (very fishy); ______________ (more fishy); _____________ (most fishy); ______________ (of the same degree of being fishy)

Now, let us practice using the affix **pang-** which means "used for." See explanations above and practice whether to use **pang-**, **pan-**, or **pam**. Remember, accuracy for this may be important only for written Filipino. In spoken Filipino, even if you make a mistake and say, for example, **pangbulalo** instead of **pambulalo**, it is not a problem. Even native speakers, including myself, make such mistakes.

Attach the affix **pang-**, **pam-**, or **pan** to the following words:

1. **sinigang** – **pansinigang** (used for **sinigang**)

2. **bulalo** – _____________________________

3. **sahog** – _____________________________

4. **nilaga** – _____________________________

5. **adobo** – _____________________________

6. **gisa** – _____________________________ (remember to double the "g")

Study the following shopping situations. Then, ask and answer questions. In two of the situations below, you can also practice asking for directions, which you had studied in Lesson 2. Classroom learners should work in pairs; individual learners can write down the dialogue.

Situation 1: Bianca is shopping at the poultry section of the market. She wants to buy chicken cuts for **adobo**. The chicken usually sells for ₱120 but because she is a regular customer, Mang Juan is willing to sell the chicken to her for ₱110. She changed her mind and instead of buying 2 kilos, she bought 3 kilos.

Bianca : ____.
Mang Juan : **Anong hiwa ng manok?**

Bianca : ____________________. __________ **ho ang kilo ng** __________ **?**
Mang Juan : ____.

Bianca : **Wala ho bang** ________________________ **? Suki niyo naman ako.**
Mang Juan : **Sige,** ___________ **na lang.** ____________ **ang manok sa puwesto ko. Ilang kilo ang gusto mo?**

Bianca : ____.
Mang Juan : **Heto ang** ______________ **kilo ng manok.**

Bianca : **Nagbago ho ang isip ko. Pabili ho ng** ______________ **kilo ng manok.**
Mang Juan : **Heto ang** ____________________________ **kilo ng manok.**

Situation 2: Tristan is shopping for a special dinner for his girlfriend Althea. He wants to cook beef **kaldereta** (a stew made with tomato sauce, olives, pounded liver and bell peppers). He asks for a discount, but Mang Jose says that he has given the final price. After buying the meat, he needs to ask Mang Jose where the stalls are for the **pansahog** or "other ingredients to be used for the dish." Mang Jose tells him to go straight and turn left; the stall will be on his right.

Tristan : **Magandang hapon po.** ____________________?
Mang Jose : **Anong** ____________________?

Tristan : __________. __________ **ho ang isang** __________?
Mang Jose : **Dos siyentos** ____________________.

Tristan : **Mayroon** ____________________?
Mang Jose : **Pasensiya ka na** ____________________.

Tristan : **Heto ho ang** ____________________.
Mang Jose : ____________________.

Tristan : **Gusto ko hong bumili ng** ____________________. **Saan ho ang puwesto ng nagtitinda ng oliba at tomato sauce?**
Mang Jose : ____________________
____________________.

Tristan : ____________________.
Mang Jose : **Walang anuman.**

Situation 3: It is morning. Kaegy and Joy are shopping so they can cook dinner for the meeting of their study group. They want to serve fish and vegetables. They do not have a huge budget so they want to buy relatively inexpensive fish. Fortunately, Aling Natalie has a lot of **bangus** (milkfish) which she can clean and cut up for **sinigang**. She can also give them a discount; if they buy 2 kilos, she can give it for ₱200 for 2 kilos. Kaegy wants to know where they can buy vegetables so she tells them to go straight towards the chicken stalls, and turn left at the end.

Kaegy : **Magandang**____________________.
Joy : ____________________.
Aling Natalie : ____________________.

Kaegy : **Aling isda** ____________________?
Aling Natalie : ____________________ **ngayon ang** ____________________.
Joy : **Gusto** ____________________.
Mayroon ____________________?

ALING NATALIE : **Ilang kilo** ______________________________?
KAEGY : ______________________________________.

ALING NATALIE : ______________ **na lang ang** ______________.
Anong hiwa ______________________________?
JOY : ______________________________________.
KAEGY : **Paano ho** ______________________________?

ALING NATALIE : ______________________________________.
KAEGY : ______________________________________.
JOY : ______________________________________.

ALING NATALIE : ______________________________________.

Pagsasanay Practice
Talakayan

Classroom learners should talk about either their shopping experience in the previous activity or a recent shopping experience. This can be done in two ways: one, they can form small groups; two, they can share it with the class. Each person should say at least three sentences. Then, one person in the group/class, perhaps the person sitting next to him/her, should ask a question based on the sentences. Individual learners should write down their sentences.

Here are examples of sentences one can share:

Bumili ako ng isdang pansinigang sa puwesto ni Aling Natalie. Nakatawad ako kaya dos siyentos lang ang halaga ng dalawang kilo ng bangus. Pagkatapos, pumunta ako sa puwesto ng mga nagtitinda ng gulay.

Here are examples of possible questions. Just use them as guides to make your own questions.

1. **Anong mga gulay ang binili mo?**
   What [kinds of] vegetable did you buy?
2. **Bakit ka nakatawad?**
   Why were you able to get a discount?
3. **Kailan ka bumili ng isda?**
   When did you buy fish?
4. **Bakit bangus ang binili mo?**
   Why did you buy milkfish?

Gramatika at Pagsasanay Adjectival Affixes and Other Verb Affixes

In this lesson, we are reviewing/studying two things: adjectival affixes (**napaka-**, **pinaka-**, **pang-**) and other verb affixes.

In Lesson 2, we reviewed five verb affixes: for actor focus, the affixes **um-** and **mag-**; for object focus, the affix **in-**, and the abilitative affixes **na-** and **naka-**.

Here, in Lesson 3, let us use the affix **um-** for the **infinitive** and **imperative forms** of the verb and study the affixes **in-** and **an**, used to show **benefactive focus**.

When do we use the infinitive and imperative forms of the verb? You will recall that in English, we use the infinitive form when we use the word "to." For example, we say, "want **to** buy" (in Filipino, **gusto kong bumili**), or "plan **to** sell" (**plano kong magtinda** or **magbenta**). We use the imperative form, when we give commands, for example, "Walk!" (**Lumakad ka!**) or "Run!" (**Tumakbo ka!**)

When do we use the benefactive focus? We use it when we want to bring attention to the one who "benefits" from the action. For example:

<u>Binilhan</u> ko ng bakang pangkare-kare ang kapitbahay ko.
I bought beef used for kare-kare *for my neighbor.*

Now let us compare the affixes **in-an** with the other affixes using the verb **benta** (sell). Both the verbs and the focus of the verb are underlined. The markers which give us clues about focus are in italics.

<u>Nagbenta</u> ng karne <u>*si* Mang Jose</u> kay Katie.
Mang Jose sold beef to Katie.

<u>Ibinenta</u> ni Mang Jose <u>*ang* karne</u> kay Katie.
Beef was sold by Mang Jose to Katie.

<u>Binentahan</u> ni Mang Jose ng karne <u>*si* Katie</u>.
Mang Jose sold beef to Katie.

Here are the formulas we can use:

- For both the infinitive and imperative forms: attach the affix **mag-** to the root word, thus **mag** + root, for example, **mag + tinda** = **magtinda**; and put the affix **um-** before the first vowel of the root word, thus **um** + root word (but before the first vowel), for example, **um** + **bili** = **bumili**.

- For the benefactive focus using the affixes **in-an**:
  Completed aspect, put **in-** before the first vowel of the root and then add **-an**. Place the letter **h** before the two "**a**" vowels for "ease of speaking." Thus, **in** + root word (before first vowel) + **an** = **binentahan**.
  Incompleted aspect, first two syllables of completed aspect + root word + **an** = **binebentahan**.
  Contemplated aspect: first syllable of root word + root word + **an** = **bebentahan**.

Study the chart below. Here, we have the other affixes we have reviewed in Lesson 2, although the affixes we are focusing on in Lesson 3 are in bold. This chart will help you navigate through the affixes using an example, the root **bili**.

Affix	Focus	Root	Inf/int	Completed	Incompleted	Contemplated
um	actor	bili	bumili	bumili	bumibili	bibili
-in-	object	bili	bilhin	binili	binibili	bibilhin
-in-an	benefac-tive	bili	**bilhan**	**binilhan**	**binibilhan**	**bibilhan**
naka	actor	bili	makabili	nakabili	nakabibili	makabibili
na	object	bili	mabili	nabili	nabibili	mabibili
na-an	benefactive	bili	mabilhan	nabilhan	nabibilhan	mabibilhan

Here are a few sample sentences for the root words **bili** and **benta**.

<u>Binilhan</u> ni Katie ng prutas ang kapatid niyang babae.
Katie bought fruits for her sister.

<u>Binibilhan</u> ni Katie ng prutas ang kapatid niyang babae linggo-linggo.
Katie buys fruits for her sister every week.

<u>Bibilhan</u> ni Katie ng prutas ang kapatid niya sa Sabado.
Katie will buy fruits for her sister on Saturday.

<u>Binentahan</u> ni Aling Maria ng prutas si Katie.
Aling Maria sold fruits to Katie.

<u>Binebentahan</u> ni Aling Maria ng prutas si Katie linggo-linggo.
Aling Maria sells fruits to Katie every week.

<u>Bebentahan</u> ni Aling Maria si Katie ng mga mangga sa Sabado.
Aling Maria will sell mangoes to Katie on Saturday.

Now, please complete the chart below which has the root word, **benta**.

Affix	Focus	Root	Inf/int	Completed	Incompleted	Contemplated
um	actor	benta				
-in-	object	benta				
-in-an	benefac-tive	benta				
naka	actor	benta				
na	object	benta				

Mga Talang Pangkultura: Sa Palengke At the Public Market

Talakayan/Pagsusulat: Saan ka namamalengke?
Which market do you go to?

Based on the culture notes, ask and answer questions with your partner or your small group. You may choose to ask answer one, two or all the questions below. Classroom learners may work in pair or form small groups. Individual learners should write down a short paragraph based on answers to the guide questions.

Here are some questions you may want to ask and answer. Remember, sometimes there are many ways of saying the same thing. For example, you can say **bumibili** (buying), **namimili** (shopping), or **namamalengke** (going to the market).

1. Where do you shop for the freshest fish/meat/vegetables?
   Saan ka namimili ng pinakasariwang isda/karne/gulay?
2. Have you been to a market in the Philippines? What was your experience like?
   Nakapunta ka na ba sa isang palengke sa Pilipinas? Ano ang naging karanasan mo?
3. Do you go shopping at a farmers' market? When do you go? What do you buy?
   Namimili ka ba sa isang farmers' market? Kailan ka pumupunta roon? Ano ang binibili mo?
4. Do you like haggling? Narrate an experience.
   Gusto mo bang tumawad? Ikuwento mo ang isang karanasan.

Gawain Activity
Tinda-tindahan Playing store

Classroom learners can form small groups of 2–3 people in a group. All groups should be given a number. Each group is assigned (or they can draw lots) a food group (for example, fish and other seafood, vegetables, poultry, beef or pork, fruits). The students then decide on what they are selling and the adjectives to describe their products (for example, **pansigang** or **napakalaking isda**). Then, they could either use cut-outs or drawings.

All groups with even numbers become sellers first, and all groups with odd numbers are the buyers. The group buyers also draw lots to determine the amount they have (for example, ₱200, ₱300, etc.). Each group determines the dish they are cooking and go shopping for it. Then the groups exchange roles, and the sellers become the buyers. At the end of the activity, each group gives a report.

Pakikinig: Excerpt from Dagdag-sahod na Makabuluhan, Kailangang Ipaglaban Struggle for Substantial Wage Increase

Pagbabasa Reading
Ang Suweldo sa Kanyang Bulsa The Salary in Her Pocket

Read the following short short story and then answer the questions below. To prepare, review/study the following words: **nakangiti** (smiling); **sobre** (envelope); **pabrika** (factory); **koryente** (electricity); **utang** (debt); **baon** (money/food one brings from home); **nagkuwenta** (counted; computed), **kangkong** (water spinach); **kampana** (bells); **iniisip** (thinking); **bulsa** (pocket).

Can you guess the meaning of the following words derived from English/Spanish: **matematika**; **suma total**?

Ang Suweldo sa Kanyang Bulsa[1]

Kriiing!

Alas-singko na ng hapon, Biyernes, araw ng suweldo. Nakangiting kinuha ni Nitz ang sobre ng suweldo para sa isang linggo na trabaho.

Araw-araw, pumapasok si Nitz sa pabrika ng bag. At araw-araw, gumagawa siya ng bulsa ng bag. Ganoon sa pabrika—may mga manggagawa na gumagawa ng bulsa, may gumagawa ng katawan ng bag, may gumagawa ng bag straps, may naglalagay ng buckle.

Parang lesson sa matematika ang araw ng suweldo kay Nitz. Suweldo bawat araw, apat na raan at apatnapu't anim na piso. Limang araw sa isang linggo. Suma total, dalawang libo, dalawang daan at tatlumpung piso raw. Pero kapag nabawas na ang buwis, ang SSS, Philhealth, at iba pang dapat bayaran, halos isang libo limang daan na lang ang natitira.

Binuksan ni Nitz ang sobre. Kinuha niya ang walong daan at inilagay sa isa pang sobre – bayad ito para sa bahay, sa koryente, sa tubig, sa utang, sa baon sa eskuwelahan ng dalawang anak na nasa high school. Pitong daang piso na lang ang nasa sobre ng suweldo. Ipinasok niya sa bulsa ng pantalon ang sobre.

May malapit na palengke sa pabrika. Bibili lang ako para sa hapunan mamayang gabi, naisip ni Nitz. Ano kaya ang masarap?

Pumunta si Nitz sa mga puwesto ng isda. Ay, pansigang na bangus. Ang sarap ng sinigang. Bangus, siyento beinte; isang tali ng kangkong, beinte pesos. Sandali, magkano ang tilapia? Tilapia na lang, sandaang piso lang. Kangkong na pang-adobo, beinte. Pero hindi. Kung sinigang, may sabaw; puwede na kahit konting sabaw lang at kanin. Pinakamurang bigas, trenta pesos. Suma total, siyento sitenta.

Nagkuwenta uli si Nitz. Pitong daang piso minus siyento sitenta. Limang daan at tatlumpung piso.

Paano na kaya ang iba pang araw sa susunod na linggo?

Kleng kleng kleng… Alas-sais ng hapon, at tumutunog na ang mga kampana sa simbahan.

Sa dyipni pauwi sa bahay, iniisip ni Nitz ang lahat ng bulsa ng bag sa pabrika, ang lahat ng trabaho araw-araw, ang pinamili niya para sa hapunan, at ang lumiliit, lumiliit, lumiliit na suweldo sa kanyang bulsa.

1. What is Nitz's job?
2. How much does she earn in a week?
3. After deducting taxes, payments for rent, electricity, water, and money for her children to go to school, how much is left?
4. What did Nitz want to buy at the market? What did she buy?
5. What was Nitz thinking of as she was riding the jeepney home?

---

[1] This story was inspired by Roland Tolentino's short story about a teacher counting her salary. Nitz is the name of a labor organizer in the Philippines.

Pagsusulat Writing: Grocery List

Write a short paragraph on one of the following situations. Practice the contemplated aspect of the verb.

1. You are planning to host a dinner party for three friends on Friday night. However, you have a limited budget of 15 dollars for the party. What will you buy? Start your paragraph with the words, "**Sa Biyernes....**"
2. You live alone. You want to cook several dishes on Sunday to prepare for the following week. What can you buy at the farmers' market this Saturday? Start your paragraph with the words, "**Sa farmers' market...**"
3. You invited your boyfriend/girlfriend to dinner at your home. You are planning a romantic dinner menu and need to go shopping. Start your paragraph with, "**Nagpaplano ako ng romantikong hapunan...**"

Paglalagom Summing Up

In this lesson, we have:

- Reviewed/Studied words and phrases related to shopping in a market;
- Studied adjectival affixes (**magka-**, **magkasing-**, **napaka-**, **pinaka-**) as well as affixes used to show benefactive focus (**in-an**);
- Practiced role-plays related to shopping;
- Read/wrote about the relation of wages and buying capacity.

Aralin 4
Lesson

Pag-order ng Pagkain sa Restawran
Ordering Food in a Restaurant

This is our fourth review and expansion lesson. Review words and phrases for food, utensils, and ordering at a restaurant, as well as verb affixes used in causative sentences.

Diyalogo Dialogue
Malamig na ang Sabaw! The Soup is Cold!

Study the following dialogue by reading it aloud. Armael and Katie are having dinner in a restaurant.

WAITER : **Ano ho ang gusto niyong orderin?**
What would you like to order?

ARMAEL : **Pakibigyan ho ninyo kami ng lechong kawali, sweet and sour lapulapu, bulalo, at kanin.**
Please give us pan-fried pork with crispy skin, sweet and sour lapulapu *[a kind of fish], beef soup, and rice.*

WAITER : **Ano ho ang inumin niyo?**
What [are] your drinks?

ARMAEL : **Buko juice na lang ho.**
Just coconut juice.

KATIE : **Meron ho ba kayong mainit na kalamansi juice?**
Do you have hot native lemon juice?

WAITER : **Meron ho. Sandali lang ho.**
We do. Just a moment please.

(Pagkatapos ng ilang minuto.) (*After a few minutes.*)

WAITER : **Heto na ho ang order niyo.**
Here is your order.

KATIE : **Pahingi naman ho ng isa pang mangkok, dalawang kutsilyo, dagdag na sarsa para sa lechong kawali at sawsawan para sa bulalo.**
Please give us another bowl, two knives, additional sauce for the pan-fried pork with crispy skin, and some dipping sauce.

WAITER : **Ano hong klaseng sawsawan ang gusto ninyo?**
What kind of sauce would you like?

KATIE : **Patis ho.**
Fish sauce.

WAITER : **Heto ho.**
Here you are.

KATIE : **Ang sarap ng lapulapu!**
The lapulapu *is delicious!*

ARMAEL : **Naku, malamig na ho ang sabaw!**
Oh no, the soup is cold.

WAITER : **Pasensiya na ho kayo.**
Sorry.

ARMAEL : **Pakibalik niyo na lang ang bulalo dahil hindi namin ito makakain.**
Please return the bulalo *because we cannot eat this.*

WAITER : **Ipapainit ko ho ito sa kusinero namin.**
I will have it reheated by our cook.

Bokabularyo Vocabulary

Review/study the following groups of vocabulary words:

WORDS RELATED TO FOOD AND DRINK: lechong kawali (pan-fried pork with crispy skin); sweet and sour **lapulapu** (a kind of fish cooked with vinegar and sugar); **bulalo** (beef soup made using bones with marrow); **litson/lechon** (roasted whole pig known for its crispy skin); **kanin** (cooked rice); **nilaga** (boiled); **inihaw** (grilled); **pinirito** (fried); **pinasingaw** (steamed); **gisado** (sauteed); **pinausukan** (smoked); **kilawin** (method of cooking raw food, usually fish, using vinegar); **sarsa** (sauce); **sawsawan** (dipping sauce); **suka** (vinegar); **toyo** (soy sauce); **patis** (fish sauce); **bagoong** (salty anchovies or shrimp paste); **pagkain** (food); **putahe** (dish); **inumin** (accent on the second syllable – drink); **alak** (wine); **katas** (juice); **yelo** (ice); **sopas** (soup); **sabaw** (broth/soup); **ensalada** (salad); **ulam** (viand; anything eaten with rice); **panghimagas** (dessert)

WORDS FOR UTENSILS, COOKWARE, AND TABLEWARE: **kutsara** (spoon); **kutsarita** (teaspoon); **tinidor** (fork); **kutsilyo** (knife); **plato** (plate); **platito** (saucer); **baso** (glass); **tasa** (cup); **mangkok** (bowl); **pitsel** (pitcher); **kawali** (wok-like frying pan); **kaldero** (pot); **siyanse** (cooking utensil used for sauteeing)

ADJECTIVES THAT DESCRIBE FOOD AND DRINK: **mainit** (hot); **maligamgam** (tepid); **malamig** (cold); **masarap** (delicious); **maalat** (salty); **maanghang** (spicy); **matamis** (sweet); **maasim** (sour); **malasa/malinamnam** (tasty); **mapait** (bitter); **matigas** (hard/ tough, used for example to describe tough meat); **malambot** (soft/tender); **makunat** (tough; difficult to chew); **malabnaw** (thin, referring to soup); **malutong** (crispy)

VERBS: **orderin** (to order in); **pakibigyan** (please give us); **pahingi** (ask; literally, [I] ask; please); **pakibalik** (please return); **ipapaluto** (will ask [someone] to cook)

OTHER WORDS: **kusinero** (male cook); **kusinera** (female cook)

Mga Pangungusap Sentences

Review/Study sentences that use the imperative or command form of the verb, that indicate requests. Note the use of the affixes **paki-** and **pa**, which are used to mean "please." Also, note that sometimes there are two ways by which we can say the same thing.

1. **<u>Pakibigyan</u> ho ninyo kami ng lechong kawali, sweet and sour lapulapu, bulalo, at kanin.** *Please give us pan-fried pork with crispy skin, sweet and sour* lapulapu *[a kind of fish], beef soup, and rice.*
2. **<u>Pahingi</u> naman ho ng isa pang mangkok, dalawang kutsilyo, dagdag na sarsa para sa lechong kawali, at sawsawan para sa bulalo.** *Please give us another bowl, two knives, additional sauce for the pan-fried pork with crispy skin, and some dipping sauce.*
3. **<u>Pakibalik</u> niyo na lang ang bulalo dahil hindi namin ito makakain.** *Please return the* bulalo *because we cannot eat this.*
4. **<u>Ipapainit/ipaiinit</u> ko ho ito sa kusinero namin.** *I will have it reheated by our cook.*

Pagsasanay Practice

First, practice the words **pakibigyan** (please give), **pahingi** (literally, [I] ask), and **pakibalik** (please return). Do not be confused with the words **pakibigyan** and **pahingi** which have similar meanings, and which you can sometimes interchange. Both words mean "please give [me];" however, the root word **bigay** means "give," while the root word **hingi** means "ask [for something]." Moreover, remember that although grammarians prefer to duplicate the root word, for example, **ipinatitimpla**, in conversational Filipino, **ipinapatimpla** is commonly used. Choose whatever is convenient to you.

Here are a few situations wherein you may use the following words. Classroom learners should work with a partner and take turns giving the situation and giving the dialogue in Tagalog/Filipino. Individual learners should write down the dialogue in Tagalog/Filipino. Also, practice using the words you have reviewed/learned in the Vocabulary section.

1. You want the waiter to give you fried fish, broiled pork, and steamed vegetables.
   You say: ______________________________ .

2. You ask the waiter for a glass of water and a spoon.
   You say: ______________________________ .

3. You ask the the waiter to return the fried chicken because it is too salty.
   You say: ______________________________ .

4. You want the waiter to give you boiled pork, steamed fish, and broiled vegetables.
   You say: ______________________________ .

5. You ask the waiter to return the sauteed vegetables because they are too cold.
   You say: ______________________________ .

Now, let us practice the affix **pa-** which means "to ask someone to do something." This is used when the focus is on the object. In conversational Filipino, for the completed action, we use **ipina**; for incompleted action, **ipinapa**; and for contemplated, **ipapa**. The letter "i" is used for standardized language for ease of speaking, although in spoken Tagalog/Filipino, some speakers omit the letter "i." Study the following ways of using this affix:

1. **Ipapainit/Ipaiinit ko ang isda sa aming kusinero.**
   I will ask our cook to heat the fish.
2. **Ipinaluto ko sa nanay ko ang pansit.**
   I asked my mother to cook the pansit.

3. **Ipinapatimpla/ipinatitimpla ng tiyahin ko sa akin ang sawsawan para sa inihaw na isda linggo-linggo.**
   My aunt asks me to mix the dipping sauce for the broiled fish every week.
4. **Ano ang ipinapaluto/ipinaluluto mo sa kapatid mo kapag may sakit ka?**
   What do you ask your brother/sister to cook for you when you are sick?
5. **Ano ang ipinabalik mo sa waiter?**
   What did you ask the waiter to return [to the kitchen]?

Now, ask and answer the following. Choose any of the food/dishes reviewed/studied in the Vocabulary section so you can also practice those words.

1. TANONG : **Ano ang ipinainit mo sa kusinero ng restawran**?
   SAGOT : ____.

2. TANONG : **Ano ang ipinapaluto mo sa nanay mo kapag meron kang lagnat?**
   SAGOT : ____.

3. TANONG : **Anong cocktail drink ang ipatitimpla mo sa bartender?**
   SAGOT : ____.

4. TANONG : ____?
   SAGOT : **Sopas ang ipinabalik ko sa waiter.**

5. TANONG : ____?
   SAGOT : **Bulalo ang ipinaluto ko sa tatay ko para sa birthday party ko.**

Finally, practice the adjectives you have learned in the Vocabulary Section by completing the following sentences.

Here are some dishes you can use to fill in the blanks: **balat ng litson**; **bagoong**; **kimchi**; **leche** flan; **sopas/sabaw**.

1. **Maalat ang** ______________________________.
2. **Matamis ang** ______________________________.
3. **Mainit ang** ______________________________.
4. **Maanghang ang** ______________________________.
5. **Malutong ang** ______________________________.

★ **Gawain** Activity: **Role-play**

Practice restaurant situations using the menu below and the information provided. Use the dialogue you studied and the vocabulary you have reviewed/studied as a guide. Make sure to practice giving comments on the food (for example, "**ang sarap!**" [it is delicious] or "**masyadong maalat ang...**" [the ____ is too salty].)

Menu

Sopas	suam na mais *(corn soup)* sotanghong manok *(chicken and bean thread soup)* bulalo *(beef soup)*
Ensalada	ensaladang kamatis, sibuyas at hilaw na mangga na may bagoong *(salad of tomatoes, onions, green mangoes with* bagoong*)* ensaladang talbos ng kamote *(sweet potato leaves salad)*
Specials	kilawing tanguigue *(raw* tanguigue *marinated in vinegar)* lumpiang shanghai *(pork egg rolls)* crispy pata *(fried pork legs)* adobong manok *(chicken* adobo*)* rellenong bangus *(stuffed milkfish)* pritong tilapia *(fried tilapia)* kalderetang kambing *(goat meat stewed in tomatoes)* kare-kare *(beef and tripe in peanut sauce)* adobong kangkong *(swamp cabbage cooked* adobo *style)* ampalaya guisado *(sauteed bittermelon).*
Panghimagas	leche flan *(custard)* halayang ube *(sweetened purple yam)* halo-halo *(sweetened fruits with milk and ice)*
Mga Inumin	buco juice *(coconut juice)* calamansi juice *(native lemon juice)* mango juice *(mango juice)*

Classroom learners can work in groups of three; individual learners can write down a dialogue.

SITUATION 1: You are in a restaurant with your classmate. You order a fish dish and he/she orders a salad and a beef dish. You order the same kind of juice. You think that the dish is delicious, but your classmate thinks that his/her dish is too cold. You ask the waiter for another fork, and your classmate asks the waiter for more ice for his/her juice.

SITUATION 2: You are having dinner with your boyfriend/girlfriend. He/she is vegetarian and you like meat dishes. You order **buco** juice while he/she only wants water. You think that your dish is too salty. Your boyfriend/girlfriend asks for soy sauce. You also ask for a knife.

SITUATION 3: You are having lunch with your father/mother. He/she orders a chicken dish and you order a fish dish. You both order vegetables and soup. He/she thinks that the dish is too spicy. You want some vinegar as a dipping sauce. You ask the waiter to give you another glass because your glass is dirty.

Gramatika at Pagsasanay:
Affixes used in Causative Sentences

Review/Study causative sentences. In causative sentences, a person causes another person to do something. For these sentences, we use the following affixes:

- "**mag + pa**" when the focus is on the "causer" (the person giving the request)
- "**pa + in**" when the focus is on the "actor" (the person performing the request)
- "**i + pa + in**," when the focus is on the object.
- "**pa + in + an**," when the focus is on the receiver or the location of the action.

Here are the formulas you can use:

- For **magpa**: infinitive/imperative, **magpa** + root word; completed, **nagpa** + root word; incompleted, **nagpa + pa** + root word; contemplated, change **n** to **m**.

- For **pa + in**: infinitive/imperative, **pa** + root word + **-in**; completed, **pina** + root word; incompleted, **pina** + first syllable of root word + root word; contemplated, **pa** + first syllable of root word + root word + **in**.

- For **i + pa + in**: infinitive/imperative, **ipa** + root word; completed, **ipina** + root word; incompleted, **ipina** + first syllable of root word + root word; contemplated, **ipa** + first syllable of root word + root word.

- For **pa + in + an**: infinitive/imperative, **pa** + root word + **an**; completed, **pina** + root word + **an**; incompleted, **pina** + first syllable of root word + root word + **an**; contemplated, **pa** + first syllable of root word + root word + **an**.

Study the following sentences to see how these affixes are used and how the root word **luto** has been changed:

1. **<u>Nagpaluto ako</u> sa kusinero ng adobo para sa kapatid ko.** *I asked the cook to cook* adobo *for my brother/sister.*
2. **<u>Pinaluto ko</u> ang kusinero ng adobo para sa kapatid ko.**
3. **<u>Adobo</u> ang <u>ipinaluto</u> ko sa kusinero para sa kapatid ko.**
4. **<u>Pinalutuan</u> ko ang <u>kapatid ko</u> ng adobo sa kusinero.**

Study the following table. Affixes studied earlier have been included to enable you to compare the resulting verbs:

Affix	Focus/ Sentence	Root	Inf/int	Completed	Incompleted	Contemplated
nag	actor	luto	magluto	nagluto	nagluluto	magluluto
-in-	object	luto	lutuin	niluto	niluluto	lulutuin
-in -an	benefac-tive	luto	lutuan	nilutuan	nilulutuan	lulutuan
naka	actor/ abilitative	luto	makaluto	nakaluto	nakaluluto	makaluluto
na	object/ abilitative	luto	maluto	naluto	naluluto	maluluto
nag-pa	causer/ causative	luto	**magpalu-to**	**nagpaluto**	**nagpapalu-to**	**magpapaluto**
pa + in	actor/ causative	luto	**palutuin**	**pinaluto**	**pinaluluto**	**palulutuin**
i + pa + in	object/ causative	luto	**ipaluto**	**ipinaluto**	**ipinaluluto**	**ipaluluto**
pa + in + an	receiver/ causative	luto	**palutuan**	**pinalutuan**	**pinalulutu-an**	**palulutuan**

Complete the following table for the verbs **gawa** (make) and **timpla**. Remember to insert the letter **h** when the affix **-an** is attached to a word ending in **a** (see example in bold).

Affix	Focus/ Sentence	Root	Inf/int	Completed	Incompleted	Contemplated
nag-pa	causer/ causative	gawa	magpaga-wa			
pa + in	actor/ causative	gawa		pinagawa		
i + pa + in	object/ causative	gawa			ipinagagawa	
pa + in + an	receiver/ causative	gawa				pagagawan
nag-pa	causer/ causative	tim-pla	magpatim-pla			

Affix	Focus/ Sentence	Root	Inf/int	Completed	Incompleted	Contemplated
pa + in	actor/ causative	tim-pla		pinatimpla		
i + pa + in	object/ causative	tim-pla			ipinatitimpla	
pa + in + an	receiver/ causative	tim-pla				**patitimplahan**

Pagsasanay Practice

Practice what you have learned about affixes used for verbs in causative sentences. Ask and answer the following.

1. TANONG : **Kanino ka nagpatimpla ng cocktail drink?**
   SAGOT : **Nagpatimpla ako ng cocktail drink sa bartender.**

2. TANONG : **Kanino ka nagpagawa ng cake sa birthday mo?**
   SAGOT : ________________ **ako ng cake sa** ________________ **Bakery.**

3. TANONG : **Anong putahe ang** ____________________ **mo ng sawsawan?**
   SAGOT : ____________________ **ang pinatimplahan ko ng sawsawan.**

4. TANONG : **Sino ang** ______________________ **mo ng cake sa Sabado?**
   SAGOT : ______________________ **ko ng cake ang mga magulang ko dahil anibersaryo nila.**

5. TANONG : **Kanino ka nagpatimpla ng kape?**
   SAGOT : ____.

6. TANONG : ____?
   SAGOT : **Apple pie ang ipinagawa ko sa kapatid ko para sa party.**

Mga Talang Pangkultura: Ang Mesang Filipino
The Filipino Table

Online PDF

Talakayan/Pagsusulat: Ang mga Paborito mong Pagkain
Your Favorite Dishes

Discuss your family's favorite dishes or dishes you like to order in a restaurant. Classroom learners should form groups of four or five, while individual learners should write down the answers.

Here are some questions you might want to ask and answer. Remember that these are just guide or suggested questions. Feel free to expand your discussions.

1. What do you and your family usually eat for breakfast?
   Ano ang madalas na kinakain ng inyong pamilya sa almusal?
2. What does your family cook on special occasions?
   Ano ang niluluto ng pamilya mo sa mga espesyal na okasyon?
3. What kind of restaurants do you like? What do you order?
   Anong klaseng restawran ang gusto mo? Ano ang inoorder mo?
4. What is your favorite Filipino food? Why?
   Ano ang paborito mong pagkaing Filipino? Bakit?

Pakikinig: Mga Pagkaing Mainit at May Sabaw, Patok Ngayong Tag-ulan Hot Food and Soups, Popular During the Rainy Season

Pagbabasa Reading
Ampalaya Bitter Melon

This exercise has two components. First, read the following poem which I had written for my Tagalog/Filipino students. Encircle the words that you know, especially those related to food—for example, **mapait**, **gulay**, **bayan**, **dose anyos**, **bata**, **estudyante**, **singtamis**, **lutong**, etc. Hint: some of the words seem to be familiar yet unfamiliar—for example, you know that **pait** means bitter. With the affix **kasim** (same)—you can guess that this means, "with the same bitterness."

Then, draw squares, around the words that are derived from English and Spanish, and try to guess the meanings of these words—for example, **aktibista** and **istorya**. Finally, look up the meaning of the words you don't know.

Read the poem and then answer the questions that come after it. More instructions follow the questions.

Ampalaya: Isang Liham Para sa Aking Mga Mag-Aaral ng Filipino

Ampalaya.
Mapait na gulay
Ang ampalaya.
Kasimpait ng mga salaysay
Mula sa tinubuang bayan:
Dose anyos na bata, nagbigti dahil sa kahirapan.
Dalawang estudyanteng aktibista,
Ginahasa at pinahirapan ng militar.
Daan-daang tao na nawalan ng tahanan dahil sa bagyong dumaan.
Pitong mangggawang magsasaka,
Binaril habang nagwewelga.

Sana'y hindi ganito kapait
Ang mga balitang natatanggap.
Sana'y maaaring ibabad
Sa asin,
Banlawan sa tubig,
Pigain hanggang sa mawala ang pait
Tulad ng pagkikibit-balikat at pagbibingi-bingihan
Ng ilang kababayan.
Tulad ng paghahanda ng ampalaya.

Kung sana'y makapagkuwento na lang ako
Ng istoryang sintamis ng leche flan,
Sinsarap at sinlutong
Ng lechon.
Ngunit walang tamis-sarap-lutong
Sa balita sa panahon
Ng panganib at panlilinlang
Sa ating bayan.

Ngunit kung makikinig kayo,
Mahal kong mga mag-aaral,
Sa mga kuwentong ampalaya
Mula sa bayan ng inyong mga ninuno,
Inyong mababatid
Na ang pagiging Filipino,
Ay wala sa dila at tiyan
Na kayang sikmurain ang pagkain
Ng ampalayang malupit ang pait.

Before reading the translation, try to answer the following questions:

1. How can we describe the vegetable **ampalaya**?
2. What news from the Philippines is shared by the poet? Give at least two news items.
3. What do cooks do to remove the bitterness from **ampalaya**?
4. What other kind of stories can one tell?
5. What is the poet's final statement?

Now, compare the original poem with the translation by Mark Pangilinan. Compared to prose, it is easier to compare original poetry with its translation because the lines are more brief.

Ampalaya: A Letter to My Filipino Language Class Students Translation by Mark Pangilinan

Ampalaya.
The bitter melon
is true to its name.
Bitter as the stories
from the land it ripens on:
Twelve-year-old girl,
Hangs herself to beat hunger.
Two student activists,
Raped and tortured by the military.
Hundreds of citizens
losing homes to a typhoon,
Seven peasant workers,
Gunned down at Hacienda picket line.

I wish the stories
were not this bitter.
That I could rub them
with salt,
Rinse them with water,
Press and wring the bitterness out,

the way many *kababayans* think
forgetting
is as easy as taking the bitterness
out of *ampalaya*.

Perhaps I could tell you stories
rich and sweet as *leche flan*,
crisp and succulent as
lechon skin.
But sweet-succulent-crispy
is not on the menu
in these times of danger and
doublespeak
in our country.
And still, if you would listen,
my darling students,
to these *ampalaya* stories
of the homeland,
You may yet learn that
being a Filipino,
is not about having the taste
or the stomach to eat
the bitter melon.
Ampalaya.

Pagsusulat Writing: Exploring Metaphors

In the reading exercise above, you learned how the **ampalaya** was used as a metaphor. Write either a short poem, story or essay using a food item or a dish as a metaphor. Here are a few options you can explore.

1. Write about a favorite food and relate it to a person in your life;
2. Write about a food that you remember from childhood and a particular incident related to it;
3. Write about a special dish that someone has prepared for you;
4. Write about a food item to talk about something abstract like love, pain, war, peace, etc.

Paglalagom Summing Up

In this lesson, we have:

- Reviewed/studied words related to food, preparing dishes, utensils, and the eating experience;
- Practiced a restaurant role-play with a problem situation;
- Studied affixes used for verbs in causative sentences.

Aralin 5
Lesson

Pagpunta sa Klinika ng Doktor
Going to a Doctor's Clinic

This is the fifth review and expansion lesson in this book. In this lesson, review/study parts of the body, words and phrases you can use to talk about illnesses, and the imperative form of the verb and adverbs.

Diyalogo Dialogue: Sa Klinika At a Clinic

Study the following dialogue. In this situation, Armael has a fever, a headache and a runny nose. He is consulting a doctor.

DOKTOR : **Ano ang maitutulong ko sa iyo?**
How can I help you?
ARMAEL : **Masama ho kasi ang pakiramdam ko.**
It's because I don't feel well.

DOKTOR : **Ano ba ang nangyari?**
What happened?
ARMAEL : **Naglalakad ho ako sa parke nang naulanan ako kahapon.**
I was walking in the park when I got rained on yesterday.

DOKTOR : **Tingnan natin ang temperatura mo.**
Let us check your temperature.

ARMAEL : **Naku, ang taas pala ng temparatura ko.**
Oh no, my temperature is so high!

DOKTOR : **Ano pa ang nararamdaman mo?**
What else do you feel?

ARMAEL : **Masakit ho ang ulo ko at kahapon pa ako ubo nang ubo.**
My head hurts and I have been coughing since yesterday.

DOKTOR : **May sipon ka rin ba?**
Do you also have a runny nose?

ARMAEL : **Oho.**
Yes.

DOKTOR : **Inumin mo ang tabletas na ito nang tatlong beses isang araw.**
Take these tablets three times a day.

ARMAEL : **Puwede na ho ba akong pumasok ng klase mamayang hapon?**
Can I go to class this afternoon?

DOKTOR : **Huwag kang pumasok sa klase ngayon. Magpahinga ka para gumaling ka agad.**
Do not go to class today. Rest so that you can get well at once.

ARMAEL : **Ano pa ho ang dapat kong gawin?**
What else should I do?

DOKTOR : **Ipinapayo kong uminom ka ng maraming tubig at juice.**
I advise you to drink a lot of water and juice.

ARMAEL : **Salamat ho.**
Thank you.

DOKTOR : **Walang anuman.**
Welcome.

Bokabularyo Vocabulary

Review/study the following words and phrases:

WORDS TO DESCRIBE THE PARTS OF THE BODY: **ulo** (head); **kilay** (eyebrow); **mata** (eyes); **pilikmata** (eyelashes); **talukap ng mata** (eyelids); **ilong** (nose); **noo** (forehead); **tenga** (ears); **pisngi** (cheeks); **bibig/bunganga** (mouth); **ngipin** (teeth); **gilagid** (gums); **baba** (chin); **buhok** (hair); **leeg** (neck); **balikat** (shoulder); **braso** (arms); **siko** (elbow); **pulso** (wrist; also, pulse); **kamay** (hands); **daliri** (fingers); **hinlalaki** (thumb); **hintuturo** (index finger); **kalingkingan** (little finger); **kuko** (nails); **dibdib** (chest); **suso** (breast); **tiyan/sikmura** (stomach); **puso** (heart); **likod** (back); **bituka** (intestines); **matris** (uterus; womb); **baywang** (waist); **balakang** (hips); **hita** (thighs); **tuhod** (knee); **binti** (legs); **paa** (feet); **talampakan** (soles); **bukongbukong** (ankle); **daliri sa paa** (toes); **puwet** (buttocks); **puki** (vagina); **titi** (penis)

WORDS RELATED TO ILLNESSES: **lagnat** (fever); **sipon** (runny nose; colds); **ubo** (cough); **ubo nang ubo** (constantly coughing); **naninikip ang dibdib** (tightening of the chest); **hindi makahinga** (cannot breathe); **nahihilo** (dizzy); **makati ang balat** (itchy skin); **pulmonya** (pneumonia); **kanser** (cancer); **alta presyon** (high blood pressure); **atake sa puso** (heart attack); **sakit sa puso** (heart ailment); **tisis/t.b.** (tubercolosis); **diyabetes** (diabetes); **sakit sa matris** (illness related to a woman's reproductive organs); **rayuma** (rheumatism/arthritis); **hika** (asthma); **sakit sa baga** (lung disease); **suka nang suka** (keeps on vomiting); **nagtatae** (diarrhea); **impeksiyon** (infection); **nana** (pus); **butlig** (cyst-like growth on the skin); **bungang-araw** (prickly heat); **pigsa** (boils); **namamaga/ pamamaga** (swelling; swelling of); **sumasakit/makirot** (painful); **pananakit** (pain); **naghihilom/paghilom** (healing/healing of, usually referring to wounds); **gumagaling/ paggaling** (getting well; to become well); **lumalala/paglala** (worsening; to become worse, usually referring to sickness)

PHRASES THAT CAN BE USED TO DESCRIBE OTHER MEDICAL CONDITIONS: **Nasunog ang balat** (flesh/skin got burned); **nasugatan ako** (I got wounded); **may mga pasa** (has bruises); **tumaas ang lagnat** (temperature became higher; literally, fever became higher); **nagkumbulsiyon** (had convulsions); **nawalan ng malay** (lost consciousness); **hinimatay** (fainted); **nabali ang buto/braso/binti** (bones/arm/leg got broken); **nagkaroon ng impeksiyon** (had an infection)

WORDS AND PHRASES TO DESCRIBE INCIDENTS OR ACCIDENTS WHICH MAY HAVE LED TO INJURY OR DEATH: **naulanan** (got rained on); **nadulas** (slipped); **nahulog/bumagsak** (fell); **nabagsakan** (have something fall on you); **may natapakan** (there was something I slipped on); **nahawaan** (got infected by); **nalunod** (drowned); **inanod** (was carried by the flow of water); **nasagasaan** (got hit or run over by a vehicle, used when people get hit); **nabangga** (get hit, used for example, when vehicles get hit by another vehicle); **nakaladkad** (was dragged); **nakagat** (was bitten); **nasaksak** (was stabbed); **nabaril** (was shot); **natamaan ng bala** (was hit by a bullet); **nadaplisan ng bala** (was grazed by a bullet); **nagpatiwakal** (committed suicide)

WORDS AND PHRASES RELATED TO CURING MEDICAL CONDITIONS: **uminom ng tabletas/ kapsula/gamot** (take tablets/capsule/medicine); **magpa-iniksiyon** (to get injected); **nagpabakuna** (to get vaccinated); **magpa-opera** (to get an operation); **magpahinga** (to rest); **magpagaling** (to work on getting well); **ilagay sa cast** (put in a cast); **kailangang tahiin** (has to be sutured); **magpa-therapy** (to get therapy); **umiwas** (avoid); **magpatingin/magpakonsulta** (to see/consult a doctor); **magpakuha ng presyon** (to ask someone to take one's blood pressure); **magpa-eksamen** (to have an examination/ test taken); **magpa-x-ray** (have one's x-ray taken); **magpasuri ng dugo** (to have one's blood examined); **lagyan ng benda** (put a bandage)

ADVERBS OF FREQUENCY: **palagi/lagi** (often); **madalas** (frequent); **paminsan-minsan** (sometimes); **bihira** (rarely); **hindi kailanman** (never); **isang beses**, **dalawang beses**, **tatlong beses isang araw** (once, twice, thrice a day); **tuwing ika-apat na oras** (every four hours); **minsan sa isang linggo** (once a week)

OTHER WORDS AND PHRASES: **dapat** (should); **kailangan** (need); **huwag** (don't); **iwasan** (avoid); **bawal** (forbidden); **ugaliin** (make it a habit); **kung kinakailangan** (as needed); **nang** (used here to mean "when"); **habang** (while); **nangyari** (happened)

Mga Pangungusap at Pagsasanay

First, let us study sentences that can describe incidents/circumstances that may have led to an illness. Note how some of the verbs in these sentences use the affixes **na- -an** (these verbs shown underlined) used for causative sentences.

1. **Naglalakad ako sa parke nang naulanan ako kahapon.**
   I was walking in the park when I got rained on yesterday.
2. **Naglilinis si Niño ng booksheves nang nabagsakan ang paa niya ng mga libro.**
   Niño was cleaning the bookshelves when his books fell on his feet.
3. **Nagluluto ang nanay ni Rochelle nang aksidenteng nabuhusan ng kumukulong tubig ang kamay niya.**
   Rochelle's mother was cooking when boiling water accidentally got poured on her hand.
4. **Nabangga si Paulene ng kotse habang nagmamaneho siya papunta sa opisina.**
   Paulene [=Paulene's car] got hit by a car while she was driving to the office.
5. **Nadulas si Kriya sa sidewalk dahil natapakan niya ang balat ng saging.**
   Kriya slipped on the sidewalk because there was a banana peel [he slipped on].
6. **Nabaril ang security guard ng bangko ng holdaper.**
   The security guard was shot by the hold-upper/robber.

Now, study the following sentences that can be used to describe one's health/medical conditions. Note the use of adverbs that describe time. Remember, there are no present perfect (use of "have been"), present perfect continuous (for example, "have been having," "have been going") and past perfect tenses in Filipino. The word **na** suffices, although literally, this is equivalent to "already." In the sentences below where **nang** is used, note that this is a contracted form of **na na** (literally, already that). The literal translations are also provided to help you understand sentence construction better.

1. **Tatlong araw na akong may sipon at ubo nang ubo.**
   I have had a runny nose and have been continuously coughing for three days.
   (literally, Three days already I LINKER have runny nose and coughing and coughing.)
2. **Nitong nakaraang linggo, palaging masakit ang ulo at may lagnat ako.**
   This past week, my head always hurts [=have been having headaches] and I have been having a fever.
   (literally, This past week, always painful MARKER head and have fever I.)
3. **Madalas na naninikip ang dibdib ko at hindi ako makahinga**
   My chest often "tightens" [=I often feel tightening in my chest] and I cannot breathe.
   (literally, Often that tightening MARKER chest my and cannot I breathe.)
4. **Isang linggo nang makati ho ang balat ko.**
   My skin has been itchy for a week now.
   (literally, One week already that itchy HONORIFIC MARKER skin my.)
5. **Dalawang linggo nang hindi gumagaling ang sugat ko.**
   My wound has not healed [in the past] two weeks.
   (literally, Two weeks already that not healing MARKER wound my.)

Finally, study sentences which may be used by a doctor/medical professional to give instructions or advice to patients. Note the use of the words **dapat** (should), **kailangan** (need), **huwag** (don't), **bawal** (forbidden), and **ugaliin** (make it a habit).

1. **Inumin mo ang mga tabletas na ito nang tatlong beses isang araw.**
   Take these tablets three times a day.
2. **Dapat kang magpahinga. Huwag kang pumasok sa opisina.**
   You should rest. Do not go to the office.
3. **Bawal kay Juan na kumain ng matatabang pagkain.**
   Fatty foods are forbidden to Juan.
4. **Ugaliin mong mag-ehersisyo nang tatlong beses sa isang linggo.**
   Make it a habit to exercise three times a week.
5. **Kailangang tahiin ang sugat ng taong nasaksak.**
   The wound [=flesh of the wound] of the person who got stabbed has to be sutured.

Pagsasanay Practice: Role-play

Study the following situations provided and review the words and phrases you have learned in the vocabulary section.

Then, fill in the blanks and complete the sentences in the first two situations and practice the role-play with your partner. For the fourth situation, make up the dialogue with your partner and practice it. You can also make up the fifth situation and give it to a partner or another group in your class.

Classroom learners should work in pairs or groups of 3 while individual learners should write down the dialogues. For classroom learners, another option is to divide the class into groups and assign each group a role-play which they can then present to the class. After the presentations, each group is assigned to talk about or summarize in a few sentences the role-play of another group.

SITUATION 1: Jesi has been sick for the past two days. She has a fever and a runny nose and has also been coughing constantly. She got infected by a virus through her sister. Her doctor advises her to drink a lot of water and juice, take capsules every four hours, and get a lot of rest. She shouldn't go to school.

DOKTOR : **Ano ang pakiramdam mo?**
JESI : ______________________________ .

DOKTOR : **Ano ang nangyari?**
JESI : **Nahawaan ako ng** ____________ **dahil sa** ____________ **ko.**

DOKTOR : ____________ **mo ang mga kapsulang ito** ____________.
JESI : **Ano pa ho ang dapat kong gawin?**

DOKTOR : ______________________________ .
JESI : ______________________________ ?

DOKTOR : **Hindi ka puwedeng pumasok sa unibersidad.**

SITUATION 2: Jordan was crossing the street when he was hit by a car. His leg got broken and he has wounds and bruises on his arms. His leg is hurting badly. The doctor wants to put his leg in a cast and have an x-ray taken of his legs. The doctor also wants him to rest for a few days and to avoid using his legs. He/she gives Jordan some tablets to take when needed for the pain.

DOKTOR : **Ano ang nangyari?**
JORDAN : ______________________________.

Doktor : **Mukhang __________ ang paa mo at may mga ______ at __________ ka sa ___________ mo. Masakit ba?**

Jordan : ____.

Doktor : **Uminom ka** ____.

Jordan : **Ano pa ho ang dapat gawin?**

Doktor : ____.

Jordan : **Puwede** ____?

Doktor : ____.

Jordan : **Puwede** ____?

Doktor : ____.

Situation 3: Maria needs to tell the doctor that she fainted yesterday. She has also been having chest pains and difficulty breathing for the past week. The doctor recommends that she get her blood pressure checked and her blood examined. He/she also wants Maria to get an x-ray taken of her lungs. During the visit, the doctor also inquires if there is a history of heart ailment in the family and Maria says that her mother has a heart condition. The doctor advises her to eat fish and vegetables and to avoid meat. He/she also advises her to exercise regularly.

Doktor : **Ano** ____?

Maria : ____.

Doktor : **Ano pa** ____?

Maria : ____**nitong nakaraang linggo.**

Doktor : **Kailangan** _______________________________________**. Mayroon bang kasaysayan ng** _______________________________________ **sa pamilya mo?**

Maria : ____.

Doktor : **Ipinapayo kong** ____.

Maria : **Puwede ho ba akong kumain ng baka at baboy?**

Doktor : ____.

Maria : **Ano pa ho ang kailangan kong gawin?**

Doktor : ____.

SITUATION 4: Your friend got hit by a stray bullet when the police officers fired at the protestors during a peaceful rally in Manila. Luckily, according to the doctor, the bullet only grazed his shoulders and he is okay. You brought him to the hospital, and because he lost consciousness, the doctor is talking to you. You want to know if you can bring him home but the doctor wants him to stay the night at the hospital. The doctor treated his wound but did not have to sew the flesh. He/she also prescribed pills which your friend can take when in pain.

DOKTOR : ____?
YOU : ____.

DOKTOR : ____?
YOU : ____.

DOKTOR : ____?
YOU : ____.

DOKTOR : ____?
YOU : ____.

DOKTOR : ____?
YOU : ____.

SITUATION 5: Write your own situation in the space provided below. For classroom learners, ask your partner or another group to make up a dialogue. For individual learners, write the dialogue.

____
____
____
____
____
____
____
____
____
____
____
____
____
____
____
____

Talakayan Discussion

Ask and answer questions about your last visit to the doctor. Classroom learners should work in pairs or groups. Individual learners should write down the questions and answers.

Here are some of the questions you can ask. They are given in English, and part of your task is to translate them into Tagalog/Filipino.

1. When did you last visit a doctor or a hospital?
2. What happened? What caused the illness/injury?
3. What did the doctor prescribe?
4. How long were you sick?

Gramatika Grammar

Review/Study the following grammar points: **na-an** affixes, location or direction focus; adverbs of time; use of modal verbs and adverbs of time.

"Na-an" affixes

Review/Study verbs using the **na-an** affix used in causative sentences with a locative or directional focus. This means that the focus is on the location or direction of the action.

In the dialogue we studied the following sentence:

Naglalakad ho ako sa parke nang naulanan ako kahapon.
I was walking in the park when I got rained on yesterday.

With the affix **na-an**, we know that the action is directed towards **ako** (I)—so the person speaking was the one who got rained on.

In the sample sentences, we studied the following sentences:

1. **Naglilinis si Niño ng booksheves nang nabagsakan ang paa niya ng mga libro.**
   Niño was cleaning the bookshelves when his books fell on his feet.
2. **Nadulas si Kriya sa sidewalk dahil natapakan niya ang balat ng saging.**
   Kriya slipped on the sidewalk because there was a banana peel he slipped on.

In these two sentences, we understand that that the books fell on Niño's feet and that Kriya stepped on a banana peel.

When does the use of the **na-an** become confusing? Most students get confused with the use of the pronouns **ko** and **ako**. Let us study two examples.

If I want to say that I stepped on someone, I can say:

Natapakan ko <u>ang</u> paa ni Kriya habang sumasayaw.
I stepped on Kriya's foot while dancing.

This means that the focus is on Kriya's foot as shown by the marker **ang**.

When do we use **ako** instead of **ko**? We use **ako** when the speaker (**ako** or I) was the one stepped on.

Natapakan <u>ako</u> ni Kriya habang sumasayaw.
Kriya stepped on me [=my foot] while dancing.

To avoid confusion, ask the following questions: Where is the action directed? Who "receives" the action?

Adverbs of Frequency

There are two ways by which we can answer the question "**Gaano kadalas**" or "How often?"

One, we can use adverbs of frequency such as **palagi** (always), **madalas** (often), **minsan**, **paminsan-minsan** (sometimes), **bihira** (rarely), and **hindi kailanman** (never).

Second, we can also use **isang beses/minsan** (once), **dalawang beses** (twice), **tatlong beses** (thrice), **apat na beses** (four times) etc. plus the time frame, for example, **sa isang araw** (in a day), **sa isang linggo** (in a week), **sa isang buwan** (in a month), **sa isang taon** (in a year).

Study the following examples, in question and answer format. Note also the use of **nang** which we use before adverbs.

TANONG : **Gaano ko kadalas dapat inumin ang gamot?**
How often should I take the medicine?
SAGOT : **Inumin mo ang gamot <u>nang</u> minsan isang araw.**
Take the medicine once a day.

TANONG : **Gaano kadalas kang nag-eehersisyo?**
How often do you exercise?
SAGOT : **Bihira akong nag-eehersisyo.**
I rarely exercise.

Equivalents of present perfect and present perfect continuous tense; use of "na"

As discussed in the sample sentences, there are no present perfect and present perfect continuous tenses in Tagalog/Filipino. Instead, we use the word **na**.

The best way to explain this is to first look at sentences in English which we want to translate into Tagalog/Filipino.

1. English: *Maria has had a fever for the past three days.*

For more conversational use of the language, start with the "time." Thus:
Tagalog/Filipino: **Tatlong araw na na may lagnat si Maria.** (literally, Three days **already that** have fever MARKER Maria.)

Now, as you can see, **na na** is awkward, so we contract this into:
Tagalog/Filipino: **Tatlong araw nang may lagnat si Maria.**

2. English: *I have been sick for a week.*

Tagalog/Filipino: **Isang linggo na ako na may sakit.** (literally, One week **already I that** have sickness.)

Now, let us contract **ako na** into **akong** for ease of speaking.
Tagalog/Filipino: **Isang linggo na akong may sakit.**

3. English: *I have been having chest pains for five days.*

Tagalog/Filipino: **Limang araw nang naninikip ang dibdib ko.** (literally, Five days already that tightening MARKER chest my.)

Note that in English, we use "having chest pains." However in Filipino, almost all nouns can be made into verbs. So instead of saying "chest pains" (**paninikip ng dibdib**), we would translate this into "**naninikip ang dibdib**" (literally, chest is tightening), which is a clear illustration. The root word here is **sikip** which means "tight."

What are we trying to learn here? For medical terms and ways to describe medical conditions, it is best to learn how to say things naturally in Filipino. While "**sumasakit ang dibdib ko**" (my chest is painful) is not wrong, the more appropriate and clearer way is to say, "**naninikip ang dibdib**." Also note that the word **dibdib** and not **puso** (heart) is used, even when it seems like one is referring to a heart ailment.

In the next exercise, practice how to translate explanations of medical conditions.

Pagsasanay sa Pagsasalin Translation Exercise

Translate the following medical conditions and medical advice from Filipino to English. Refer to the vocabulary words, sentences, and grammar notes you have just studied. This practical exercise is meant for you to practice how to translate, in case you should be asked upon to assist a patient/doctor.

1. PASYENTE : **Isang linggo na akong palaging nahihilo. Noong isang araw, hinimatay ako. Madalas ding sumasakit ang ulo ko.**

   PATIENT : ____

   ____.

2. PASYENTE : **Nabagsakan ang braso ko ng mga libro nang naglilinis ako ng kuwarto. Isang linggo na hong namamaga ang braso ko at kulay asul ang balat ko.**

   PATIENT : ____

   ____.

3. PASYENTE : **Nakagat ako ng aso ng kapitbahay ko. Isang araw na hong masakit na masakit ang sugat ko. Pakiramdam ko ay lalagnatin ako.**

   PATIENT : ____

   ____.

4. Doktor : **Kailangan mong magpa-x-ray at kailangang suriin ang dugo mo. Inumin mo ang mga tabletas na ito nang dalawang beses isang araw. Huwag kang kumain ng pagkain na maraming taba.**

   Doctor : ____

   ____

   ____.

5. Doktor : **Kailangang ilagay sa cast ang paa mo. Magpahinga ka nang isang linggo at huwag maglakad. Pagkatapos tanggalin ang cast, kailangan mong mag-therapy.**

   Doctor : ____

   ____

   ____.

6. Doktor : **Kailangang alisin ang bala sa katawan niya, tahiin ang sugat at lagyan ng benda. Kailangan niyang magpahinga ng isang linggo. Puwede siyang uminom ng gamot kapag sumasakit ang sugat niya mula sa operasyon.**

   Doctor : ____

   ____

   ____.

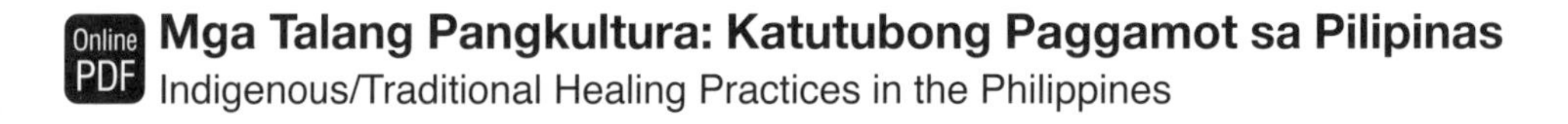

Mga Talang Pangkultura: Katutubong Paggamot sa Pilipinas
Indigenous/Traditional Healing Practices in the Philippines

Talakayan/Pagsusulat: Karanasan sa Tradisyonal na Paggamot Experiences in Traditional Medicine

Discuss your experiences with traditional healing practices. Classroom learners should form groups of four or five, while individual learners should write down the answers.

Here are some topics you might want to discuss. Remember that these are just guides or suggested questions. Feel free to expand your discussions.

1. Have you had herbal teas from the Philippines such as **pito-pito**, **banaba**, **sambong** or **lagundi**? **Naka-inom ka na ba ng mga halamang tsaa mula sa Pilipinas kagaya ng pito-pito, banaba, sambong, o lagundi?** Please share your experience.
2. Have you or any of your family members/friends experienced going to a **hilot**, **arbularyo**, **babaylan** or **espiritista**? What happened? **Nakapunta ka na ba o ang iyong mga kapamilya/kaibigan sa isang hilot, arbularyo, babaylan o espiritista? Ano ang nangyari?**

3. Have you watched the films *Himala* by Ishmael Bernal or "The Healing" by Chito Rono? What were these films about? **Napanood mo ba ang sineng "Himala" ni Ishmael Bernal o ang "The Healing" ni Chito Rono? Tungkol saan ang pelikula/mga pelikulang ito?**

Pakikinig: Mga Karaniwang Sakit sa Balat Tuwing Summer Common Skin Diseases During Summer

Pagbabasa Reading: "Diskurso ni Dok"
The Doctor's Discourse by Romulo Baquiran, Jr.

Read the following personal essay from Romulo Baquiran Jr's book *Sagad sa Buto: Hospital Diary at iba pang Sanaysay* (Manila: UST Publishing House, 2010). This book won the National Book Award (non-fiction prose) in 2011.

To prepare for this essay: review/study the following words: **maghinang** (to join together by welding; can be used metaphorically); **kalamnan** (muscles); **gilid** (side); **nabasag** (broken); **pang-aliw** (for pleasure); **katotohanan** (reality); **tiim-bagang** (literally, with clenched molars; to face something with willpower); **tantiya** (estimate); **kapangyarihan** (power); **kabado** (nervous); **panaginip** (dream)

Some of the words are derived from English. Try to guess the meaning of the following words: **diskurso**; **papet**; **operasyon**; **badyet**; **mate-tense**.

Diskurso Ni Dok

ni Romulo Baquiran Jr

Mahusay na doktor si Dr. Lai. Iyan ang larawan ng kaibigan kong nagrekomenda sa kaniya. Kung pasyente ka, dapat mong paniwalaan ang doktor mo.

Orthopedic surgery ang specialty ni Dok. Very professional ang dating. Sa teorya ni Foucault, swak na swak siya sa power discourse. Ang kilos, ang delivery ng diagnosis, ang tindig, ang salamin. Susunod ka sa kanya at maniniwala sa sinasabi niya.

Tiningnan niya ang x-ray at hindi masyadong maganda ang lagay ng sakong ko. Kakailanganin ang metal plates sa operasyon para maghinang muli ang nadurog na buto. Kailangang maghintay ng limang araw para humupa ang pamamaga ng kalamnan. Bubuksan ng parang letrang L ang gilid ng paa para maayos ang loob na nabasag.

Sana pediatrician na lang ang ipinadala. May dalang papet na pang-aliw mas maganda. Ayaw ng tao ang sobrang katotohanan, sabi nga. Pero dahil matanda na ako, kailangang harapin nang tiim-bagang itong operasyon.

Business side agad. "Magkano po ang badyet Dok?"

"Hmm, professional fee 20k, anesthesiologist 10k, metal plates 10k, plus medication and laboratory fees."

Mga 50k ang tantiya ko. Ang gastos pala. "Salamat po Dok," ang nasabi ko na lang. Diskurso ng walang kapangyarihan.

Nang kunin ng attendant ang blood pressure ko, sabi nito "Itay, ang taas po ng dugo ninyo." Itay ka diyan. Siyempre, sino ang hindi mate-tense sa nag-aabang na gastos para sa operasyon.

At kabado na ako sa trauma na idudulot ng mismong operasyon. Hindi na panaginip ito.

1. How would you describe Dr. Lai as a doctor?
2. According to the x-ray, what needs to be done to the patient/author?
3. How much would the total procedure cost?
4. Describe the feelings of the patient/author as his blood pressure was being taken.

Pagsusulat Writing: **Pagsusulat Mula sa Isang Interbyu**
Writing from an Interview

There are two steps to this exercise. First, you need to conduct an interview with a classmate, a friend, a family member or someone who you think would be an interesting subject. Second, you need to write about that person.

Pretend you are a community health worker or a doctor's assistant. You would like to ask your interviewee the following: last visit to the doctor (**huling pagbisita sa doktor**), common illnesses in the family (**mga karaniwang sakit ng pamilya**), current condition/health problems (**mga nararamdaman/mga problema sa kalusugan**). Review the vocabulary words and sentences you have studied.

Start with the line:

Ininterbyu ko si ____

____

____

____

____

Paglalagom Summing Up

In Lesson 5, we have:

- Reviewed/studied words and phrases related to body parts, illnesses, medical conditions, and treatments;
- Reviewed adverbs of frequency;
- Studied how to express in Filipino sentences that are in the past perfect and present perfect tenses in English;
- Practiced translation skills.

Aralin 6
Lesson

Isang Araw sa Buhay Ko

A Day in My Life

In this lesson, we are reviewing/learning how to talk about "daily lives" using verbs expressing habitual action. We are also learning how to make our sentences flow better using connecting words, studying plurality in verbs and question words, and practicing causative sentences.

 **Diyalogo** Dialogue**: Abala Ako!** I am Busy!

In Lesson 1, Katie was interviewing Rose and learning about her family and her work. In the continuation of the interview, Katie wants to know about Rose's day-to-day life as a caregiver. Remember, Katie is using the honorific **po** *because Rose is older than her.*

KATIE : **Puwede niyo po bang ikuwento sa akin kung paano nagsisimula ang araw ninyo?**
Can you narrate to me how your day starts?

ROSE : **Araw-araw, gumigising ako nang alas-singko y medya ng umaga dahil kailangan kong ipaghanda ng almusal ang alaga ko. Bago magluto, naliligo muna ako at nagbibihis.**
Everyday, I wake up at five thirty in the morning because I need to prepare the breakfast of my alaga *[the person I am taking care of]. Before cooking, I take a bath first and get dressed.*

KATIE : **Kayo din po ba ang nagpapakain sa kanya?**
Are you also the one feeding her?

ROSE : **Siyempre. Pagkatapos ng almusal, pinapainom ko siya ng gamot.**
Of course. After breakfast, I give her medicine.

KATIE : **Ano-ano pa po ang mga pinaggagagawa ninyo?**
What else do you do?

ROSE : **Pinaliliguan ko siya, binabasahan, at ipinapasyal sa hardin. Minsan, nanonood kami ng masasayang palabas sa telebisyon. Tuwing makalawang araw, buong maghapon kaming nasa parke. Gusto niya ng magagandang tanawin. Ipinagluluto ko siya at ako rin nagpapakain sa kanya ng tanghalian at hapunan.**
I bathe her, read [to her] and take [her] around the garden. Sometimes, we watch happy shows on television. Sometimes, we are at the park all afternoon. She likes beautiful views/sights. I also cook for her and feed her lunch and dinner.

KATIE : **Naku, abalang-abala pala kayo!**
Oh, you are so busy!

ROSE : **Oo, pero kapag tulog na siya, puwede na akong magpahinga sa kuwarto ko.**
Yes, but when she is sleeping, I can [already] rest in my room.

KATIE : **Kailan po kayo may oras para sa sarili?**
When do you have time for yourself?

ROSE : **Tuwing Linggo lang. Nagsisimba ako at nakikipagkita sa mga kaibigan ko. Kumakain kami sa labas at kung nagkakayayaan, pumupunta kami sa karaoke bar at nagsisipagkantahan. Kapag may pera ako, namimili ako para sa balikbayan box na ipinadadala ko sa pamilya ko.**
Only on Sundays. I go to church and meet my friends. We eat out and when we [end up] inviting each other, we go to the karaoke bar and sing. When I have money, I go shopping for the balikbayan *box that I send to my friends.*

KATIE : **Ano po ang pinagbibibili ninyo para sa balikbayan box?**
What [sorts of things] have you been buying for the balikbayan *box?*

ROSE : **Mga magagandang damit lang, kobre kama, at laruan.**
Just beautiful clothes, bed sheets, and toys.

KATIE : **Ano pa ho ang pinagkakaabalahan ninyo?**
What else has been keeping you busy?

ROSE : **Minsan isang buwan, dumadalo ako sa pulong ng PAWIS, iyong grupo namin ng mga tagapag-alaga at kasambahay.**
Once a month, I attend the meeting of PAWIS, the group of caregivers and domestic workers.

 Bokabularyo Vocabulary

For this lesson, focus on how affixes change the meaning of verbs. Also, observe how almost any root word and even foreign words can be transformed into verbs. Some of the words and phrases below are in the dialogue you have just read; others will be useful to you as you practice talking about your daily life. You may also remember learning some of the words in the book *Tagalog for Beginners*. Review/study these words.

VERBS THAT DESCRIBE HABITUAL ACTION OR ARE IN THEIR INCOMPLETED ASPECT (using **mag-** and **um** affixes): **nagsisimula** (starts); **gumigising** (wakes up); **bumabangon** (gets up); **naliligo** (takes a bath/shower); **nagsesepilyo** (brushes teeth); **naghihilamos** (washes face); **nagbibihis** (dresses up); **nagluluto** (cooks); **kumakain** (eats); **nag-aalmusal** (eats breakfast); **nananghalian** (eats lunch); **nagmimiminindal** (eats a snack); **naghahapunan** (eats dinner); **pumapasok** (goes to, for example, **pumapasok sa opisina**; literally, means "enters"); **pumupunta** (goes to); **sumasakay** (rides); **nagmamaneho** (drives); **naglalakad** (walks); **nagbibisikleta** (rides a bicycle); **nagbabasa** (reads); **nagsusulat** (writes); **nagpapraktis** (practices); **nag-aaral** (studies); **naglalaro** (plays, for example, **naglalaro ng tennis**); **tumutugtog** (plays, for example, **tumutugtog ng gitara** plays the guitar); **nagkokompyuter** (uses a computer); **nagpapahinga** (rests); **umuuwi** (goes home); **nanonood ng telebisyon** (watches television); **nakikinig** (listens); **natutulog** (sleeps), **naglilinis** (cleans)

VERBS USED IN THE PLURAL FORM: **pinaggagagawa** (what you have been doing); **pinagbibibili** (what you have been buying); **pinaglulululuto** (what you have been cooking); **nagsisikanta/nagsisipagkantahan** (singing); **nangagsisisayaw/nagsisipagsayawan** (dancing); **nagsisibili/nagsisipagbili** (buying). Note that in conversational Filipino, many no longer use verbs in their plural form. However, this is useful knowledge in case someone speaks/writes to you using this form.

VERBS USED WITH MODALS OR AUXILIARY VERBS (used to express ability, permission or obligation such as: **puwede** (can, used to show permission); **kailangan** (need); **gusto** (want)**; kaya** (can, used to show ability—**kaya kong ikuwento** I can narrate [to you]); **kailangan kong ihanda** (I need to prepare); **kailangan kong ipaghanda** (need to prepare [something for someone]); **gusto kong magbasa** (I want to read); **kaya kong tumugtog ng piyano** (I can play the piano)

VERBS USED IN CAUSATIVE SENTENCES (directional focus; using **in- in/-an** affixes): **pinakakain/pinapakain** (feeding someone); **pinaiinom/pinapainom** (giving someone something to drink); **pinaliliguan/pinapaliguan** (giving someone a bath); **binabasahan** (to read to someone); **ipinapasyal** (to take someone around)

Remember, both **pinakakain** and **pinapakain** mean the same. Tagalog grammar rules indicate that the correct usage is to double the root word, thus **pinakakain** should be used in writing. However, in conversational Filipino, both **pinapakain** and **pinakakain** are used. See grammar notes for more detailed explanations and examples.

Verbs used in causative sentences (directional focus; using **ipinag-**): **ipinagluluto** (to cook for someone); **ipinagsasaing** (to cook rice for someone); **ipinagpaplantsa** (to iron for someone); **ipinaglilinis** (to clean for someone)

Question words used in the plural form: ano-ano (what); **sino-sino** (who); **saan-saan** (where)

Adjectives in the plural form: masasaya (happy); **magaganda** (beautiful); **malulungkot** (sad)

nouns: pinagkakaabalahan (something/things that keep you busy); **kobre kama** (bed sheets; bed covers); **tagapag-alaga** (caregiver); **kasambahay** (domestic workers)

words and phrases that express frequency, time and duration: tuwing (every time); **tuwing Lunes** (every Monday); **tuwing umaga** (every morning); **araw-araw** (everyday); **tuwing makalawang araw** (every other day); **kapag** (when); **habang** (while); **linggo-linggo** (every week); **buwan-buwan** (every month); **taon-taon** (every year); **bago magluto** (before cooking), **pagkatapos kumain** (after eating); **buong umaga** (all morning); **maghapon** (all afternoon); **buong gabi/magdamag** (all evening); **araw at gabi** (day and night); **buong linggo** (all week); **buong buwan** (all month); **buong taon** (all year)

useful connecting words: at (and); **dahil/kasi** (because)

Mga Pangungusap Sentences

Study how the following sentences are constructed. Most of these sentences are from the dialogue we have just learned.

In *Tagalog for Beginners*, you learned how to make simple sentences that described your daily life. In the intermediate level, let us practice making sentences with two or more clauses.

Also, study how modals or auxiliary verbs such as **kailangan** (need); **gusto** (want); and **kaya (**"can", for ability); **puwede (**"can", for possibility) are used—these verb phrases are underlined.

1. **Araw-araw, gumigising ako nang alas-singko y medya ng umaga dahil kailangan kong ipaghanda ng almusal ang alaga ko.**
   Every day, I wake up at five thirty in the morning because I need to prepare the breakfast of my alaga *[the person I am taking care of].*

2. **Pero kapag tulog na siya, puwede na akong magpahinga sa kuwarto ko.**
   But when she is sleeping, I can [already] rest in my room.

3. **Kung niyayaya ako ng mga kaibigan ko, nagkakaraoke kami.**
   When my friends invite me, we do karaoke (singing in a special room equipped with microphones and other karaoke equipment.)

Now, let us study how verbs are used in causative sentences. In previous lessons, you have practiced using **nagpa-** and **pina-** (for example, **nagpaluto** and **pinaluto**, used when you asked someone to cook something for you). In this lesson, practice the use of affixes **in-an**, **in-** and **ipinag-**.

4. **Pinaliliguan ko siya, binabasahan ko siya, at ipinapasyal ko siya sa hardin.**
   I bathe her, read to her and take her around the garden.

5. **Ipinagluluto ko siya at ako rin ang nagpapakain sa kanya ng tanghalian at hapunan.**
   I also cook for her and feed her lunch and dinner.

Finally, study how question words, adjectives, and verbs are used in the plural form. Here are some examples:

6. **Ano-ano ang pinaggagagawa mo?**
   What [sorts of things] have you been doing?

7. **Ano-ano ang pinagbibibili mo?**
   What [sort of things] have you been buying?

8. **Kung nagkakayayaan, pumupunta kami sa karaoke bar at nagsisipagkantahan.**
   When we [end up] inviting each other, we go to the karaoke bar and sing.

9. **Gusto niya ng magagandang tanawin.**
   She likes beautiful views/sights.

Pagsasanay Practice

Study the following situations and make up a schedule. Use the words and verb phrases you have learned. Write at least four sentences in response to the question. Say/write at least one verb in a causative sentence and at least one verb in the plural form.

In some descriptions, you will notice the use of the past perfect progressive and present perfect progressive in the English sentences.

Remember that there is no past perfect progressive (for example, *She had been sleeping until her dog woke her up.*) or present perfect progressive (*She has been sleeping for ten hours*). In Filipino, the translations of these sentences are: **Natutulog siya hanggang sa ginising siya ng aso niya.**, and **Sampung oras na siyang natutulog.** Note the use of the incompleted aspect and the use of **na** in the second sentence.)

Situation 1: Your two friends are visiting and they have been staying with you for the past five days. You have been cooking breakfast for them in the morning. Then you usually eat, take a shower and get dressed. At around ten o'clock you usually drive them around and/or take them around the tourist attractions in your city. Sometimes, you go shopping. After dinner last night, you and your friends went dancing.

Tanong : **Ano-ano ang pinaggagagawa mo?**

Sagot : ______________________________

____

____

____

____

____

Situation 2: Your grandmother has been sick so you visited her in your hometown. You are giving your aunt a break and have volunteered to care for your grandmother. For the past week, you have been giving your grandmother her medicine three times a day and have been cooking her meals. You also give her a bath daily and sometimes take her out to the garden. On Sundays, your cousins come over to play the piano and sing songs to your grandmother.

Tanong : **Ano-ano ang pinagkakaabalahan mo ngayon?**
Sagot : ____________________

____

____

____

____

____

Situation 3: You and your siblings have been busy preparing for your trip to the Philippines. Every other day, you talk to your relatives in the Philippines to give them the latest news about your trip and ask them what they want you to bring as gifts. You and your siblings have been shopping for clothes, shoes, bags, and toys. You have also been checking travel sites on the internet to check on travel deals to nearby Southeast Asian countries. In the evenings, you have been working extra hours after five o'clock so you can earn more money for the trip.

Tanong : **Ano-ano ang pinaggagagawa mo ngayon?**
Sagot : ____________________

____

____

____

____

____

Gramatika at Pagsasanay

Study how verbs and questions words can be made plural and how to conjugate verbs with receiver focus in causative sentences.

Plurality

As mentioned earlier, you do not have to use verbs, adjectives and questions in the plural form, but it is an option, and it is useful to know this because someone might speak to you this way or you might read something in the plural form.

For **question words**, only **ano** (what), **sino** (who) and **saan** (where), are used in the plural form. Simply double the question words. Thus, we say **ano-ano**, **sino-sino** and **saan-saan**. Study the following sample sentences:

Ano-anong mga putahe ang niluto mo?
What dishes did you cook?
Sino-sino ang mga pumunta sa party mo?
Who came to your party?
Saan-saan kayo namasyal?
Where did you go around?

Note that you if you say, "**Anong mga putahe ang niluto mo?**" or "**Sino ang mga pumunta sa party mo**," or "**Saan kayo namasyal**," these sentences are perfectly fine as well.

For **adjectives**, double the first syllable of the root word. For example:

(Singular)	(Plural)
Maganda ang bulaklak.	**Magaganda ang mga bulaklak.**
The flower is beautiful.	*The flowers are beautiful.*
Masarap ang putahe.	**Masasarap ang mga putahe.**
The dish is delicious.	*The dishes are delicious.*

Let's practice:

Can you give the plural form of the following words?

Masaya (happy) — ____________________________

Malungkot (sad) — ____________________________

Mabango (fragrant) — __________________________

Maluwang (wide) — ___________________________

Malaki (big) — ______________________________

What did you notice with the adjectives above? They all use the affix **ma-**. Note that adjectives that do not use the affix **ma-**, such as **bago** (new), **mahal** (expensive; **ma** here is not an affix but part of the root word), and **luma** (old) do not have plural forms. Again, remember that this a choice. Some native speakers do not use the plural form.

For **verbs**, we use the affixes **nagsi-**, **nangagsi-** and to show social action, **nagsipag-an**.

For example:

(Singular)	(Plural)
Bumili ako ng bestida.	**Nagsibili kami ng mga damit.**
I bought a dress.	*We bought dresses.*
	Nangagsibili kami ng mga damit.
	We bought dresses.

With verbs that show social action, usually the **nag-an** affixes are enough and hardly anyone uses the **nagsipag-** and **nangagsipag-** affixes. However, you may still find them in some literary texts, so it is good to know them even if you don't use them in everyday conversations. For example:

Nagkantahan kami sa karaoke bar.
We sang with each other at the karaoke bar.
Nagsipagkantahan kami sa karaoke bar.
We sang with each other at the karaoke bar.
Nangagsipagkantahan kami sa karaoke bar.
We sang with each other at the karaoke bar.

As you can see, you can say the same thing in different ways.

Practice by writing down the plural form of the following verbs; the first ones have been done for you:

Kain — nagsikain; nagsipagkain

Laro — nagsilaro; nangagsilaro; nagsipaglaro; nangagsipaglaro

Sayaw; sayawan — nagsisayaw, nangagsisayaw; nagsipagsayawan; nangagsipagsayawan

Tugtog; tugtugan — ______________________

Inom — ______________________

Langoy — ______________________

Nood — ______________________

Lakad — ______________________

Takbo — ______________________

Verbs in Causative Sentences

We use the affixes **ipinag-** and **pina- -an** for the receiver or goal focus in causative sentences. Compare the following sentences.

Use **ipinag-** when there is a recipient or goal of the action in the sentence. In this first sentence, the focus is on the receiver of the action, the sister:

Ipinagluto ni Maristelle ng sopas ang kapatid niya. *Maristelle cooked soup for her sister/brother.*

In this second sentence, the focus is on the doer of the action, Maristelle:

Nagluto si Maristelle ng sopas para sa kapatid niya.

In this third sentence, the focus is on the object, the soup.

Sopas ang niluto ni Maristelle para sa kapatid niya.

Do not be confused. You may remember at this point the affixes **nagpa- ang pina/ ipina-** and **pina-an**. You use these affixes only when you want to say that you asked someone else to do something and **you are not doing it yourself**. For example:

Nagpaluto si Maristelle ng sopas para sa kapatid niya sa kusinera.
Maristelle asked the cook to make soup for her sister/brother.
Pinalutuan ni Maristelle ng sopas ang kapatid niya sa kusinera.
Soup is what Maristelle asked the cook to make for her sister/brother.

Use **pina-an** when the verb can stand whether or not there is a direct object. Here are some examples:

Pinaliguan ni Simon ang sanggol.
Simon gave the baby a bath.
Pinakain ni Fia ang aso.
Fia fed the dog.
Pinakain ni Fia ang aso ng dog treats.
Fia fed the dog dog treats.

Practice by translating the following sentences. Use the affixes **ipinag-** and **pina-**:

1. I gave my youngest sister a bath.

   ____

2. The nurse gave the patient his/her medicine this morning.

   ____

3. Clyde will take his cousins [sightseeing] around the city.

____

4. Katrina cooked pansit for her friend because it was her friend's birthday.

____

5. Mari's grandmother is preparing lunch for him.

____

Online PDF

Mga Talang Pangkultura
Maynila Manila

Interbyu/Talakayan Interview/Discussion
Pangkaraniwang Araw sa Buhay ng Isang Tao
An Ordinary Day in the Life of a Person

There are two parts to this discussion exercise: first, a discussion on the culture notes you have just read; and second, a discussion on the childhood everyday life of a person you know.

Here are some guide questions based on the culture notes. Remember that these are just suggested questions. Feel free to expand your discussions, but remember to practice Filipino (I need to emphasize this because even some of my students sometimes think they can discuss in English):

1. How did the privileged Spaniards, mestizos, and Filipinos mentioned in the article lead such leisurely lives? In your opinion, what enabled them to do so?
   Paanong nagkakaroon ng buhay na may layaw ang mga Kastila, mestizo at Filipino? Sa inyong opinyon, ano ang nagbibigay sa kanila ng ganitong pribilehiyo?

2. Is it true that domestic workers are poor because they are lazy? Why or why not?
   Totoo ba na mahihirap ang mga kasambahay dahil tamad sila? Bakit o bakit hindi?

For the second part of this exercise, you need to interview someone. Whether you are a classroom learner or an individual learner, try to communicate with someone either by phone or text (text is advised for classroom learners). Choose someone older who was a child during the 50s, the 60s or the 70s, or a decade you are not familiar with. This can be a parent, a grandparent, an aunt/uncle or a friend.

1. When he/she was a child, what time did he/she wake up? What did he/she do in the morning after getting up?
   Noong bata siya, anong oras siya gumigising? Ano-ano ang mga ginagawa niya pagkabangon?

2. What things did he/she do after school?
   Ano-ano ang mga ginagawa niya pagkatapos ng eskuwela?

Then, if you are a classroom learner, share the information that you got with your partner or group mates. If you are an individual learner, write down as much as you can remember from your interview.

Pagsasanay sa Pagsasalin Translation Practice

Practice your translation skills by translating some accounts of life during the Japanese Occupation of the Philippines. These short paragraphs are from some of the transcribed interviews found in the book *Kuwentong Bayan: Noong Panahon ng Hapon: Everyday Life in a Time of War* by Thelma B. Kintanar, Clemen C. Aquino, Patricia B. Arinto and Ma. Luisa T. Camagay (UP Press, 2006).

You know most of the words used by the interviewees because these are common words, and most of them can be found either in this book or in *Tagalog for Beginners*. Should there be words you are not familiar with, consult a dictionary. This is part of your learning experience as a translator.

Remember that after your first draft, you need to read your translation to edit it. Does it sound natural? How can you make it sound more natural in your target language—English? You may want to change the word order or the structure of the sentence.

Text 1: Excerpt from an interview with Marcelo San Diego, p. 362
San Diego: Alam ninyo, noong panahon ko, ako'y magsasaka. Meron ho akong kapirasong lupa na ginagawa, na tinatamnan ko ng mga vegetables saka palay. Kaya kami ng pamilya namin ay hindi masyadong nahirapan na kumain kami nang hindi karapat-dapat. Hirap kami. Ang kahirapan, pag nagkulang ka ng ani, mais ang aming kinakain [o] kaya niyog.

Translation: ____

____

____

____

____

____

____.

TEXT 2: Except from an interview with Leonarda Chico, p.384

Chico: ... Ako nga, hindi halos nakakatulog sa gabi dahil baka walang ano-ano, may raid sa gabi, hindi ka na makaalis ng bahay. Kaya madalang ang tao na nakakatulog noon. Ang tenga mo ay palaging nakataas. Pagka halimbawa e dito sa lugar na ito tumahol ang aso, nandoon ako sa may lugar na iyon, e di madidinig mo. E nagtaas na ng ulo ang taong iyon.

TRANSLATION: ____

____

____

____

____

____

____.

TEXT 3: Excerpt from an interview with Vicente Capalad, p. 279

Capalad: ... Ako ay alas-singko pa lang e nandiyan na sa palaisdaan, namamansing na ako. Awa naman ng Diyos, pagka ako ay sinusuwerte, yung pambigas at saka nakakapagtabi pa ko ng ulam. Naitatawid namin yung maghapong ulam. Nakabili ka ng isang salop ng bigas. E di maghapon na kakanin na iyon. Ganyan ang trabaho namin. Ang misis ko naman, walang lubay sa labada 'yan. Labada doon, labada dine, labada roon, mga kapitbahay.

TRANSLATION: ____

____

____

____

____

____

____.

Pakikinig: Excerpt from *Reporter's Notebook*
Mukha ng Gutom The Face of Hunger

Pagbabasa/Gawain: Ang mga Kagila-gilalas na Pakikipag-sapalaran ni Juan de la Cruz

The Amazing Adventures of Juan de la Cruz

Read the following poem by Jose F. Lacaba. In this poem, Juan de la Cruz stands for the ordinary Filipino struggling to survive. The poem became popular in the 1970s in Manila when it was made into a poem-play by a university theater group, UP

Repertory Company, led by Professor Behn Cervantes. It was possible to make it into a play because the poem had a lot of verbs or action words. Through the years, the play has been performed by many generations of UP Rep members, and the company, as well as other theater groups, have been inspired to write their own "poem-plays."

Study/review the following vocabulary words before reading the poem. Then, answer the comprehension questions below.

Vocabulary words: **kagila-gilalas** (amazing); **pakikipagsapalaran** (adventures); **pangamba** (fear); **pusturang-pustura** (well-dressed); **minura** (cursed); **tinitigan** (stared); **takilyera** (ticket seller); **diputado** (congressman/congresswoman; also deputy); **kamanyang** (incense); **libog** (desire); **pusali** (swamp); **bugaw** (pimp); **higop** (gulp); **humikab** (yawned); **malunok** (swallow); **gulok** (**bolo**; native knife); **gula-gulanit** (torn); **Arayat** (a mountain in Luzon); **sinulsulan** (urged; prodded)

Ang mga Kagila-gilalas na Pakikipagsapalaran ni Juan de la Cruz

ni Jose F. Lacaba

Isang gabing madilim
puno ng pangambang sumakay sa bus
si Juan de la Cruz
pusturang-pustura
kahit walang laman ang bulsa
BAWAL MANIGARILYO BOSS
sabi ng konduktora
at minura
si Juan de la Cruz.

Pusturang-pustura
kahit walang laman ang bulsa
nilakad ni Juan de la Cruz
ang buong Avenida
BAWAL PUMARADA
sabi ng kalsada
BAWAL UMIHI DITO
sabi ng bakod
kaya napagod
si Juan de la Cruz.

Nang abutan ng gutom
si Juan de la Cruz
tumapat sa Ma Mon Luk
inamoy ang mami siopao
hanggang sa mabusog.
Nagdaan sa Sine Dalisay
tinitigan ang retrato ni Chichay
PASSES NOT HONORED TODAY
sabi ng takilyera
tawa nang tawa.

Dumalaw sa Kongreso
si Juan de la Cruz
MAG-INGAT SA ASO
sabi ng diputado.
Nagtuloy sa Malakanyang
wala namang dalang kamanyang
KEEP OFF THE GRASS
sabi ng hardinero
sabi ng sundalo
kay Juan de la Cruz.

Nang dapuan ng libog
si Juan de la Cruz
namasyal sa Culiculi

at nahulog sa pusali
parang espadang bali-bali
YOUR CREDIT IS GOOD BUT WE NEED CASH
sabi ng bugaw
sabay higop ng sabaw.

Pusturang-pustura
kahit walang laman ang bulsa
naglibot sa Dewey
si Juan de la Cruz
PAN-AM BAYSIDE SAVOY THEY SATISFY
sabi ng neon.
Humikab ang dagat na parang leon
masarap sanang tumalon pero
BAWAL MAGTAPON NG BASURA
sabi ng alon.

Nagbalik sa Quiapo
si Juan de la Cruz
at medyo kinakabahan
pumasok sa simbahan
IN GOD WE TRUST
sabi ng obispo
ALL OTHERS PAY CASH.

Nang wala nang malunok
si Juan de la Cruz
dala-dala'y gulok
gula-gulanit na ang damit
wala pa ring laman ang bulsa
umakyat
sa Arayat
ang namayat
na si Juan de la Cruz.
WANTED DEAD OR ALIVE
sabi ng PC
at sinisi
ang walanghiyang kabataan
kung bakit sinulsulan
ang isang tahimik na mamamayan
na tulad ni Juan de la Cruz.

1. What were some of the things that Juan de la Cruz was forbidden to do?
2. What were some of the images that Lacaba used in his poem?
3. What does "**umakyat sa Arayat**" mean in the context of rebellion during the days of Martial Law and the Marcos government (1972–1986)?
4. Who were blamed by the authorities?
5. In your opinion, what is the poem about?

If you are a classroom learner, you might want to dramatize this poem. You may want to divide the class into groups with each group dramatizing a stanza or two. Or you might form groups with each group having their own interpretation of the same poem. Traditionally, there are only 3 performers in the **dula-tula**: a reader, and two movers. The reader reads the poem while the two movers act out the play. One of the two movers plays the main character while the other mover plays all the other characters. The second mover (also known as Mr./Ms. Ellaneous) changes character through props/costumes that can easily be worn or held: for example, a white coat to play a doctor; a cap to play a police officer; a book to play a teacher.

Pagsusulat Writing

Write your own play. In the history of the **dula-tula** or poem-play, several writers/theater groups/organizations wrote their own versions. For example, Richie Valencia's "Iskolar ng Bayan," which narrates the experiences of students at the University of the Philippines, has been performed for the past forty years. Other poem-plays were on the lives of peasants, teachers, and journalists.

What are some of the techniques that can help you write your own poem-play?

1. Choose a character. For example, a student (which university?); a worker (be specific; for example, factory worker, caregiver; domestic worker; construction worker etc.), or a professional.

2. Write an outline. In many poem-plays, the main character (representing a group of people) usually embarks on a kind of journey as he/she goes through a series of challenges. Think of 4 or 5 significant experiences/challenges that this character may experience.

3. Think of 4–5 characters that your main character would encounter and include these characters in your poem-play. Think of the settings where your main character would meet these other characters.

4. Write the text of your poem-play. Make sure you include a lot of action words.

5. Ensure that there is conflict in your poem-play because conflicts/contradictions create action, and allow your play to move forward. If your character has no problems, there is no "drama" in your poem-play.

6. Think of what action your character will take towards the end of the play.

7. Review and revise your play.

Paglalagom Summing Up

In lesson 6, we have:

- Reviewed and expanded vocabulary on verbs that talk about our daily activities;
- Practiced the use of auxiliary verbs;
- Studied plural forms;
- Read a poem-play; written a poem-play.

Aralin
Lesson

7

Pagkukuwento ng Bakasyon/Pagpaplano

Talking about a Vacation/Making Plans

This is the seventh and last review and expansion lesson. In this lesson, review and practice completed and contemplated aspects of the verb, review and practice **nagpa-** and **pina-** affixes, and conditional words **kung** and **kapag**.

Diyalogo Dialogue: Paanyaya sa Bohol

An Invitation to Go to Bohol

Study the following dialogue. Armael and Katie have just returned from their vacations.

ARMAEL : **Saan ka nagbakasyon?**
Where did you spend your vacation?

KATIE : **Nagpunta ako sa Boracay dahil hindi pa ako nakakapunta roon.**
I went to Boracay because I haven't been there.

ARMAEL : **Talaga? Ano ang ginawa mo sa Boracay?**
Really? What did you do in Boracay?

KATIE : **Lumangoy ako, nagpamasahe, at nag-scuba diving. Ang saya-saya namin ng mga pinsan ko!**
I went swimming, had [someone give me] a massage, and went scuba-diving. My cousins and I were so happy.

ARMAEL : **Balita ko, maraming restawran sa Boracay.**
I heard [that] there are a lot of restaurants in Boracay.

KATIE : **Oo. Kumain ako ng pagkaing Hapon at pagkaing Indian. Pero isang beses, bumili kami ng isda sa dalampasigan at pinaluto namin sa kusinero ng hotel.**
Yes. I ate Japanese food and Indian food. However, one time, we bought fish at the seashore and asked the hotel cook to cook [=prepare] it.

ARMAEL : **Saan kayo tumitira kapag pumupunta kayo sa Boracay?**
Where do you stay when you go to Boracay?

KATIE : **Tumitira kami sa Seashells Resort dahil nakakakuha kami ng diskuwento.**
We stay at Seashells Resort because we can get a discount.

ARMAEL : **Ano-ano ang mga pinamili mo?**
What did you shop for?

KATIE : **Bumili ako ng sarong. Ikaw, saan ka nagpunta?**
I bought sarongs. [What about] you, where did you go?

ARMAEL : **Pagkatapos kong mamasyal sa Cebu, pumunta naman ako sa Bohol.**
After going sightseeing in Cebu, I went to Bohol.

KATIE : **Hindi pa ako nakararating sa Bohol. Maganda ba?**
I haven't been to Bohol. Is it beautiful?

ARMAEL : **Ang ganda-ganda! Nagpunta ako sa Chocolate Hills. Namasyal ako sa ilog at nakinig sa Loboc Children's Choir. Nakakita din ako ng mga tarsier.**
It's so beautiful! I went to Chocolate Hills. I went sightseeing at the river and listened to Loboc Children's Choir. I was also able to see tarsiers.

KATIE : **Kung hindi sana ako abala, gusto ko rin sanang makapunta sa Bohol.**
If I were not busy, I would also like to be able to go to Bohol.

ARMAEL : **Bibisita uli ako sa lola ko sa isang buwan. Magdiriwang siya ng kaarawan. Kung libre ka sa Disyembre, gusto mo bang sumama?**
I will visit my grandmother again next month. She will celebrate her birthday. If you are free in December, would you like to go with me?

KATIE : **Sige, sasama ako kapag naka-ipon ako ng pamasahe.**
Yes, I will go with you if I am able to save [money] for my [plane] fare.

Bokabularyo Vocabulary

Review/Study the following words and phrases:

NOUNS: **pinamili** (items shopped for); **diskuwento** (discount); **pamasahe** (fare)

Adjectival phrases: Ang ganda-ganda! (So beautiful!); **Ang saya-saya!** (So happy!)

Verbs: nagbakasyon (went on vacation); **lumangoy** (swam); **nagpamasahe** (had a massage given by someone); **nag-scuba diving** (went scuba diving); **tumitira** (stay; literally, live); **nakararating** (have reached; literally, have arrived at; note use of root word **dating/rating**); **namasyal** (went sightseeing); **nakinig** (listened); **nakakita** (was able to see); **bibisita** (will visit); **magdiriwang** (will celebrate); **sasama** (to go with); **nakaipon** (able to save)

Consider how words are used in different ways. This is the reason why you shouldn't translate sentences literally.

For example, study the words **tumitira** and **nakararating** as used in the dialogue:

The root word **tira** (accent on the second syllable) means "to live." You are probably familiar with this because in *Tagalog for Beginners*, you use it when saying "**Nakatira ako sa Los Angeles** (I live in Los Angeles)" or "**Tumitira ako sa Daly City kapag bakasyon** (I live in Daly City during vacation [months])." Do not confuse this with **tira** (accent on the first syllable, meaning "to hit") nor with the noun **tira** (also with the accent on the first syllable) meaning "leftovers."

In the dialogue, we find the sentence:
Tumitira kami sa Seashells Resort dahil nakakakuha kami ng diskwento.

Translated literally, we might say: "We dwelled at Seashells Resort because we can get a discount." This is wrong because "dwell" means to "reside."

The correct translation is: "We stayed at Seaside Resort."

Now, what happens if we are thinking in English and we want to say "We stayed at Seaside Resort" in Tagalog/Filipino?

Some would translate this as "**Tumigil kami sa Seaside Resort.**" Google Translate translates this into: "**Nagtutulog namin sa Seashells Resort dahil maaari naming makakuha ng isang discount.**" This is obviously wrong because of the word **namin** meaning "our" instead of "we" and **nagtutulog** uses the verb **tulog** (sleep) in a wrong way—it should be **natutulog**.

The most common way of saying this is: "**Tumira kami sa Seaside Resort dahil nakakakuha kami ng diskuwento.**"

Now, consider the verb **nakararating** and its use in the sentence: **Hindi pa ako nakararating sa Bohol.**

The verb **dating/rating** literally means "arrive" or "reach." Google Translate translates this to "I have not come to Bohol."

However, the best translation for the sentence above is "I haven't been to Bohol."

Conjunctions used for time and conditional clauses: kapag/pag (when); **kung** (if/when); **kung sakali man** (in case); **habang** (while); **hanggang sa/hangga't** (until); **oras na** (when; literally, at the time that); **basta't** (as long as); **tuwing** (each/each time); **bago** (before); **pagkatapos** (after).

Mga Pangungusap Sentences

Review/Study how to use conjunctions in making time and conditional sentences. This is useful so that you can practice making compound and complex sentences. Also review/study the use of **naka** and **nakapag** affixes.

In English, we use "if" and "when" to express conditionality. Study how the following sentences were constructed:

1. **Kung libre ka sa Disyembre, gusto mo bang sumama?**
   If you are free in December, would you like to come with me?

2. **Kapag libre ka sa Disyembre, gusto mo bang sumama?**
   If you are free in December, would you like to come with me?

Notice that in the sentences above, **kung** and **kapag** are used interchangeably. Thus, you might ask—what is the difference in the use of **kung** and **kapag**?

According to Paul Schacter and Fe Otanes in the book *Tagalog Reference Grammar*, we use **kung** when we express a condition that is contrary to a fact or if we use the contemplated aspect. In all other cases, **kung** and **kapag** are interchangeable (466–469). Here are more examples; note the use of **sana** (literally, hopefully; used here to mean "would be") and **hindi** (no).

3. **Kung hindi lang sana ako abala, gusto ko rin sanang makapunta sa Bohol.**
   If I were not busy, I would also like to be able to go to Bohol.

4. **Kung sumama ka sa akin sa Bohol, ang saya sana natin.**
   If you had gone with me to Bohol, we would have been so happy [=had so much fun].

5. **Kung hindi naatraso ang eroplano, dumating sana tayo nang mas maaga.**
   If the plane had not been delayed, we would have arrived earlier.

In these sentences, it would have been wrong to use **kapag**. Here is an example of the use of **kung** with a verb in the contemplated aspect. Again, also review **naka-** and **nakapag-** affixes used to mean "was able to."

6. **Kung pupunta ka sa Cebu, makabibili ka ng maraming mangga.**
   If you are going to Cebu, you will be able to buy a lot of mangoes.

Should you wish to use the conjunctor **kapag**, the verb should be in the infinitive/ imperative form:

7. **Kapag pumunta ka sa Cebu, makabibili ka ng maraming mangga.**
   If you go [=Should you go] to Cebu, buy a lot of mangoes.

Moreover, use **kung** when pairing it with another subordinating conjuction (Schacter and Otanes, 466). For example, let us use **kung** with **sakali** (in case) in this next example.

8. **Kung sakaling bibili ka ng tiket bukas, bilhan mo na rin ako.**
   In case you buy a ticket tomorrow, buy one for me as well.

Now, let us study how we can use other conjunctions for conditional clauses.

9. **Makapupunta/Makakapunta ka na sa maraming probinsiya habang nasa Pilipinas ka.**
   You will be able to go to many provinces while you are in the Philippines.

10. **Makakapagpraktis/Makapagpapraktis ako ng Filipino samantalang nasa Pilipinas ako.**
    I will be able to practice Filipino while I am in the Philippines.

11. **Hindi makaaalis/makakaalis ang eroplano hangga't malakas ang bagyo.**
    The plane can't leave as long as the typhoon is strong.

Sometimes, words that are used for time and conditional clauses seem to be used metaphorically. For example:

12. **Sa oras na makaipon ako, bibili ako ng tiket.**
    At a time [=When] I am able to save (money), I will buy a ticket.

13. **Sa sandaling makaipon ako, bibili ako ng tiket.**
    At the moment [=When] I am able to save (money), I will buy a ticket.

14. **Tuwing umuuwi ako ng Pilipinas, nabibisita ko ang lola ko.**
    Each time I go home to the Philippines, I can visit my grandmother.

15. **Bago ako pumunta sa Bohol, pumunta muna ako sa Cebu.**
    Before going to Bohol I went to Cebu first.

16. **Pagkatapos kong mamasyal sa Cebu, pumunta naman ako sa Bohol.**
    After going sightseeing in Cebu, I went to Bohol.

Pagsasanay Practice
Mga Tanong at Sagot

Ask and answer the following questions: make sure you use the conjunctors studied.

1. Tanong : **Kung libre ka sa Agosto, saan ka magbabakasyon?**
   Sagot : ____.

2. Tanong : **Kapag nakaipon ka na ng pera, ano ang bibilhin mo?**
   Sagot : ____.

3. Tanong : **Kung sakaling makapunta ka sa Pilipinas, sino ang bibisitahin mo?**
   Sagot : ____.

4. Tanong : **Sa oras na makarating ka sa bahay, ano ang gagawin mo?**
   Sagot : ____.

5. Tanong : **Ano ang ginawa mo kagabi bago ka matulog?**
   Sagot : ____.

6. Tanong : ____?
   Sagot : **Kung pupunta ako ng New York, titira ako sa bahay ni Nikki.**

7. Tanong : ____?
   Sagot : **Ibibigay ko sa kapatid ko ang cellphone ko kapag nakabili na ako ng bagong cellphone.**

8. Tanong : ____?
   Sagot : **Bibili ako ng gulay kung sakaling makadaan ako sa Farmers' Market.**

9. Tanong : ____?
   Sagot : **Gagawa ako ng tsaa pagkatapos kong kumain.**

10. Tanong : ____?
    Sagot : **Nakikinig si Edmundo ng musika hanggang sa makatulog siya.**

Pagsasanay Practice

Write the dialogues for the following situations. Feel free to expand or alter the situations.

SITUATION 1: Ralph, Lina and eight other friends are planning to go to Lobo, Batangas to spend a few days at the beach. However, they can only do so if Lobo Beach Resort has five (5) vacant rooms for three (3) days. Also, they will only be able to go in one vehicle if they can rent a ten-seater van. They plan to reserve the rooms as soon as they can confirm the schedule with their friends. They plan to drop by Tagaytay after going to Lobo.

RALPH : **Lina, ________________________ ka na ba ng mga kuwarto sa Lobo Beach Resort?**

LINA : **Hindi pa. Tatawag sa akin ang resort manager bukas. ______________________ tayo _________________ may bakanteng ________________ para sa ______________________.**

RALPH : **Salamat. __________ nakapag-reserba ka na ng kuwarto, tawagan mo ako.**

LINA : **_________________________ ka na ba ng ten-seater na van?**

RALPH : **______________ makakakuha tayo ng reserbasyon ngayon o bukas, ____________________ na ako ng van.**

LINA : **Saan tayo pupunta ___________________ nating magbakasyon sa Lobo?**

RALPH : **Dumaan tayo sa Tagaytay.**

SITUATION 2: Cynthia, Romanlito, and Beth spent one week in Baguio for their teachers' seminar. They were able to get a discount. They are now planning to go further north in Sagada to spend two nights at Sagada Mountain Inn and go sightseeing. They are not sure they can do this because there had been a landslide and they are waiting for word that the roads are now safe (**ligtas**). They also need to buy five bus tickets for themselves and two other friends.

Cynthia : ____

____

____.

Romanlito : ____

____

____.

Beth : ____

____

____.

Cynthia : ____

____

____.

Romanlito : ____

____

____.

Cynthia : ____

____

____.

Romanlito : ____

____

____.

Beth : ____

____

____.

Situation 3: Julia, Lia, Rose, Robert, and Edmundo have just spent the past four days in Paris, France. They were able to travel because they got discounted tickets and discounted reservations. They were able to go sightseeing and eat good French food. They plan to go to Spain because they want to watch flamenco dancers and eat authentic paella. They can only do this if they can get cheap train tickets and if Julia's aunt lets them stay in her house in Madrid. Write a dialogue with 2, 3 or 4 or 5 characters.

Gramatika at Pagsasanay

In this lesson, we are reviewing verbs in the completed and contemplated aspects, particularly the use of **naka-** and **nakapag-** with these verbs. However, it is useful to review the other ways by which we use **naka-** and **nakapag-** affixes. We are also practicing the use of conjunctors so that we can practice making compound and complex sentences.

"Naka-" and "nakapag-" affixes

Let us review the ways by which we use the **naka-** affixes:

First, we use **naka-** *to indicate a position, state or condition.* Here are a few examples:

1. **Nakaupo ang babaeng nakasuot ng salamin.**
   The woman wearing glasses is sitting.

2. **Nakatayo ang lalaking nakapayong.**
   The man with an umbrella is standing.

Second, we use **naka-** *to form adjectives*:

For example, to show irritation at something, you might say: "**Nakakainis!**" or "**Nakaiinis!**" While both are correct, speakers would usually utter the former wherein it is the syllable **ka** that is duplicated, but an editor would tend to favor the duplication of the first syllable of the root word.

You may also expand this by referring to something you are particularly irritated at:

Nakakainis ang librong binasa ko. *I was irritated by the book I read.*

Here are other examples:

1. **Nakakalungkot/Nakalulungkot ang balitang natanggap ni Martha.**
   The news that Martha received was saddening.

2. **Nakakasuka/Nakasusuka ang pagkaing kinain ko sa restawran.**
   The food I ate at the restaurant makes me want to vomit.

Third, we use **naka-** and **nakapag-** *to indicate ability*. In general, most words that begin with vowels use **naka-** while words that begin with consonants use **nakapag-**, although there are many exceptions to this. Sample sentences are:

1. **Nakakapagbasa at nakakapagsulat na ang anak niyang si Sophie, na tatlong taong gulang.**
   His/Her daughter, Sophie, who is only three years old, can (already) read and write.

2. **Nakakausap niya ang kasintahan niyang nasa Pilipinas sa pamamagitan ng Skype.**
   She/He is able to talk to her boyfriend/girlfriend, who is in the Philippines, through Skype.

3. **Mahusay na nakakatugtog/nakatutugtog si Nancy ng piyano.**
   Nancy can play the piano well.

Fourth, **naka-** and **nakapag-**, as reviewed in this lesson, can be used *to form the equivalent of the past and present perfect tenses in English*. As explained in earlier lessons and in *Tagalog for Beginners*, there are no tenses in Tagalog/Filipino, just aspects. Review/study how the following sentences are constructed to mean "have you ever (verb)…" or "I have (verb)…" Note the use of the word **na**, roughly equivalent to "already." (Note: This also explains the Filipino's fondness for using the word "already." For example: *I have eaten already.*)

1. **Nakakain ka na ba ng prutas na durian?**
   Have you ever eaten durian fruit?

2. **Nakapaglaro ka na ba ng squash?**
   Have you ever played squash?

3. **Hindi pa ako nakakapunta sa Barcelona.**
   I have never been to Barcelona.

At this point, some learners get confused with **nakapag-** and **nakipag-**. Use **nakipag-** to mean "with." Review the following sentences.

1. **Nakapag-usap na kami ng nanay ko kagabi nang tumawag ang kapatid ko.** *My mother and I had finished talking last night when my brother/sister called.*
2. **Nakipag-usap na ako sa nanay ko nang tumawag ang kapatid ko.** *I had finished talking with my mother when my brother/sister called.*
3. **Nakapagsayaw na kami ni Roman ng tango nang dumating ang madalas kong kapareha sa tango.** *Roman and I had finished dancing the tango when my usual tango partner arrived.*
4. **Nakipagsayaw na ako kay Roman ng tango nang dumating ang madalas kong kapareha sa tango.** *I had finished dancing the tango with Roman when my usual tango partner arrived.*

Conjunctions for Time and Conditional Clauses

As you know, conjunctions are used to connect words, phrases, and clauses. In the Vocabulary section of this lesson, you reviewed sentences using the conjunctions **kung** (if *or* when), **kapag** (if *or* when), **kung sakali** (in case), **habang** (while), **kung sakali man** (in case), **habang** (while), **hanggang sa/hangga't** (until), **oras na** (when; literally, at the time that), **basta't** (as long as), **tuwing** (each/each time), **bago** (before), and **pagkatapos** (after). You also learned that **kung** and **kapag** are interchangeable, except in two instances: first, when we express a condition that is contrary to a fact; second, when we use the contemplated aspect. In these two instances, we can only use **kung**.

Practice these conjunctions by filling in the blanks. Remember, in some instances, there may be more than one correct answer.

1. **Nanonood si Larry ng telebisyon ___________________ kumakain siya ng hapunan.**
2. **Tuwing umaga, kumakain ako ng almusal _______________ ko magbihis.**
3. **Bibili ako ng tiket papuntang Pilipinas ______________ makaipon ako ng pera.**
4. **Hindi tayo dapat lumabas ng bahay ________________ malakas ang bagyo.**
5. **____________________ makita mo si Millicent, sabihin mo sa kanyang tumawag siya sa akin.**
6. **Tutulungan kita _____________________ makakaya ko.**
7. **___________________ pupunta ka sa kusina, pakidala ang mga platong ito.**

8. __________________ **nakahiram ka na ng libro, tawagan mo ang kaklase mo.**

9. **Hugasan mo muna ang mga mansanas** __________________ **mo kainin.**

10. **Dadaan ako sa groseri** __________________ **may oras ako mamaya.**

Pagsasanay Practice
Pagsasalin mula sa Ingles tungo sa Tagalog/Filipino
Translating from English to Tagalog/Filipino

Pretend you are a healthcare volunteer at a free medical clinic that serves Filipinos and Filipino Americans. To be able to serve your clients better, you want to translate the following form. Enter your translation in the parenthesis or in the line provided immediately after the English word/phrase/sentence.

Patient Information (Impormasyon Tungkol sa Pasyente)

Name (____________________):.. Age (______):...............
Address (____________________):..
.... Telephone (______________):............................
Occupation (______________):.................... Employer (______________):....................

When was your last check-up/visit to the doctor?

____?

Have you been vaccinated in the last six months? Yes / No

____?

Have you ever suffered from any of the following: high blood pressure, diabetes, heart condition? Yes / No

____?

What medical examinations such as mammograms, colonoscopies, etc. have you had in the past two years?

____?

What are the common illnesses in your family?

____?

What surgeries and/or operations have you had?

____?

What allergies do you have?

____?

Have you been treated in the clinic? If yes, when and for what?

____?

Mga Talang Pangkultura: Mga Manlalakbay Travelers

Pakikinig: Ulat Tungkol sa Paglalakbay Travel Report

Talakayan: Mga Paboritong Bakasyunan Favorite Vacation Places

For classroom learners, form groups or pairs and discuss your favorite vacation places. Individual learners can write a paragraph about your favorite vacation place. Here are some talking points:

1. What is your favorite vacation place? **Ano ang paborito mong bakasyunan?**
2. When did you last go there? **Kailan ka huling pumunta roon?**
3. What kinds of things do you do there? **Ano-ano ang mga bagay na ginagawa mo roon?**
4. If you can choose to go anywhere and you have no issues about budget and time, where and when would you go? Why? **Kung puwede kang pumunta kahit saan at wala kang problema sa badyet at oras, saan at kailan ka pupunta? Bakit?**

Pagbabasa Reading
Kaarawan Birthday

Read this short short story about Sarahbelle's birthday. At the end of the story, answer the comprehension questions. Note the use of time and conditional conjunctions.

To prepare for this reading exercise, review/study the following words: **mamahalin** (expensive); **siglo** (century); **talon** (waterfalls); **dala-dala** (being carried); **nakakulong** (in jail); **detenidong pulitikal** (political detainees).

Kaarawan

Kaarawan ni Sarahbelle ngayong araw na ito, ika-11 ng Nobyembre, at 36 na taong gulang na siya.

Maraming puwedeng gawin sa isang kaarawan. Kapag marami kang pera, puwede kang mag-imbita ng mga kaibigan sa isang mamahaling restawran o magpa-cater ng party sa sarili mong bahay. Kung marami kang oras, puwede kang mag-biyahe sa isang malayong lugar—bundok, dalampasigan, o lungsod na hindi mo pa napupuntahan.

Maagang gumising si Sarahbelle. Alas-siyete ng umaga ang alis ng eroplano niya papuntang Tacloban, Samar. Sayang, naisip niya, kung maaga lang sana siyang nakabili ng tiket, makakasakay sana siya ng diretsong eroplano papunta ng Calbayog, Samar. Wala nang diretsong tiket nang magdesisyon siyang pumunta ng Calbayog kaya pupunta na lang siya ng Tacloban, at sasakay ng bus.

Maganda ang Samar. Nakalista pa nga sa tourism website ng probinsiya ang mga lugar na pinupuntahan ng mga turista. Naroon ang Sohoton National Park na may mga kuweba, limestone boulders at underground rivers. Naroon din ang simbahan ng Tinago na itinayo pa noong ika-15 na siglo. Maraming malilinis na dalampasigan at talon, at siyempre, naroon ang pinakamahabang tulay ng Timog Silangang Asya, ang San Juanico Bridge, na nagdudugtong sa mga probinsiya ng Samar at Leyte.

Sayang, kung mas marami lang sana akong oras, makakapasyal ako, naisip ni Sarahbelle habang naghihintay ng flight sa airport. Pero hindi bale, nakapag-ayos naman siya nang mabuti at nakapaghanda. Espesyal na damit. Check. Black and white floral na V ang neckline at may dilaw na ribbon sa ilalim ng dibdib; simple pero elegante. Libro at ipod para malibang sa biyahe at mga pasalubong na libro. Check uli. Higit sa lahat, birthday cake. Birthday naman niya talaga, di ba? Check check check.

Isang oras at dalawampung minuto ang biyahe sa eroplano mula Maynila hanggang Tacloban. Pagkatapos, tatlo at kalahating oras ang bus mula Tacloban hanggang Calbayog. Sampung minuto ang traysikel mula paradahan ng bus hanggang Calbayog sub-provincial jail.

"Ano ito?" tanong ng guwardiya sa dala-dalang puting kahon ni Sarahbelle.

"Birthday cake ho. Birthday ko kasi."

Binuksan ng guwardiya ang kahon. May dalawang numero sa ibabaw ng cake –3 at 6. May mga rosettes pa at sprinkles. Ang nakasulat, "Free Ericson Acosta!"

Tama. Palayain si Ericson Acosta, dating editor ng pahayagang pang-unibersidad na Philippine Collegian, manunulat at aktibista, at dating kaklase ni Sarahbelle. Labing-walong buwan nang nakakulong si Ericson. Kabilang siya sa apat na raan at isang detenidong pulitikal sa ilalim ng pamahalaang Aquino.

Maligaya at makabuluhang kaarawan, Sarahbelle!

1. What did Sarahbelle do on her birthday?
2. Why was Sarahbelle unable to book a direct flight to Calbayog?
3. What are the choices one has to celebrate a birthday?
4. What places can one visit in Samar?
5. Who is Ericson Acosta? How long has he been in prison?

Pagsusulat Writing
Mga Payo sa Paglalakbay Travel Advice/Tips

Pretend that you are writing a travel blog. Write a paragraph giving advice on a destination—where to stay, what to do, best means of transportation, how to save money. Make sure you use conjunctions such as **kung**, **kapag**, **kung sakaling**, **bago**, **pagkatapos**, and others.

____
____
____
____
____
____
____
____

Paglalagom Summing Up

In lesson 7, we have:

- Reviewed verbs in the completed and contemplated aspect;
- Reviewed/studied the use of conjunctions in time and conditional clauses;
- Learned about travel accounts on the Philippines;
- Listened and read about travel, testing our vocabulary and comprehension skills;
- Practiced writing skills.

Aralin
Lesson
8

Paglalarawan ng Tao
Describing a Person

Lesson 8 marks the second part of our book where we develop skills essential in learning a language: describing people, places and emotions; telling a story, explaining and formulating arguments. In this Lesson, we will focus on describing a person, expanding our vocabulary to describe sizes and shapes, making comparisons and practicing **maging** (to become) and **magkaroon** (to have).

 **Diyalogo** Dialogue: **Nakita ko Sila!** I Saw Them!

Katie is in Manila on a six-week Intensive Philippine Studies course at the University of the Philippines. On Sundays, she takes the jeepney to go to her aunt's house in Fairview, Quezon City. Unfortunately, she and her fellow passengers got held up by two men. In this dialogue, she describes the two hold-uppers to a police officer and a sketch artist.

PULIS : **Puwede niyo ho bang ilarawan sa amin ang dalawang holdaper?**
Can you describe the two hold-uppers to us?

KATIE : **Oho. Iyon hong isang holdaper, maiksi ang buhok na may kulay, malaki ang mata at malaki rin ang tenga. Malapad ho ang noo niya, pango ang ilong, at makapal ang labi. Maitim na maitim ho siya.**
Yes. One hold-upper had short colored hair, big eyes and big ears. He had a wide forehead, a flat nose and thick lips. He was very dark.

PULIS : **May napansin ba kayong mga palantandaan?**
Did you notice any distinguishing marks?

KATIE : **May napansin ho akong mga tatu sa mga braso niya at saka may malaking nunal ho siya sa mukha.**
I noticed some tattoos on his arms and he also had a big mole on his face.

PULIS : **Mga gaano ho siya katangkad?**
Approximately how tall was he?

KATIE : **Pandak ho. Siguro ho mga limang talampakan at dalawang pulgada lang.**
He was short. Perhaps only five feet and two inches.

PULIS : **Kumusta ho ang pangangatawan niya?**
What was his body build like?

KATIE : **Matipuno ho siya.**
He was muscled [=he had a muscular built].

PULIS : **E iyon naman hong isang holdaper?**
What about the other hold-upper?

KATIE : **Iyon hong isa, matangkad. Mga anim na talampakan ho siguro.**
The other one was tall. Perhaps around six feet.

PULIS : **Ano ho ang hitsura niya?**
What did he look like?

KATIE : **Maputi ho. Kalbo ho siya, singkit ang mga mata, at matangos ang ilong. Pahaba ho ang mukha.**
He was fair-skinned. He was bald, had small/slanted eyes, and a high-bridged nose. He had an oblong-shaped face.

PULIS : **Ang pangangatawan ho?**
What about his build?

KATIE : **Payat ho siya.**
He was thin.

PULIS : **Salamat ho sa tulong ninyo.**
Thank you for your help.

Bokabularyo Vocabulary

In this dialogue, we are reviewing/studying words that describe a person's physical characteristics. You learned some of these descriptive words in *Tagalog for Beginners*. Review the words you learned and expand your vocabulary by learning new words:

Describing Hair (Buhok): mahaba (long); **maiksi** (short); **hanggang sa balikat** (shoulder-length); **hanggang sa puwet** (very long hair reaching up to one's backside); **kalbo** (bald); **may kulay** (colored hair; in the Philippines, this refers to "lightened hair"); **itim** (black); **brown** (brown); **kulay mais** (blonde); **puti** (gray/white); **abuhin** (salt and pepper); **kulot** (curly); **tuwid** (straight); **alon-alon** (wavy)

Describing the Face (Mukha): bilugan (round); **pahaba** (oblong-shaped); **kuwadrado** (square-shaped); **hugis-puso** (heart-shaped)

Describing Parts of the Face (Bahagi ng Mukha): malapad ang noo (wide forehead); **makapal ang kilay** (has thick eyebrows); **manipis ang kilay** (has thin eyebrows) **malaki ang mata** (huge eyes); **singkit ang mata** (small or slanted eyes); **malapad ang ilong** (wide nose); **matangos ang ilong** (has a high-bridged nose); **pango ang ilong** (has a flat-bridged nose); **malaki/maliit ang tenga** (has big/small ears); **makapal/manipis ang labi** (has thick/thin lips); **may bigote** (has a mustache); **may balbas** (has a beard)

Describing Skin (Balat) and Complexion (Kutis): morena/moreno, **kayumanggi/kulay kape** (brown-skinned); **maputi** (fair); **mestisa/mestiso** (fair-skinned; used to refer to people of mixed race, usually people of Filipino and Caucasian or Filipino and East Asian descent); **maitim** (dark-skinned); **mala-sutla ang balat** (skin as smooth as silk); **magaspang** (rough skin); **makinis ang balat/pino ang balat** (smooth-skinned); **maraming tagiyawat** (has a lot of pimples); **maraming pekis ang balat** (has a lot of scars on the face)

Describing Body Build (Pangangatawan): malaki ang pangangatawan (heavily built); **maskulado** (well-muscled); **mataba** (weight-challenged); **katamtaman** (medium build); **balingkinitan** (has a small waist); **payat** (thin); **taas** (height); **timbang** (weight)

Describing Height (Taas): matangkad (tall); **pandak** (vertically challenged; used pejoratively—sometimes it is better to say **maliit**); **katamtaman ang taas** (average height)

Describing Body Marks (Palatandaan): nunal (mole); **pilat** (scar); **tatu** (tattoo)

Mga Pangungusap Sentences

Let us focus on expressing changes in appearance. Study the following sentences that will enable you to talk about how your appearance has changed or will change. Also, study the use of the words **naging** (became) and **nagkaroon** (had; meaning "possessed") and review the use of **nagpa-**, **pina-** and **pina-an** affixes

1. **Gustong maging maskulado ni Rojo kaya pumupunta siya sa gym araw-araw.**
   Rojo wants to be muscled so he goes to the gym everyday.

2. **Nagkaroon si Kawayan ng malaking bukol sa binti dahil sa impeksiyon.**
   Kawayan's calf got swollen because of an infection.

3. **Ayaw niyang maging kalbo kaya nagsusuot siya ng wig.**
   He/she doesn't want to be bald so he/she wears a wig.

4. **Nagkaroon ako ng pilat sa braso dahil malalim ang sugat ko.**
   I developed a scar on my arm because my wound was deep.

5. **Pinakulayan ng lola ko ang buhok niya para itago ang mga puti niyang buhok.**
   My grandmother had her hair colored to hide her gray hair.

6. **Nagpatatu si Diwa ng pangalan niya sa mga titik ng baybayin.**
   Diwa had her name tattooed using baybayin *letters.*

7. **Gusto niyang magpapayat kaya nagdidiyeta siya.**
   He/she wants to be leaner so he/she is dieting.

Now, let us practice asking questions. Here are some helpful ways to ask questions about another person's appearance:

1. **Gaano ka katangkad/kabigat?**
   How tall/heavy are you?

2. **Ano ang hugis/kulay ng iyong ______________________________?**
   What is the shape/color of your ______________________________?

3. **Paano nagbago ang itsura mo?**
   How did your appearance change?

4. **Bakit/paano ka nagkaroon ng ______________________________?**
   Why/how did you have a ______________________________?

5. **Ano ang pangangatawan ni ______________________________?**
   What is ______________________________ body built?

6. **Ano ang itsura ng mata/ilong/bibig ni ______________________________?**
   What does ______________________________'s eyes/nose/lips look like?

Mga Tanong at Sagot

Ask and answer the following questions so that you can practice describing yourself, members of your family, and your friends and classmates. Classroom learners can form pairs to do this orally, while individual learners can write down their answers. Please remember to answer in complete sentences.

1. TANONG : **Ano ang hugis ng mukha mo?**
   SAGOT : ______________________________.

2. TANONG : **Ano ang taas at timbang mo?**
   SAGOT : ______________________________.

3. TANONG : **Ano-ano ang mga kulay ng buhok ng mga kaklase o kaibigan mo?**
   SAGOT : ______________________________.

4. TANONG : **Gaano ka katangkad?**
   SAGOT : ______________________________.

5. TANONG : **Gaano ka kabigat?**
   SAGOT : ______________________________.

6. TANONG : ______________________________?
   SAGOT : **Asul ang kulay ng mata ng anak ko.**

7. TANONG : ______________________________?
   SAGOT : **Pango ang ilong niya.**

8. TANONG : ______________________________?
   SAGOT : **Pinakulayan niya ang buhok niya dahil gusto niya ng buhok na itim na itim.**

9. TANONG : ______________________________?
   SAGOT : **Katamtaman ang pangangatawan ng nanay ko.**

8. TANONG : ______________________________?
   SAGOT : **Gusto kong magpataba dahil ang payat-payat ko na.**

Pagsasanay Practice

Practice the words and sentences you have learned by writing dialogues or paragraphs for the situations below. In each of the situations, someone is describing another person's physical appearance.

Situation 1: Amir is describing the thief he saw robbing a convenience store to the police. The thief is dark-skinned, has black hair and brown eyes, around five feet ten inches tall, and heavy-built. He has short hair, huge eyes, and a wide nose. He has a huge mole above his lips. He had a beard.

Amir: ____

____

____

____

____

Situation 2: Amaya is describing herself over the phone to her cousin Timyas who will be meeting her at the Ninoy Aquino International Airport in Manila. She has not seen her cousin for ten years because she last visited Manila when she was 12 years old. Amaya is fair-skinned and has long wavy blonde hair that reaches up to her backside. She used to have brown hair but she had her hair colored recently. She has green eyes, a high-bridged nose, and wears glasses. She is around five feet five inches tall and of medium build. She has a tattoo on her left shoulder.

Timyas is also describing herself to Amaya. She is brown-skinned and has short and curly brown hair, and black eyes. She has big eyes, a small nose and thin lips. In the last picture she sent Amaya, she was heavy because she just gave birth. Since then she has lost weight because of diet and exercise.

Amaya: ____

____

____

____

____

____

Timyas: ____

____

____

____

____

____

Situation 3: Mrs. Espino is looking for her daughter Karen. Karen was last seen in Hagonoy, Bulacan where she was abducted while working as an agriculture specialist and peasant organizer for a non-government organization helping farmers. Mrs. Espino is being interviewed on television and she is describing both Karen and Karen's abductors.

Karen is five feet two inches tall. She is fair-skinned but has a lot of pimples. She has a well-muscled body because she used to be in the university's volleyball team. Her waist is small. She has shoulder-length straight hair, brown eyes, and big ears. The three men who abducted her were all tall and heavily-built. They had very short hair and were wearing sunglasses. One was bald and another had a mustache.

Mrs. Espino: ____

____

____

____

____

____

____

Gramatika Grammar

Review/Study the use of **naging** (became) and **nagkaroon** (got; developed; acquired) as well as the affixes **nagpa-**, **pina**, and **pina-an**. Also, study how culture influences the way we choose words and construct sentences grammatically—some notes on culture, vocabulary, and grammar are given towards the end of this section.

As you know, there are many ways to say the same thing. Explore your options, and the words and phrases you can use.

"Naging/Nagiging/Maging" with adjectives

You have practiced the use of **naging**, **nagiging** and **maging** earlier in Lesson 1 when you practiced speaking/writing about life histories and milestones.

In this lesson, we are focusing on the use of **naging** and **maging** with adjectives as related to changes in one's physical appearance. However, in some instances, one can skip the use of **naging** and simply conjugate the verb. Here are a few examples:

1a. **Magiging malusog ka kung kakain ka ng maraming gulay.**
You will be healthy if you eat a lot of vegetables.

However, another way of saying the same thing is to just take the root word **lusog** and use it as a verb in the contemplated aspect.

1b. **Lulusog ka kung kakain ka ng maraming gulay.**
You will be healthy if you eat a lot of vegetables.

Here are other examples:

2a. **Naging matangkad ang mga anak ni Nina dahil matangkad ang asawa niya.**
Nina's children became tall because her husband is tall.
2b. **Tumangkad ang mga anak ni Nina dahil matangkad ang asawa niya.**
Nina's children became tall because her husband is tall.

3a. **Ayon sa advertisement sa telebisyon, nagiging makinis ang kutis kapag nagpapahid ng cream sa mukha gabi-gabi.**
According to the advertisement on television, your skin complexion will be smoother (=you will be smooth-skinned) if you apply cream on your face nightly.
3b. **Ayon sa advertisement sa telebisyon, kumikinis ang kutis kapag nagpapahid ng cream sa mukha gabi-gabi.**
According to the advertisement on television, your skin complexion will be smoother (=you will be smooth-skinned) if you apply cream on your face nightly.

4a. **Hindi totoong magiging kalbo ka kung matutulog ka nang basá ang buhok mo.**
It is not true that you will be bald if you sleep with wet hair.
4b. **Hindi totoong makakalbo ka kung matutulog ka nang basá ang buhok mo.**
It is not true that you will be bald if you sleep with wet hair.

However, there are exceptions, especially when the adjective is not formed by the affix **ma-** and the root word (such as **matangkad** and **makinis**). Two examples are **pandak** (short) and **balingkinitan** (with a short but narrow waist.)

"Nagkaroon/Magkaroon"

Similarly, you can use the words **nagkaroon**, **nagkakaroon** and **magkakaroon** to express "got, developed or acquired." Alternatively, you can form a verb by using the affix **nagka-** with the root word of the verb. Here are some examples:

1a. **Nagkaroon ako ng pilat dahil malalim ang sugat ko.**
I developed a scar because my wound was deep.
1b. **Nagkapilat ako dahil malalim ang sugat ko.**
I developed a scar because my wound was deep.

2a. **Nagkakaroon ng bungang-araw ang maraming bata sa Pilipinas tuwing tag-araw.**
Many children in the Philippines get heat rashes [or prickly heat; literally, fruit of the sun] every summer.

2b. **Nagkakabungang-araw ang maraming bata sa Pilipinas tuwing tag-araw.**
Many children in the Philippines get heat rashes [or prickly heat; literally, fruit of the sun] every summer.

3a. **Ayon sa mga doktor, hindi totoong magkakaroon ka ng tagiyawat dahil sa pagkain ng tsokolate.**
According to doctors, it is not true that you will develop pimples from eating chocolate.

3b. **Ayon sa mga doktor, hindi totoong magkakatagiyawat ka dahil sa pagkain ng tsokolate.**
According to doctors, it is not true that you will develop pimples from eating chocolate.

"Nagpa-", "pina-" and "pina-an" affixes

We have studied **nagpa-**, **pina-**, and **pina-an** affixes in previous lessons. Let us practice these affixes again in this lesson by using them in speaking/writing about appearances.

Earlier, we used **nagpa-**, **pina-** and **pina-an** to express "having someone do something for us." For example:

English: *I asked my mother to cook pansit for Joseph.*
Actor Focus: **Nagpaluto ako ng pansit sa nanay ko para kay Joseph.**
Object Focus: **Pinaluto ko ang pansit para kay Joseph sa nanay ko.**
Receiver Focus: **Pinalutuan ko ng pansit si Joseph sa nanay ko.**

Study how to use these affixes when speaking/writing about changing one's physical appearance.

English: *Sandino had the* baybayin *(indigenous Filipino script) tattooed on his back at the Filipino Tattoos Center.*
Actor Focus: **Nagpatatu si Sandino ng baybayin sa likod niya sa Filipino Tattoos Center.**
Object Focus: **Baybayin ang pinatatu ni Sandino sa likod niya sa Filipino Tattoos Center.**
Location/Receiver Focus: **Pinatatuan ni Sandino ang likod niya sa Filipino Tattoos Center.**

Moreover, we can also use these affixes even when we do something for ourselves. Note that when the English translation is awkward, the better English equivalent is inside the brackets. Here are some examples.

1. English: *Kawayan is making his muscles bigger [=developing his muscles] for the weight lifting competition.*

Actor Focus: **Nagpapalaki ng mga masel si Kawayan para sa weight-lifting competition.**

Object Focus: **Pinapalaki ni Kawayan ang mga masel niya para sa weight-lifting competition.**

2. English: *Roselie is trying to be thinner [=trying to lose weight] because she wants to wear her old clothes.*

Actor Focus: **Nagpapapayat si Roselie dahil gusto niyang isuot ang luma niyang mga damit.**

Object Focus: **Pinapapapayat ni Roselie ang katawan niya dahil gusto niyang isuot ang luma niyang mga damit.**

3. English: *He grew a mustache to look old [=older].*

Actor Focus: **Nagpatubo siya ng bigote para magmukhang matanda.**

Note the following: In the second and third examples, we do not need an "object" (the body or **katawan**). Also, the second sentence, with the "object" as the focus, in this case the body (**katawan**), is not something a native speaker would usually say. Thus, in the third example, a sentence with the object as the focus is no longer given.

Notes on grammar and culture

As you may have noticed, Filipinos like to greet each other by making comments on one's physical appearance. People from other cultures find this offensive and politically incorrect, especially when Filipinos give comments on body weight or skin color, for example, "**Tumaba ka!**" (You became fat [=weight challenged]!) or "**Ang itim-itim mo ngayon**." (You are so dark now [=these days]!)

There are several things we need to bear in mind. First, the preference for fair skin can be attributed to colonial history (the fair skin of the colonizer, and according to culture historian Nicanor Tiongson, religious sculptures), and a privileged status (in precolonial times, those who did not have to work in the fields such as the **binukot**, or storytellers). Second, body weight preferences are flexible because they can signify abundance/lack of food, discipline/lack of discipline, healthy/unhealthy lifestyle—depending on the speakers and the circumstances of the conversation.

Our concern in this section is vocabulary and grammar. Here is what we need to remember:

1. Although **morena/moreno** and **kayumanggi** are used to describe brown-skinned people, these words are not used to talk about change in color. We just use the verb forms of **itim** (black; used to mean "dark") and **puti** (white; used to mean "fair"). For example, we say, "**Umitim siya**" (He/She became darker) and "**Pumuti siya**." (He/she became fairer.)

2. There is no indigenous concept of "tanning" or going to the beach/tanning salon to be tanned. The word **nagpapaitim** is used.

3. When talking about body size and weight, unless one is speaking as a medical professional, we do not say "**Bumaba yata ang timbang mo**" (You seem to have lowered your [=lost a lot of] weight.) We simply say **tumaba** or **pumayat**.

Pagsasanay Practice

Practice what you have reviewed/studied in the grammar portion of this lesson by asking and answering questions:

1. TANONG : **Paano ka naging balingkinitan?**
   SAGOT : ______________________________.

2. TANONG : **Ano ang pinatatu mo noong kaarawan mo?**
   SAGOT : ______________________________.

3. TANONG : **Bakit siya nagpakalbo?**
   SAGOT : ______________________________.

4. TANONG : **Ilang tao ang nagpapaitim sa beach?**
   SAGOT : ______________________________.

5. TANONG : **Bakit niya gustong magpahaba ng buhok?**
   SAGOT : ______________________________.

6. TANONG : ______________________________?
   SAGOT : **Nagpapataba siya ngayon dahil pumayat siya noong nagkasakit siya.**

7. TANONG : ______________________________?
   SAGOT : **Nagkapilat siya sa braso noong naimpeksiyon ang sugat niya.**

8. TANONG : ______________________________?
   SAGOT : **Naging maputi ang mang-aawit dahil sa pag-inom ng tabletas.**

9. TANONG : ______________________________?
   SAGOT : **Nagpatubo siya ng balbas para magmukhang matanda.**

10. TANONG : ______________________________?
    SAGOT : **Pangalan ng nobya niya ang pinatatu niya.**

Diyalogo Dialogue
Sa Lamay ng Patay At a Funeral Wake

In this dialogue, review/study words and idiomatic expressions that you can use to describe a person's character or personality. Encircle the adjectives you can find in this dialogue. Then, answer the comprehension questions. You may want to check the meaning of some words in the Vocabulary section that follows.

Armael is at a funeral wake with his friend, Raquel. They are talking about their friend who passed away. Many people are at the wake because Maita was the director of a women's shelter and she had helped many women.

ARMAEL : **Dakilang tao si Maita.**
Maita is/was a great [and noble] person.

RAQUEL : **Tama ka. Napakamatulungin niya kaya ang daming tao sa lamay.**
Maita was so nice and helpful; that's why [=so] many people are [here] at the wake.

ARMAEL : **Kung minsan, akala ng mga tao, masungit siya.**
Sometimes, some people thought she was ill-tempered.

RAQUEL : **Seryoso kasi sa trabaho. Pero mabait siya. Akala rin ng mga tao hindi siya makabasag-pinggan pero palaban siya.**
Because she's serious with work. But she is kind. People also thought she was very prim and proper but she was a fighter.

ARMAEL : **Gusto raw lagi niyang mapag-isa nitong nakaraang mga buwan. Nagkasakit kasi siya. Ang tigas ng ulo, trabaho nang trabaho kahit may sakit.**
They say she often wanted to be alone these past few months. That was because she got sick. She was hard headed, she kept on working even when she was sick.

RAQUEL : **Oo. Lagi siyang nasa bahay niya sa maliit na isla. Pero masayahin naman daw, ang sabi ng mga bumisitang kaibigan.**
Yes. She was often in her house in a small island. But she was always happy, said [=according to] the friends who visited her.

ARMAEL : **Malungkot ang lahat ng tao rito.**
All the people here are sad.

RAQUEL : **Oo nga.**
Yes [=That's right].

ARMAEL : **Bakit ka umiiyak?**
Why are you crying?
RAQUEL : **Mababaw talaga ang luha ko.**
I cry easily.

1. What were some of the adjectives used to describe Maita?
2. What was she like the past few months?
3. What was the atmosphere like at the funeral parlor?

Bokabularyo Vocabulary

Review/study the following vocabulary words and phrases that are used to describe a person's character or personality:

POSITIVE TRAITS: mabait (good; kind); **matulungin** (helpful); **masipag** (industrious); **mabuti ang kalooban** (has a good heart); **mapagkawanggawa** (charitable); **mapagkumbaba** (humble; modest); **maganda ang ugali** (has a good personality); **maalalahanin** (thoughtful); **mapagmahal** (loving); **matapang** (brave); **malambing** (affectionate); **matapat** (honest)

NEGATIVE TRAITS: masungit (ill-tempered; surly); **mainitin ang ulo** (hot-tempered); **mapagbasag-ulo** (always fighting with others); **masamang tao** (bad/evil person); **makasarili** (selfish); **mayabang** (boastful); **mapagmataas/arogante** (arrogant); **matapobre** (looks down on the poor); **maitim ang budhi** (literally, has an evil soul; evil); **duwag** (cowardly)

OTHER TRAITS: masayahin (always happy); **malungkutin** (always sad); **mapag-isa** (wants to be alone); **masunurin** (obedient); **madasalin** (likes to pray; always praying); **mapangarapin** (dreamy); **antukin** (always sleepy); **relihiyoso** (religious); **ulyanin** (forgetful); **palaban** (a fighter)

IDIOMATIC EXPRESSIONS: balat-sibuyas (sensitive; easily hurt; literally, onion-skinned); **makapal ang mukha** (shameless; literally, thick-faced); **di-makabasag pinggan** (prim and proper; fragile looking); **halang ang bituka** (a person with no moral compass; literally, possessing horizontal intestines); **magaan ang kamay** (easily provoked to hurt another person); **malikot ang kamay** (a person who steals things); **matamis ang dila** (honey-tongued); **mababaw ang luha** (easily cries; literally, has shallow tears)

Gawain Activity: Sketch Artist

In this exercise, try to describe someone you know. Start with the physical attributes and then with the personality of the person. Not all the information is prompted, so fill in the details. Use the words you have learned, especially the idiomatic expressions.

For classroom learners, work in pairs. One person describes his/her "character," while the other sketches. Think of details. For example, what kind of shoes would this person have? What kind of blouse/shirt would this person wear? What flavor of ice cream would he/she have?

To make your characters more interesting, think of possible contradictions. For example, can you think of ...

1. A classmate/former classmate who looks mean but is actually a nice person?
2. An aunt/older woman friend who is very careful with her appearance?
3. A cousin/friend who is chatty and friendly but has certain quirks?
4. Someone you have read about or know who looks fragile but is actually fierce?

Pagsasanay sa Pagsasalin: Isang Liham A Letter

Translate the following text—a letter on the passing of Horacio "Boy" Morales (1943–2012), former underground activist and political prisoner (1982–1986) during Martial Law (1972–1986), then President of the Philippine Rural Reconstruction Movement and Secretary of Agrarian Reform (1998–2001). This excerpt from a statement by revolutionary leader Jose Ma. Sison, shows how Morales was respected by many, even those he no longer worked with.

In translating this text, do not do a word-for-word translation. Instead, get the essence of the text. Then try your best to say it in Filipino. You can break up or combine sentences as you wish or say things in a simpler way. Use the adjectives you learned earlier; and remember, some of those adjectives can be used as adverbs. Here are some words that can be useful to use: **rebolusyonaryong kilusan** (revolutionary movement); **pananaw** (views); **rebolusyonaryong puwersa** (revolutionary forces); **ilang isyu** (certain issues); **hindi pagtanggap** (not accepting); **ambag** (contribute); **makakaya** (what one could).

A fill-in-the-blanks translation is below, but try to do this on your own first. The fill-in-the-blanks translation is there so that you can compare your own translation and study translation techniques.

Text for Translation:
"Boy was never arrogant towards anyone in the revolutionary movement even when he held his high position in government. He was approachable and helpful...

"Boy had a high capacity for achievement and expressed his political views clearly, honestly and modestly. Even when he had views different from those of the revolutionary forces, he never sought to impose his views on the whole or any part of the revolutionary movement and certainly he never attacked the movement for not accepting his views on certain issues. He was ever ready to find a common ground and contribute what he could to the revolutionary movement."

____

____

____

____

____

____

____

____

Checking your Translation:
Here is a fill-in-the blanks translation of the passage. Study how the sentences are constructed and fill in the blanks with the vocabulary you have learned.

Hindi kailanman naging ________________ si Boy sa ________________ sa ______________________ kahit na nasa ____________________ na siya sa __________________. Madali siyang lapitan at ____________ .

Naging ____________ si Boy sa buhay. Ipinahayag niya ang kanyang mga ____________ nang __________, ___________, at ___________. Kahit na iba ang kanyang _________ sa _________ ng mga ____________, hindi niya ipinilit ang kanyang mga ________ sa kabuuan o sino mang bahagi ng _________. Sigurado akong hindi niya kailanman _________ ang ________________ sa hindi nito pagtanggap sa kanyang mga ____________ sa ________________. Lagi siyang ______________ na makahanap ng mapagkakasunduan at mag-ambag ng makakaya sa ________________________.

Mga Talang Pangkultura: Mga Tatu at Palamuti
Tattoos and Ornaments

Talakayan: Paglalarawan ng mga Tao Describing People

After reading the culture notes (found in the CD), choose among the following questions to discuss. Classroom learners should form pairs or small groups of four or five. Individual learners can write a paragraph.

1. How can you describe the indigenous people of the Philippines before colonization? **Paano mo mailalarawan ang mga katutubo sa Pilipinas bago ang kolonisasyon?**
2. How can you describe your family members? **Paano mo mailalarawan ang mga miyembro ng iyong pamilya?**

Pakikinig: Nawawala: Remedios Velasquez
Missing: Remedios Velasquez

Pagbabasa Reading
Ang Nagbabagong Kuwento nina Malakas at Maganda
The Changing Story of *The Strong and The Beautiful*

This story is an adaptation of the **Malakas at Maganda** (The Strong and The Beautiful) creation myth. Read the story and answer the comprehension questions.

REVIEW WORDS RELATED TO NATURE THAT YOU ALREADY KNOW: **dagat** (ocean); **langit** (sky); **isla** (island); **agila** (eagle); **ibon** (bird); **amihan** (northeast wind); **habagat** (south wind); **kawayan** (bamboo); **lindol** (earthquake); **lawin** (hawk); **daigdig** (world)

Now, study the following nouns, adjectives, verbs that were used to have more specific descriptions and action in the story. Some of these words are familiar to you: **magtapon** (throw); **lumilipad** (flying); **pigilan** (prevent); **humapon** (perched); **iwan** (leave); **mapayapa** (peaceful); **lumulutang-lutang** (floating); **natamaan** (got hit); **tinuka** (pecked); **kahoy na pamalo** (wood used to hit something/someone); **nagtago** (hid); **lahi** (race); **kubling kuwarto** (concealed room); **pinuno** (leader; chief); **alipin** (slave); **pugon** (fireplace; stove); **habang buhay** (forever); **nag-iiba-iba** (changing); **naghahangad** (aspires); **giting** (valor); **kasarian** (gender); **uri** (class); **pang-aapi** (oppression).

Ang Nagbabagong Kuwento nina Malakas at Maganda

Unang Bersiyon[1]:
Sa kuwento na nasa libro ng isang Amerikana na tumira sa Pilipinas, walang lupa noon sa daigdig, dagat lang at langit. Isang araw, napagod ang isang agilang lumlipad, kaya't ginulo niya ang dagat hanggang sa magtapon ang dagat ng tubig paakyat sa langit. Upang pigilan ang dagat, nagtapon din ang langit ng mga isla sa dagat. Pagkatapos, inutusan nito ang agila na humapon sa isa sa mga isla, gumawa ng pugad, at iwang mapayapa ang langit at dagat.

Samantala, ikinasal naman ang hanging amihan sa habagat, at nagkaroon sila ng anak—si kawayan. Isang araw, lumulutang-lutang ang kawayan at natamaan ang agila. Nagalit ang agila, at tinuka nito ang kawayan, at lumabas ang unang babae at ang unang lalaki.

[1] *Philippine Folk Tales*. Compiled and Annotated by Mabel Cook Cole. 1916. Project Gutenberg Ebook #12814. Released March 27, 2008. http://www.gutenberg.org/files/12814/12814-8.txt

Tinawag ng lindol ang lahat ng ibon at isda, at sila ang nagdesisyon na dapat ikasal ang unang babae at lalaki. Nagkaroon sila ng maraming anak, at galing dito ang lahat ng lahi.

Dumami ang mga anak, at naging magulong-magulo sa bahay, kaya nagalit ang ama, at kumuha ito ng kahoy na pamalo. Natakot ang mga anak at nagtago sila. Ang mga nagtago sa mga kubling kuwarto ay naging mga pinuno; ang mga nasa dingding, ang naging alipin. Ang mga tumakbo sa labas ay mga malayang tao, ang mga nagtago sa pugon, ang lahing itim, at ang mga nagpunta sa dagat at nagbalik, ang mga lahing puti.

Ikalawang Bersiyon:
Sa kuwentong naging popular, ang lalaki at ang babae ay naging sina Malakas at Maganda. Ang ibon ay naging lawin, at pagkatapos ng maraming taon, naging Sarimanok, isang ibon na maraming kulay, ngunit nasa isip lang.

Isang araw, may isang Pangulo na gustong maging hari habambuhay. Kumuha siya ng pintor para gumawa ng dalawang larawan. Ang una'y kamukha niya – si Malakas; ang ikalawa'y kamukha ng kanyang asawa—si Maganda.

Ang Malayang Bersiyon:
Ang malayang bersiyon ay bersiyon na nag-iiba-iba. May mga nagsasabing si Malakas ay babae. May nagsasabi na lumabas sa kayawan ang dalawang lalaki o dalawang babae, na parehong Malakas at Maganda.

Ang aking bersiyon ay bersiyong walang pangalan—na naghahangad ng lakas at ganda at higit pa rito, ng giting at tapang. Ang mga anak ay hindi nahahati sa lahi o sa uri, kundi nagkakaisa sa layunin—isang daigdig na malaya sa pang-aapi, at mayroong tunay na pagkakapantay-pantay, ano man ang kasarian at uri at lahi.

1. What did the ocean and the sky do when the eagle caused them to fight?
2. What caused the first man and woman to come out of the bamboo?
3. Where did the children hide?
4. What did the President who wanted to be king forever do?
5. Narrate one of the many "free versions" of the story.

Pagsusulat Writing
Ang Bolang Crystal The Crystal Ball

Pretend that you have a crystal ball. Using the new words you have learned from this lesson you can choose to:

1. describe yourself and your family 20 years from now;
2. describe a fictitious person 20 years from now;
3. describe one of the people in the photo 20 years from now.

Paglalagom Summing Up

In Lesson 8, you have:

- Learned how to describe people in greater detail;
- Practiced **naka-**, **naging** and **nagkaroon**;
- Learned about descriptions given to inhabitants of the Philippine islands before colonial rule;
- Read a creation myth;
- Practiced your writing skills in describing people.

Aralin 9
Lesson

Paglalarawan ng Lugar
Describing a Place

In this lesson, study how to describe places—in particular, vocabulary related to houses, space, and geography. Also, study adjectival affixes and phrases as well as comparatives and superlatives so that you can write better sentences. Practice natural speech patterns.

 Diyalogo Dialogue: Pagbili ng Bahay Buying a House

Rose is buying a house in Manila for her parents and her three siblings. She has asked her real estate agent Joy, to help them in their search for a suitable home. In Manila, lots are measured through square meters.

JOY : **Ano ho bang klaseng bahay ang gusto niyong bilhin?**
What kind of house would you like to buy?

ROSE : **Iyong hindi masyadong malaki at hindi naman masyadong maliit. Mas maganda ho siguro kung dalawang palapag ang bahay.**
Something that is not too big but is also not too small. Perhaps it would be good if the house has two floors.

JOY : **Ilang kuwarto ho at ilang banyo?**
How many bedrooms and how many bathrooms?

ROSE : **Siguro, tatlong kuwarto lang ho at dalawang banyo. Pero ang gusto ko sana, iyong malalaki ang bintana para presko at lagusan ang hangin.**
Perhaps, just three bedrooms and two bathrooms. However, I would like [a house] that has huge windows so it would be cool and air could circulate.

JOY : **Gaano ho ba kalaking lupa ang gusto ninyo?**
How large a lot would you like?

ROSE : **Puwede na ako sa hindi kalakihan, mga 200 square meters lang.**
I am fine with something not too large, just around 200 square meters.

JOY : **Saan niyo ho ba iniisip bumili ng bahay?**
Where are you thinking of buying a house?

ROSE : **Sa Quezon City ho sana, pero ayaw ko ho doon sa lugar na mababa at bumabaha.**
I am hoping [to buy] in Quezon City, but I don't want a place that is low and where it floods [=a low-lying area that is in a flood zone].

JOY : **Doon ho tayo bumili sa mataas na lugar. Gusto ho ba ninyo ng bagong tayong bahay o lumang bahay?**
Let us buy at a "higher" place. Would you like a newly built house or an old house?

ROSE : **Ano ho ba ang mas mainam?**
Which is better?

JOY : **Kung lumang bahay ho, baka maraming kailangang kumpunihin. Kung bagong bahay naman, wala masyadong dapat ayusin, pero mas mahal.**
If it is an old house, you might have a lot of repairs [to do]. If it's a new house, you don't have to do a lot of repairs, but it will be more expensive.

ROSE : **May mairerekomenda ka ba?**
Can you recommend something?

JOY : **Meron hong ibinibentang bahay ang kaopisina ko sa ahensiya. Medyo luma na ang bahay pero moderno ang disenyo, at maraming punong-kahoy sa paligid. 20 porsiyento ho ang paunang bayad at 30 libong piso hulugan buwan-buwan.**
My co-worker at the [real estate] agency is selling a house. It is a little bit old, but it has a beautiful garden and there are many trees around [the house]. The downpayment is 20 percent and the monthly payment is 30 thousand pesos every month.

ROSE : **Malapit ba sa sakayan ng bus, jeepney, o tren?**
Is it near bus, jeepney or train stops?

JOY : **Meron naman hong masasakyang traysikel papasok ng subdibisyon. Heto ho ang larawan. Ano ho sa tingin niyo?**
There is a tricycle you can ride going inside the subdivision. What do you think?

ROSE : **Aba, maganda ang bahay na ito!**
So, this house is beautiful!

Bokabularyo Vocabulary

Review/study words that describe houses and places. Some of these words are in the previous dialogue and previous lessons; others are useful in conversations about houses, communities and cities. Note how some adjectives have flexible meanings.

Also, note the use of the affix **-ma** with most root words to form adjectives.

WORDS AND PHRASES THAT DESCRIBE HOUSES/CONDOS/APARTMENTS: malaki (huge); **maliit** (small); **katamtaman** (neither big nor small; just right); **maluwang** (roomy; means "wide" when used to describe clothes); **masikip** (not roomy enough; depends on the number of people occupying a house); **maaliwalas** (bright; sunny; open; spacious); **lagusan ang hangin** (air flows all throughout; **hangin** refers to both wind and air); **may isang, dalawang, tatlong palapag** (has one, two, three floors/stories); **moderno ang disenyo** (has a modern design); **bilang ng kuwarto** (number of rooms/bedrooms; note that **kuwarto** can mean either a room or a bedroom); **mataas ang kisame** (has high ceilings); **mababa ang kisame** (has low ceilings); **bahay kubo** (literally, cube house; house made of bamboo and **nipa**, a kind of palm tree); **bahay na bato** (literally, stone house; architectural style during the Spanish colonial period, two-story house made of stone and wood); **bahay bakasyunan** (vacation house); **maraming kailangang kumpunihin** (many things need to be fixed); **nasa ika-_ na palapag** (on the __th floor); **pinakamataas na palapag** (highest floor); **yari sa kahoy** (made of wood); **metal** (metal); **semento** (cement); **marmol** (marble)

WORDS AND PHRASES THAT DESCRIBE PLACES (HOUSES, STREETS, COMMUNITIES, CITIES): palaging binabaha tuwing bumabagyo (always flooded when there is a storm); **mataas na lugar** (high place); **mababang lugar** (low-lying place); **mapuno** (place where there are many trees); **matarik** (steep); **madilim** (dark); **maaraw** (has a lot of sun); **malapit sa pinagtatrabahuhan** (close to place of work); **malapit sa baybayin** (near the seashore); **nalalakad ang sakayan ng bus** (the bus stop can be reached by walking); **malapit sa palengke** (close to the market); **maganda ang tanawin** (has a good view); **malinis** (clean); **madumi/marumi** (dirty); **matrapik** (has a lot of traffic); **matao** (has a lot of people); **malawak** (expansive)

USE OF "HINDI" (NO/NOT) WITH ADJECTIVES: hindi kalakihan (not too big); **hindi kagandahan** (not too beautiful)

WORDS THAT SHOW FLEXIBILITY/UNCERTAINTY: siguro (perhaps); **mga** (approximately); **bandang** (around)

OTHER WORDS: mairerekomenda (can recommend); **mainam** (good); **mas mainam** (better); **paunang bayad** (downpayment); **hulugan** (periodic payments); **buwanang hulog** (monthly payments)

EXPRESSIONS: **ang mabuti ho siguro** (perhaps it would be good if...); **puwede na ako sa...** (I am fine with...); **aba** (so!; expression showing surprise)

Mga Pangungusap Sentences

Review and practice natural speech. In the following examples, practice the following: the use of of **siguro** (perhaps); **mga** (used to mean "approximately"); **bandang** (around) to indicate flexibility of meaning (remember how the word **bayan** means "town, country, and people"?); **iniisip** (thinking of); **sa tingin ko** (in my opinion); and **puwede na ako** (I am fine with); and **aba** (so!)

1. **Mas maganda ho siguro kung dalawang palapag ang bahay.**

OR **Siguro, mas maganda kung dalawang palapag ang bahay.**

Perhaps it would be good if the house has two floors.

You can put **siguro** either at the beginning or the middle of the sentence.

2. **Puwede na ako sa hindi kalakihan, mga 200 square meters lang.**

I am fine with something not too large, just around 200 square meters.

Use **puwede na ako** with **sa** followed by the adjective, in this case, **hindi kalakihan**.

3. TANONG : **Saan niyo ho ba iniisip bumili ng bahay?**

Where are you thinking of buying a house?

SAGOT : **Iniisip kong bumili ng bahay doon sa mataas na lugar.**

I am thinking of buying a house in a high place [=a place on higher gorund].

OR **Sa mataas na lugar ko iniisip bumili ng bahay.**

(literally, At high LINKER place I am thinking buying MARKER house.)

You can use **iniisip** with the verb in the infinitive form: **iniisip kong** + verb = **iniisip kong bumili**.

4. **Ano ho sa tingin niyo?**

What do you think?

(literally, What HONORIFIC in view your?)

In this sentence, we do not use the word **iniisip** when asking for an opinion, which in English, can be expressed as "What do you think?." Instead, we use the word **tingin** (meaning "look; viewpoint").

5. SPOKEN FILIPINO: **Sa Quezon City ho sana, pero ayaw ko sa lugar na mababa at binabaha.** *I am hoping [to buy] in Quezon City, but I don't want a place that is low and where it floods [=a low-lying area that is in a flood zone].* (literally, In Quezon City HONORIFIC hope, but don't want I in place that low and flooded.)
   WRITTEN FILIPINO: **Sa Quezon City ko ho sana gustong bumili ng bahay, pero ayaw kong bumili ng bahay sa lugar na mababa at binabaha.** *I am hoping to buy a house in Quezon City, but I don't want to buy in a place/area that is low and flooded [=in a flood zone].* (literally, In Quezon City I HONORIFIC hope want to buy MARKER house, but don't want I to buy MARKER house in place/area that low and flooded [=in a flood zone].)

Study how spoken Filipino differs from written Filipino. In more natural speech, you can just attach the word **sana** (hope/wish) before or after your preference, in this case, **Sa Quezon City sana** (In Quezon City, hopefully) or alternatively, **Sana, sa Quezon City** (Hopefully, in Quezon City). The written version is more complete, as it includes the phrase **gustong bumili ng bahay** ([where] I would like to buy a house).

Pagsasanay Practice: Mga Tanong at Sagot

Practice natural speech by responding to the following questions and providing the questions to the given answers. In parenthesis, find the word/phrase/question word that you need to practice (questions 1–5). Refer to the vocabulary words you have just learned.

SITUATION 1: You are speaking to a real estate agent. You want to buy a condo that is: small; has two-bedrooms; one bathroom; near your place of work; top floor; around 100 square meters. You think that the condo in the picture he/she showed to you is beautiful.

1. TANONG : **Ano ho ang gusto ninyong bilhin?**
   SAGOT : **(sana)** ____________________.

2. TANONG : **Saan niyo ho iniisip bumili?**
   SAGOT : **(iniisip)** ____________________.

3. Tanong : **Ilang kuwarto ho ang gusto niyo?**
   Sagot : **(siguro)** ______________________________.

4. Tanong : **Gaano kalaki ho ang gusto niyo?**
   Sagot : **(puwede na ako)** ______________________________.

5. Tanong : **Ano ho ang tingin niyo sa condo na ito?**
   Sagot : **(aba)** ______________________________.

Situation 2: You are selling your grandparents' house. Your realtor asks you questions about the house:

6. Tanong : **(klase)** ______________________________?
   Sagot : **Bahay ho na may dalawang palapag.**

7. Tanong : **(gaano)** ______________________________?
   Sagot : **Mga 500 square feet ho.**

8. Tanong : **(iniisip)** ______________________________?
   Sagot : **Iniisip ko hong ibenta ng mga 40 milyong piso.**

9. Tanong : **(masyadong mura)** ______________________________?
   Sagot : **Kasi ho, maraming dapat kumpunihin sa bahay.**

10. Tanong : **(tingin)** ______________________________?
    Sagot : **Maaliwalas ho ang bahay.**

Pagsasanay Practice
Talking About A Real Estate Property/ Writing Advertisements

Pretend that you are a real estate agent. For classroom learners, create dialogues that will help you sell a house to your customer. Teachers may want to divide the class into two: buyers and sellers (who might work in pairs or groups of three), with sellers and buyers provided the same information until they can find their "match." Individual learners should write advertisements that describe the property they are selling.

Real Estate Property 1: Three-bedroom, two-bathroom house with a beautiful garden; 350 square meters; has huge windows for good airflow; bright and sunny; priced competitively because it is near a river that tends to overflow during the rainy season; modern architectural style; has two floors; close to the public market.

REAL ESTATE PROPERTY 2: One-bedroom, one bathroom condominium unit on the eighth floor of a high-rise building; close to a train station and bus stops; close to a shopping mall; has a good view of the city; 90 square meters.

REAL ESTATE PROPERTY 3: Four-bedroom, two-bathroom vacation house near the beach; has high ceilings; property comes with a **nipa** hut which serves as a playhouse for kids; 15 percent downpayment, and 40 thousand pesos monthly payment; made of wood and stone; has an expansive lot of 500 square meters.

REAL ESTATE PROPERTY 4: Two-bedroom, one bathroom with marble tiles, two-story townhouse; has small windows; close to a shopping mall, property is in a flood-free area but has a lot of traffic; 120 square meters.

Gramatika Grammar
Adjectives and Adjectival Affixes[1]

In Lessons 8–10, the focus is on describing people, places and feelings, so this is a good time to have an overview on the use of adjectival affixes. This will help you guess the meaning of an unfamiliar word as long as you can guess the root word; also, most dictionaries will probably have only the root word, so you might not find the meaning of a word with an uncommon affix.

As you may know, there are also some adjectives such as **pandak** (short); **pagod** (tired) that do not have affixes.

Here is a list of affixes with usage in mind: forming words that describe people, objects and places; outlining how they are used; and providing examples of adjectives used in describing people, objects, and places. You are familiar with many of these affixes as they have been introduced in previous lessons.

For example, the adjectival affix **pang-** (with variations of of **pam-** and **pan**) was introduced in Lesson 3. For other adjective formations (for example, intensification such as **malungkot na malungkot** [very sad]), more examples will be given in succeeding lessons.

The chart next page, however, enables you to have an overview of affixes which can be used to form adjectives. The first column features the affix; the second, third, and fourth columns provide you with one or two examples each. Note that some affixes are not used for objects and places, only for people. Also, in the latter half of the chart, you will find words that are verb participles used as adjectives.

[1] In listing the affixes and examples, I was guided by the grammatical explanations in the book *Tagalog Reference Grammar* by Paul Schachter and Fe T. Otanes.

Your task is to study the adjective by analyzing how the word is constructed using the affix and the root word, and in some cases, the duplication of syllables.

Affix	Usage	Adjectives describing a person	Adjectives describing a place	Adjectives describing an object or other nouns
Ma-	Used to show abundance of a certain quality	**maganda** (beautiful); **matalino** (intelligent)	**matao** (crowded); **matrapik** (has a lot of traffic)	**malaki** (big); **makulay** (colorful)
Ma- in	Used to show inclination or habit	**matulungin** (helpful); **madasalin** (prays a lot)		**mainitin** (for example, **mainitin ang ulo** [hot-headed] – the object being "**ulo**" (or head))
Naka-	Used to show condition or state	**nakaupo** (sitting); **nakatayo** (standing)	**nakalubog sa tubig-baha** (immersed in flood waters); **nakakabit** (attached to)	**nakabaon** (embedded); **nakaangat** (lifted)
-an	Used to mean "full of" or "covered with"	**sugatan** (covered with wounds); **bayaran** (a person that can be "bought")		**duguan** (covered with blood, for example, referring to clothes); **putikan** (covered with mud)
-in	Used to show abundance of a certain quality; being susceptible to something	**sipunin** (susceptible to colds); **bigatin** (heavy; used metaphorically to refer to an important person)	**bahain** (susceptible to floods)	**dumihin** (susceptible to dirt, for example, **damit** [clothes] **na dumihin**)
Mala-	Used to show similarity to something	**malareyna** (like a queen)	**malapalasyo** (like a palace)	**malasutla** (like silk), for example, **mala-sutlang kutis** (silken complexion)
Mapag-	Used to mean inclination or "being fond of"	**mapagmataas** (haughty); **mapagmarunong** (someone who thinks he/she knows best)		**mapaglaro**, for example, **mapaglaro ang tadhana** (equivalent to the English idiom "fate plays its tricks")
Mapang- (see exceptions below where one uses **mapan-** or replaces the first letter of root word)	Used to mean "inclination" or "being fond of"	**mapanghamak** (fond of putting others down); **mapang-api** (oppressive towards others)	**mapang-api** (oppressive), for example, a country that is oppressive towards its people	

Affix	Usage	Adjectives describing a person	Adjectives describing a place	Adjectives describing an object or other nouns
Maka-	Used to show inclination or "being in favor or fond of something"	**makabayan** (nationalistic); **makasarili** (individualistic; selfish)		
Pala-	Used to show something that one usually does	**palangiti** (always smiling); **palaaway** (always fighting with someone)		
Pang- (with variations **pam-** used for labial consonants **p**, **b**, **m**, **w**; **pan-** used for dental consonants **t**, **d**, **n**, **l**, **r** and **s** (see Lesson 3)	Used to mean "used for"		**pambakasyon** (used for vacations)	**pambahay na damit** (clothing used for the house); **panluto** (used for cooking)
Pang- -an **Pang-** + root word + **-an** (with same variations as above)	Used to mean "used for"			**pandalawahan** (for two)
Pa- **Pa + root** word or **Pa +** duplication of root word	Used in three ways: to show intermittent activity; to mean "was starting to"; to show "manner"	**papunta-punta** (sometimes goes to…); **pakanta-kanta** (sometimes sings); **papunta** (was about to go); **paalis** (was about to leave); **patalikod** (by turning one's back); **paharap** (face to face)		
Ka- + duplication of root word	Used to mean "very" or "highly"	**kanais-nais** (very delightful); **kagalang-galang** (very respectable)	**kaakit-akit** (highly enticing); **kapuri-puri** (very commendable)	**katuwa-tuwa** (very pleasant); **kapana-panabik** (very exciting)
Ka-/magka-	Used to show relationship or commonality	**kakuwentuhan/ magkakuwentu-han** (someone one trades stories with); **kaututang-dila** (used metaphorically, to mean "someone one is close to")	**kalapit/ magkalapit** (nearby); **kakabit**; **magkakabit** (attached to)	**kauri/magkauri** (of the same kind); **kakulay/magkakulay** (of the same color)

Affix	Usage	Adjectives describing a person	Adjectives describing a place	Adjectives describing an object or other nouns
Kasing/ mag-kasing with variations **pam-** used for labial consonants **p, b, m, w**; **pan-** used for dental consonants **t, d, n, l, r** and **s** (see Lesson 3)	Used to show comparisons	**kasingkisig/ magkasingkisig** (equally handsome); **kasimbait/ magkasimbait** (equally kind)	**kasinggulo/ magkasinggulo** (equally chaotic); **kasinlinis/ magkasinlinis** (equally clean)	**kasingkinis/ magkasingkinis** (equally smooth); **kasinsarap/ magkasinsarap** (equally delicious)
Magka-	Used to show commonality between two people, objects, or places	**magkalapit** (near each other); **magkabanggaan** (clashing with each other)	**magkalayo** (far from each other); **magkakatabi** (beside each other)	**magkakulay** (of the same color); **magkahugis** (of the same shape)
Magkaka-	Used to show commonality between 3 or more people, objects, places	**magkakalapit** (near each other); **magkakabanggan** (clashing with each other)	**magkakalayo** (far from each other); **magkakatabi** (beside each other)	**magkakakulay** (of the same color); **magkakahugis** (of the same shape)
Pinaka-	Used to show superlatives	**pinakamabait** (nicest); **pinakamahirap** (poorest)	**pinakamalapit** (nearest); **pinakamalawak** (most expansive)	**pinakamaliit** (smallest); **pinakamagaan** (lightest in weight)
Nakapang + first syllable of root word + root word; sometimes "**ka**" is duplicated	Used to refer to effect	**nakapanghihinayang/ nakakapanghinayang** (makes one regret)		**nakapanghihina/ nakakapanghina** (makes one weak)
Ma- –an Ma + root word + **an**	Used to mean "characterized by"			**matagalan** (for a long time); **malaliman** (deep)
Na- + first syllable or root word + root word	Used to mean "can"	**nakakausap** (someone one can talk to); **naaapi** (can be oppressed)	**nalalakad ang estasyon ng tren** (the train station is within walking distance); **naaabot** (can be reached)	**nakakain** (can be eaten); **nabibili** (can be bought)

Affix	Usage	Adjectives describing a person	Adjectives describing a place	Adjectives describing an object or other nouns
Na –an **Na** + first syllable of root word + root word + **-an**	Used to mean "can"	**natatapakan** (used metaphorically to describe a person that can be stepped on)	**natataniman** (can be planted on); **nababakuran** (can be fenced)	**nasusuotan** (can be dressed); for example, **nasusuotan ng damit ang manyika** (doll); **napakikinggan** (can be heard; listened to)
Naka+ first syllable of root word + root word; in conversational Filipino, sometimes "**ka**" and not the first syllable of the root word is duplicated	Used in two ways: one, to show effect; two, refers to ability or to mean "can"	**nakaiinis/ nakakainis** (irritating); **nakaka; nakatutugtog** (has the ability to play an instrument); **nakasasayaw** (has the ability to dance)	**nakahahalina** (fascinating); **nakahihikayat** (has the ability to attract or persuade)	**nakaluluto** (has the ability to cook); **nakagagamot** (has the ability to heal)
Nakapag- first syllable of root word + root word; sometimes "**ka**" is duplicated	Used to refer to ability	**nakapaglalaro** (can play a game or sport); **nakatutugtog** (can play an instrument)	**nakapag-aangkat** (can import); **nakapagaani** (able to harvest)	**nakapagdadala** (has the ability to bring); **nakapagsasakay** (has the ability to transport)
Napa- **Napa** + first syllable of root word + root word	Used to refer to something that can be caused to a person, object or place	**napagalit** (was made angry); **napaluhod** (was made to kneel)	**napaganda** (was made beautiful)	**napalaki** (was made big); **napaliit** (was made small)

Some points to remember when using adjectival affixes are:

1. Variations in "pang-," "kasing/magkasing," and "mapang-"

As discussed in Lesson 3, **pang-** is used with variations: **pam-** for labial consonants **p**, **b**, **m**, **w**; and **pan-** used for dental consonants **t**, **d**, **n**, **l**, **r** and **s**. For example, we say **damit pambahay** (to refer to clothes or footwear worn inside the house) and **damit panlakad** (clothes worn outside the house).

Similarly, we say **kasingkisig/magkasingkisig** (equally handsome); **kasimbait/ magkasimbait** (equally nice); and **kasinlinis/magkasinlinis** (equally clean).

2. The affix "pa-"

As explained in other lessons, the affix **pa-** is used in several ways: first, to show intermittent activity; second; to describe an action that one is about to do; and third; to show manner. These uses of **pa-** can sometimes be confusing to the learners because **pa-** is also used to form verbs and adverbs. For example:

Masaya ang pakanta-kantang si Maria.
Maria, who is singing intermittently, is happy.
Pakanta-kanta si Maria habang nagtatrabaho.
Maria sings intermittently while she works.

Tinawagan ni Suzette ang patulog nang si Jorge.
Suzette called Jorge, who was about to sleep.
Patulog na si Jorge nang tawagan siya ni Suzette.
Jorge was about to sleep when Suzette called him.

Patalikod ang bata sa gusali.
The child had his back to the building.
Patalikod na naglakad ang bata papunta sa gusali.
The child walked backwards towards the building.

Note that the word examples above can be used as adjectives, verbs, or adverbs.

3. Using "kasing-" and "magkasing-"

The affix **kasing-** (with variations **kasin-** and **kasim-**) is used to mean "as . . . . as" while **magkasing-** (with variations **magkasin-** and **magkasim-**) is used to mean "equally ... ." For example:

Kasinlinis ng bahay ko ang bahay ng kapatid ko.
My sister/brother's house is as clean as my house.
(literally, As clean as my house MARKER house of sister/brother my.)

Magkasinlinis ang bahay ko at ang bahay ng kapatid ko.
My house and my sister/brother's house are equally clean.
(literally, Equally clean MARKER house my and MARKER house of sister/brother my.)

4. Affixes used for adjectives and verbs—using "mag-an", "na-+," "na--an," "naka-," "nakapag-," and "napa-"

You might ask: are these affixes used for adjectives, verbs or adverbs? The answer would be: it depends on how the words/phrases are used.

Compare how they are used in the sentences below:

• Affixes **mag- an** used to form an adverb:
Magdamagan silang nagtrabaho sa call center.
They worked all night at the call center.

• Affix **mag- -an** used to form an adjective:
Magdamagan ang trabaho nila sa call center.

Their [kind of] work at the call center is an all-nighter.

- Affix **na-** used to form a verb:
  Nalalakad ko ang buong baryo sa isang araw.
  I can walk [around] the whole village in a day.

- Affix **na-** used to form an adjective:
  Maliit lang ang baryo, kaya nalalakad ito sa isang araw.
  The village is small, so one can walk [around it] in a day.
  (literally, Small only MARKER village, so can walk it in one day.)

- Affixes **na- -an** used to form a verb:
  Natataniman ko ng gulay ang bakuran ko buong taon.
  I can plant vegetables in my backyard all year.

- Affixes **na-an** used to form an adjective:
  Maliit lang ang buong taon kong natatanimang bakuran ng gulay.
  The backyard, on which I plant vegetables all year, is just small.

- Affix **naka-** used to form a verb:
  Nakagagamot ng diyabetis ang halamang ito.
  This plant can cure diabetes.

- Affix **naka-** used to form an adjective:
  Bumili ka ng halamang nakagagamot ng diyabetis.
  Buy a plant that can cure diabetes.

- Affix **nakapag-** used to form a verb:
  Nakapagsasakay ang dyipni ng 16 na pasahero.
  The jeepney can take 16 passengers.

- Affix **nakapag-** to form an adjective:
  Inirehistro niya ang dyipni niyang nakapagsasakay ng 16 na pasahero.
  He/she registered his/her jeepney that can take 16 passengers.

- Affix **napa-** used to form a verb:
  Napaganda nang husto ni Mabelle ang bahay niya.
  Mabelle was really able to make her house beautiful.

- Affix **napa-** used to form an adjective:
  Ipinakita sa akin ni Mabelle ang napaganda niyang bahay.
  Mabelle showed me the house she had made beautiful.

Pagsasanay Practice
Mga Tanong at Sagot

Practice the affixes you have learned by asking and answering questions:

1. Tanong : **Aling lugar sa lungsod mo ang matao?**
   Sagot : ______________________________.

2. Tanong : **Sino sa mga kaibigan mo ang matulungin?**
   Sagot : ______________________________.

3. Tanong : **Bakit nakalubog sa baha ang Compostela Valley?**
   Sagot : ______________________________.

4. Tanong : **Kaninong T-shirt ang duguan?**
   Sagot : ______________________________.

5. Tanong : **Ano ang kulay ng palda mong dumihin?**
   Sagot : ______________________________.

6. Tanong : ______________________________?
   Sagot : **Malapalasyo ang bahay ni Ginang Cruz.**

7. Tanong : ______________________________?
   Sagot : **Ayaw ng mga kaklase ni Lance sa kanya dahil mapagmataas siya.**

8. Tanong : ______________________________?
   Sagot : **Galit ang mga magsasaka sa asyenda dahil mapang-api ang sistema nito.**

9. Tanong : ______________________________?
   Sagot : **Binaril si Jose Rizal dahil isa siyang makabayan.**

10. Tanong : ______________________________?
    Sagot : **Marami siyang kaibigan dahil palangiti siya.**

11. Tanong : ______________________________?
    Sagot : **Nakasuot siya ng damit na pambahay.**

12. Tanong : **Anong mesa ang gusto ninyo, pandalawahan o pantatluhan?**
    Sagot : ______________________________.

13. Tanong : **Ano ang kulay ng paalis nang bus?**
    Sagot : ______________________________.

14. TANONG : **Ano-ano ang mga katuwa-tuwang lugar sa inyong lungsod?**
    SAGOT : ______________________________.

15. TANONG : **Sino-sino ang mga kakuwentuhan mo sa klase?**
    SAGOT : ______________________________.

16. TANONG : **Aling mga gusali ang magkasinlinis sa unibersidad mo?**
    SAGOT : ______________________________.

17. TANONG : **Ano-ano ang magkakatabing bayan o lungsod sa inyong lugar?**
    SAGOT : ______________________________.

18. TANONG : **Gaano kalayo ang pinakamalapit na restawran sa bahay mo?**
    SAGOT : ______________________________.

19. TANONG : ______________________________?
    SAGOT : **Ang sakit niya ang nakapanghihina sa kanya.**

20. TANONG : ______________________________?
    SAGOT : **Napagod siya dahil magdamagan ang trabaho.**

21. TANONG : **Aling estasyon ng tren ang nalalakad mo mula sa bahay mo?**
    SAGOT : ______________________________.

22. TANONG : ______________________________.
    SAGOT : **Isang ektarya ang lupang nataniman ng mga magsasaka ng gulay.**

23. TANONG : ______________________________.
    SAGOT : **Maraming turista sa isla dahil nakahihikayat ang mga dalampasigan nito.**

24. TANONG : ______________________________.
    SAGOT : **Bumili siya ng dalawang dyipni na nakapagsasakay ng labing-anim na tao.**

25. TANONG : ______________________________.
    SAGOT : **3000 square feet na ang sukat ng napalaki niyang bahay.**

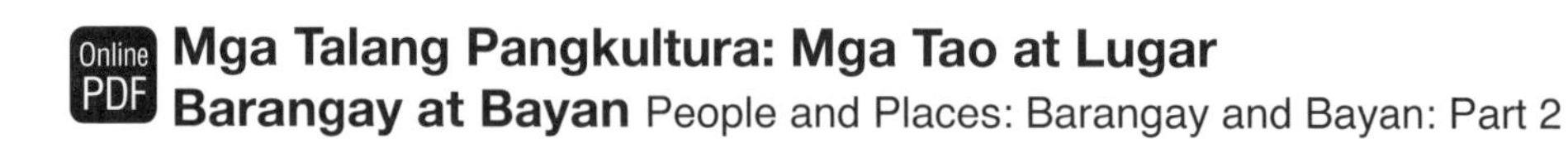

Mga Talang Pangkultura: Mga Tao at Lugar Barangay at Bayan People and Places: Barangay and Bayan: Part 2

Talakayan: Ano ang iyong bayan/mga bayan?
What is/are your town/s, or country/countries/ or people/s?

Classroom learners can form small groups to discuss one or more questions below. Individual learners can write a paragraph or two in response to one or more prompts.

1. When did you first encounter the word ***bayan***? What was the first meaning/s you associated with this word?
   Kailan mo unang nabasa o narinig ang salitang bayan? Ano ang mga kahulugan na una mong naiugnay sa salitang ito?
2. What is/are your town/s, country/countries, or people?
   Ano ang iyong bayan/mga bayan?
3. In your conversations with other Filipinos (including your family members), what do they think of the term **bayan**?
   Sa inyong pakikipag-usap sa ibang Filipino, [kasama na ang inyong mga kapamilya), ano ang tingin nila sa terminong "bayan"?
4. List and discuss words related to **bayan**—for example, **kababayan** and **Inang Bayan**. You can also do an internet search for the word.
   Talakayin ang mga salitang may kaugnayan sa bayan—halimbawa, kababayan, and Inang Bayan. Puwede rin kayong mag-search sa internet.

Pakikinig: New Bataan, Compostela Valley, sinalanta nang husto ng bagyong Pablo New Bataan, Compostela Valley, totally damaged by typhoon Pablo

Dagdag na Gawain Additional Activity
Pananaliksik Research

As an additional activity, do research on what happened in Compostela Valley in Mindanao, southern Philippines in December 2012. Classroom learners should work in small groups and try to discuss or write about the incident. Individual learners can write a paragraph.

Here are some talking points/questions which you might want to address.

1. **Ano ang nangyari sa Compostela Valley?**
   What happened in Compostela Valley?
2. **Ano ang ugat ng problema?**
   What is the root of the problem?

3. **Ano ang dapat gawin ng pamahalaan?**
   What should be done by the government?

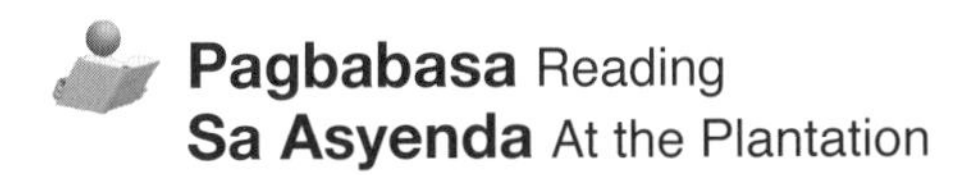

Pagbabasa Reading
Sa Asyenda At the Plantation

Read the following passage on an unnamed plantation. Then, answer the comprehension questions found below. As an added activity, you may want to encircle the adjectives in this passage. Review/study the following vocabulary words: **bumati** (greeted); **balikan** (return); **panahon ng kolonyalismo** (colonial period); **ipinagmamalaki** (boasts of); **huni** (chirping); **lawiswis** (swishing sound made by bamboo); **karatula** (sign); **biglang-bigla** (suddenly).

Sa Asyenda

Sintamis ng asukal ang ngiti ng real estate agent na bumati sa akin. “Magandang umaga po. Maiksi lang po ang biyahe natin papuntang Tarlac. Sigurado akong magugustuhan ninyo ang subdibisyong ito,” sabi niya.

“Sabi mo, perfect sa amin ang subdivision?” tanong ko sa kanya.

“Gusto niyo kasi ang makalumang bahay na bakasyunan. Ang asawa niyo naman, mahilig mag-golf,” sagot niya na parang siguradong-sigurado na makabebenta siya ngayong araw na ito.

Inabot niya ang brochure na “Las haciendas.” Ingles siyempre, dahil English-speaking naman ang mga mamimiling may middle-class aspirations. “Experience the Spanish countryside at the Hacienda,” ang sabi ng brochure, na parang ang lahat ng tao, gustong balikan ang panahon ng kolonyalismo. Tahimik na buhay sa kanayunan, ngunit abot-kamay ang lahat ng conveniences ng lungsod. May mga mapa at larawan ng clubhouse, golf course, swimming pool, gazebo, lugar para makapag-piknik, mga hardin, kapihan, at kalapit na shopping mall. Parang paraiso raw ito—pulang-pula ang fire trees at luntiang-luntian naman ang mga puno at damo. Bukod rito, kalapit ng asyenda ang shopping mall, mga sinehan, ang industrial park, at isang mamahaling otel.

Ipinagmamalaki rin ng brochure na magiging ligtas ang mga residente. Eksklusibo ang pasukan at labasan ng mga residente at may mga guwardiya sa limang subdibisyon ng "Las Haciendas." Mahalagang feature daw ang perimeter wall, sabi ng real estate agent na may ngiting kasintamis ng asukal. Samakatuwid, bawal ang mga pagala-galang magsasaka, manggagawa at kung sino-sino pang mahihirap na tao. Hindi para sa kanila ang subdibisyon.

Maiksi lang ang biyahe sa highway; hindi matrapik ang daan. Sa wakas, nakarating din kami sa probinsiya, at sa romantiko kong isipan, parang naririnig ko na ang huni ng ibon, ang lawiswis ng kawayan, at ¾ beat ng tinikling music. Ang lapit ko na sa pangarap kong bahay bakasyunan, kaya napangiti ako—sintamis ng asukal.

But no, no, no. Ano itong nadadaanan namin? Sa bakod malapit sa refinery ay may nakasabit na mga mahahabang karatula: "Ituloy ang laban!" "Katarungan para sa mga pinatay na magsasaka!" "Ipamahagi ang lupa sa asyenda!"

Ito ang hindi nasabi ng brochure at ng real estate agent na may ngiting kasintamis ng asukal: pitong magsasaka ang binaril ng mga pulis at sundalo sa piketlayn; kahit pumanig na sa mga magsasaka ang Korte Suprema, hindi pa rin ipinapamahagi ang lupa; ang pinakaluntian at pinakamasaganang bahagi ng asyenda ay ang mga lupang binawi ng mga magsasaka sa pamamagitan ng bungkalan—sama-samang pagtatanim ng lupa kahit walang pahintulot.

Biglang-bigla, naging pinagsamang pelikulang aksiyon, drama, horror, at suspense ang aking romantikong dream movie.

1. What is the main character's dream house like?
2. Why does the agent think that the property is ideal for the couple?
3. How is the village community described in the brochure?
4. What did the main character imagine rural life to be?
5. Why did the author's dream movie become a horror story?

For students who would like to know more about land disputes, agrarian reform and the peasant struggle in the Philippines, you may want to start by checking out these links: http://bulatlat.com/main/tag/hacienda-luisita/; http://kilusangmagbubukid.org/ and http://www.eiler.ph/another-world-is-possible/.

Pagsusulat Writing

Write a short piece on any of the following topics. You can choose to write an essay or a short short story (about 100 words). Make sure you use a lot of adjectives. Here are a few topics you might find interesting:

1. Your favorite place;
2. Your dream place;
3. Your childhood vacation place.

Before proceeding to write, think of a metaphor that you can use to describe this particular place.

Paglalagom Summing Up

In Lesson 9, you have learned:

- Words and phrases that describe houses, places, and geography;
- Affixes used for adjectives;
- The many meanings of the word **bayan**.

Aralin
Lesson
10

Paglalarawan ng Damdamin
Describing One's Feelings

In this lesson, review/study words and phrases that you can use to describe feelings, direct and indirect object focus, more idiomatic expressions, and sing a song in Filipino.

Diyalogo Dialogue**: Despedida** Farewell Party

Read the following dialogue aloud. Pay attention to the idiomatic expressions used. You may want to encircle these words/phrases. After reading the dialogue, classroom learners can ask and answer questions, while individual learners can write a paragraph about it.

It is Saturday evening. Katie and Armael is at Katie's **despedida** or farewell party. Katie is on her way to Manila, and then to Davao in southern Philippines, as part of a medical mission assisting flood victims in Compostela Valley. Katie is especially excited about the mission because her family is from Davao City, a few hours from Compostela Valley.

KATIE : **Salamat at binigyan niyo ako ng despedida, ha?**
Thanks for giving me a despedida.

ARMAEL : **Kumusta, Katie? Handa ka na ba sa biyahe mo sa Lunes?**
How are you, Katie? Are you ready for your travel [=flight] on Monday?

KATIE : **Sabik na sabik na nga ako. Para akong pusang hindi mapaanak. Dalawang tulog na lang.**
I am [already] so excited. I am like a cat who could not give birth [=about to give birth]. Just two more [nights of] sleep.

ARMAEL : **Masayang-masaya siguro ang lola mo, ano?**
Perhaps your grandmother is very happy, right?

KATIE : **Oo, kasi magkakasama kami sa Pasko. Mahal na mahal ako ng lola ko, alam mo? Nag-iisa kasi akong apo na babae.**
Yes, because we will be together during Christmas. My grandmother loves me very much, you know. [That's] because I am her only granddaughter.

ARMAEL : **Hindi ba nagdaramdam ang nanay at tatay mo?**
Do your mother and father not feel hurt?

KATIE : **Ilang araw na ngang mukhang Biyernes Santo ang nanay at tatay ko. Bagong Taon na kasi ang balik ko sa Oakland.**
They have looked as though it's Good Friday [=been sad] for several days now. [That's] because I will be back in Oakland only during New Year's Day.

ARMAEL : **Kumusta pala ang mga nasalanta ng bagyo? Ano ang balita?**
How are the [people] devastated by the typhoon? What is the news?

KATIE : **Naku, ang daming namatay at nawalan ng tirahan. Lugaming-lugami nga raw ang Pasko nila.**
Oh, so many [people] died and [others] lost their homes. [They] say their Christmas is very depressing.

ARMAEL : **Kawawa naman sila. Hindi ba marami namang relief efforts?**
Poor them! [=I feel bad for them!] Aren't there a lot of relief efforts?

KATIE : **Oo, pero ang problema, nagrereklamo na rin ang mga tao. Namumuti na raw ang mga mata nila sa kahihintay sa tulong. Sira kasi ang mga daan kaya mahirap ang biyahe.**
Yes, but the problem is, the people are also complaining. Their eyes are turning white [=they have been waiting for a long time] for assistance. [It's] because the roads have been destroyed so travel is difficult.

ARMAEL : **Sana makatulong ang na-fund raise natin.**
I hope what we have [fund-]raised can help.

KATIE : **Makakatulong talaga. Natutuwa nga ako at maraming doktor at nars na nagboluntaryo para sa medical at relief mission.**

[It] can certainly help. I am happy that many doctors and nurses volunteered for the medical and relief mission.

ARMAEL : **Bakit ba nagkaroon ng landslide at baha?**
Why did the landslide and the floods happen?

KATIE : **Iyan ang nakakagalit. Napakasakim kasi ng mga malalaking minahan na sumira sa bundok.**
That's what makes [me] angry. The huge mining [companies] that destroyed the mountain[s] are so greedy.

ARMAEL : **Naku, matagal nang ikinagagalit iyan ng mga tao, lalo na ng mga katutubo.**
Oh, that has long made the people angry, especially the indigenous people.

KATIE : **Maiba ako… Ikaw, saan ka magpa-Pasko?**
On another [topic]... [What about] you, where will you [spend] Christmas?

ARMAEL : **Uuwi ako sa Los Angeles. Dadalo ako sa kasal ni Melissa.**
I will go home to Los Angeles. I will attend Melissa's wedding.

KATIE : **Abay ka ba?**
Are you a wedding sponsor?

ARMAEL : **Oo. Baka magsaulian kami ng kandila kapag hindi ako pumunta.**
Yes. We might exchange candles [=part ways] if I don't come.

KATIE : **Pakisabi kay Melissa, binabati ko siya.**
Please send my greetings to Melissa.

Bokabularyo Vocabulary

Study the following words that can help you express feelings and use idiomatic expressions. In *Tagalog for Beginners*, you learned basic words to express feelings—for example, **masaya** (happy), **malungkot** (sad), **galit** (angry) etc. For Intermediate Filipino, study synonyms of these words and also new words, phrases and idiomatic expressions that show how intensity of emotion differs.

WORDS/PHRASES/IDIOMS EXPRESSING HAPPINESS: masaya/maligaya/nagagalak (happy); **masayang-masaya/napakasaya/lubhang nagagalak/maligayang-maligaya** (very happy); **natutuwa** (pleased); **ikinalulugod** (makes me pleased); **walang pagsidlan ang tuwa** (very happy; literally, there is no container that can hold [my happiness]); **abot-tenga ang ngiti** (smiling from ear to ear; literally, smile reaches one's ear); **sabik na sabik** (excited); **nakakataba ng puso** (gives pleasure; something one might say when given a compliment)

WORDS/PHRASES/IDIOMS EXPRESSING SADNESS: nagdaramdam (feels hurt); **malungkot/malumbay** (sad); **naaawa** (pities; feels sad for someone); **napakalungkot/malungkot na malungkot/napakalumbay/malumbay na malumbay** (very sad); **nanlulumo** (feeling devastated); **nakapanlulumo** (tragic); **lugami** (feeling sad; feeling of failure); **naghihinagpis** (grieving; feeling resentful); **nananaghoy** (feeling of lament; mourning); **nagluluksa** (mourning); **mukhang Biyernes Santo** (looks sad; literally, looks like Good Friday); **dumaraing** (grieves; complains); **sugat sa dibdib** (heartache; literally; wound in heart); **mabigat ang loob** (with a heavy heart; literally, heavy inside)

WORDS/PHRASES/IDIOMS EXPRESSING FEAR: natatakot/nangangamba (feels afraid); **nasindak** (felt fear, terror and shock); **nagulat** (was surprised); **nakapanghihilakbot** (evokes a feeling of fear; hair-raising); **nakaduduwag** (makes one feel cowardly); **may daga sa dibdib** (afraid; worried; literally, mouse in chest)

WORDS/PHRASES/IDIOMS EXPRESSING ANGER: naiinis (irritated); **nagagalit** (angry); **nasusuklam/napopoot** (feeling intense anger/hatred); **nagdilim ang paningin** (became really angry; literally, vision became black); **nagngingitngit** (angry; feeling of indignation); **nag-aalimpuyo ang dibdib** (very angry; literally, has a whirlpool in one's chest)

WORDS/PHRASES/IDIOMS EXPRESSING LOVE, DESIRE, COURTSHIP AND MARRIAGE: mahal/minamahal (loves); **iniibig** (loves; used only for the "beloved" or the country); **sinisinta/iniirog/pinipintuho** (loves; adores); **gusto** (likes); **malapit na malapit** (very close); **ninanasa** (desires); **nalilibugan** (lusts for); **nililigawan** (courts); **sinusuyo** (shows affection to); **namanhikan** (asked for a woman's hand in marriage from her parents, as part of traditional courtship customs); **pag-iisang dibdib** (wedding; marriage; literally; having one heart); **kabiyak ng dibdib** (husband, wife or partner; literally, partner of one's heart); **pulot-gata** (honeymoon; literally honey cream or honey coconut milk)

OTHER IDIOMATIC EXPRESSIONS USED IN THE DIALOGUE: parang pusang hindi mapaanak (restless, either because of excitement or tension; literally, like a cat waiting to give birth); **namumuti ang mata** (waiting for a long time); **magsaulian ng kandila** (part ways; cease to be friends; literally, exchanging candles)

OTHER WORDS: nasalanta (devastated by); **pagguho ng lupa** (landslide); **baha** (floods); **kahihintay** (waiting; similar to another noun form, **paghihintay**); **abay** (wedding sponsor)

EXPRESSIONS ONE CAN USE TO GREET/CONDOLE ANOTHER PERSON: Binabati kita! (Congratulations!); **Natutuwa ako para sa iyo.** (I am happy for you.); **Ikinalulungkot ko.** (I am sad for you.); **Nakikiramay ako.** (My condolences.); **Taos-pusong pakikiramay.** (My heartfelt condolences.); **Binabati kita sa iyong pagtatapos.** (I congratulate you on your graduation); **Karapat-dapat ka talaga.** (You are well deserving.); **Binabati kita sa iyong kasal.** (I congratulate you on your wedding.); **Kawawa!/ ka naman!** (Poor you! [=I feel bad for you!])

Mga Pangungusap Sentences

In this lesson we want to: first, continue our study of natural speech; and second, look at how sentences that express emotions differ when the focus shifts.

You have learned that spoken Tagalog/Filipino varies vastly from both written Tagalog/Filipino and the English language. In this lesson, pay attention to three things: shorter sentences in dialogues (something to remember in case you want to be a playwright or a scriptwriter, needed for actors' ease of speaking); choice of words; and sentence structure.

In the dialogue above, you find the following sentences:

1. **Masaya nga kasi magkakasama kami sa Pasko. Mahal na mahal ako ng lola ko, alam mo? Nag-iisa kasi akong apo na babae.**
   Happy because we will be together during Christmas. My grandmother loves me very much, you know. [That's] because I am her only granddaughter.

Note the use of **alam mo** (you know), which we find in conversations, and **kasi** (because) in the middle of the sentences (again, not recommended for written sentences in Tagalog/Filipino.)

If we were to write these sentences in a short story, for example, we would replace **kasi** with **dahil** and make the sentences more complete. For example:

2. **Masaya nga <u>dahil</u> magkakasama kami sa Pasko. Mahal na mahal ako ng lola ko <u>dahil</u> nag-iisa akong apo na babae.**

Now, let us look at other choices of words. Study examples 3 (which comes from the dialogue) and 4. Notice the use of **ba** (used for yes-and-no questions, and also for emphasis in natural speech). Also, in conversations, most people will use the word "landslide" instead of **pagguho**.

3. **Dialogue: Bakit ba nagkaroon ng landslide at baha?**
   Why did the landslide and the floods happen?

4. **News Report: Bakit nagkaroon ng pagguho ng lupa at baha?**
   Why did the landslide and the floods happen?

Next, let us look into sentence structure and tenses. Look at the literal translation of the sentence in Tagalog/Filipino.

5. **Spoken Filipino: Sira kasi ang mga daan kaya mahirap ang biyahe.**
   Literal translation: Destroyed because MARKER roads so difficult MARKER travel.

Natural English translation: *It's because the roads had been destroyed that travel is difficult.*
Written Filipino: Dahil sira ang mga daan, mahirap ang biyahe. (*Because the roads had been destroyed, travel is difficult.*) (literally, Because destroyed MARKER roads, difficult MARKER travel.)

In example no. 5, the English translations needed to use the past perfect tense to be grammatically correct. This was not necessary in the Tagalog/Filipino sentences. As you know, there are no tenses in Tagalog/Filipino, only aspects.

Let's move on. Study the following sentences from the dialogue and study the affixes that are used for the root word **galit**. Sentences 6 and 7 are from the dialogue, while sentences 8 and 9, show more clearly the shift from actor focus to object focus.

6. **Iyan ang nakakagalit.**
   That's what makes [me] angry.
   (Note: **nakakagalit** here is used as an adjective—something that makes one angry.)

7. **Naku, matagal nang ikinagagalit iyan ng mga tao, lalo na ang mga katutubo.**
   Oh, that has long made the people angry, especially the indigenous people.

8. **Nagagalit ako sa mga sakim na mga minahan.**
   I am angry because the mining companies are greedy.

9. **Ikinakagalit ko ang mga sakim na minahan.**
   It is the greedy mining companies that make me angry.

Here are more examples:

10. **Nagbigay ang mga kaibigan ni Katie ng despedida para sa kanya.** (actor focus)

11. **Despedida party ang ibinigay ng mga kaibigan ni Katie para sa kanya.** (object focus)

12. **Binigyan si Katie ng despedida party ng mga kaibigan niya.** (receiver focus or benefactive focus)

13. **Sumaya si Katie dahil sa despedida party na ibinigay sa kanya ng mga kaibigan niya.** (actor focus)

14. **Ikinasaya ni Katie ang despedida party na ibinigay sa kanya ng mga kaibigan niya.** (object focus)

Finally, be careful with the use of words for love. As mentioned earlier, use **mahal** in a more general way, because words such as **iniibig, sinisinta** and **pinipintuho** are used only for the "beloved" or for the country. However, the noun form **pag-ibig** can also be used in a general way.

15. **Mahal ko ang pusa ko dahil malambing siya.**
    I love my cat because he/she is affectionate.
    —Do not say "**Iniibig ko ang pusa ko**."

16. **Iniibig ko ang Pilipinas dahil ito ang lupain ng aking mga ninuno.**
    I love the Philippines because it is the land of my ancestors.

Pagsasanay Practice
Mga Tanong at Sagot

Practice the words, phrases, and idiomatic expressions you have learned that can be used to express feelings. Some of the following questions/answers are from the dialogue you have just read and some can be answered/asked based on your own personal experience.

1. TANONG : **Ano ang ikinasaya ni Katie?**
   SAGOT : ______________________________.

2. TANONG : **Ano ang ikinagalit ng mga katutubo?**
   SAGOT : ______________________________.

3. TANONG : **Ano ang ikinalungkot mo?**
   SAGOT : ______________________________.

4. TANONG : **Sino sa iyong mga kaibigan ang abot-tenga ang ngiti?**
   SAGOT : ______________________________.

5. TANONG : **Bakit walang pagsidlan ang tuwa niya?**
   SAGOT : ______________________________.

6. TANONG : **Ano ang ikinatatakot ng mga tao sa bagyo?**
   SAGOT : ______________________________.

7. TANONG : ______________________________?
   SAGOT : **Naghihinagpis ang mga tao sa Compostela Valley dahil marami ang nasawi.**

8. TANONG : ______________________________?
   SAGOT : **Nasusuklam si Katie sa mga kompanyang sumira sa bundok.**

9. TANONG : ____?
   SAGOT : **Ikinasasabik ni Armael ang pagpunta sa kasal.**

10. TANONG : ____?
    SAGOT : **Para siyang pusang hindi maihi dahil nag-aalala siya na baka makansela ang flight niya.**

Pagsasanay Practice
Paggamit ng mga Ekspresyon ng Pagbati/Pakikiramay
Using Expressions to Greet or Congratulate/Give One's Condolences

Here are a few situations. Your friend has just told you some news. Please respond to the news by choosing one of the expressions you have just learned.

1. KAIBIGAN : **Ako ang magbibigay ng commencement address sa pagtatapos namin.**
   IKAW : ____.

2. KAIBIGAN : **Yumao na ang lolo ko dahil sa katandaan.**
   IKAW : ____.

3. KAIBIGAN : **Ikakasal na ako sa Hunyo.**
   IKAW : ____.

4. KAIBIGAN : **Naaksidente ang kapatid ko.**
   IKAW : ____.

5. KAIBIGAN : **Nanalo ako sa kontest para sa pagsulat ng maikling kuwento.**
   IKAW : ____.

Role-Play/Pagsusulat
Ang Nararamdaman Ko! What I Feel!

Review/use the words, phrases and idiomatic expressions you have just learned. Study the three situations below. For the first part of this exercise, complete/write a dialogue expressing the feeling of both characters. In the second part, write a short paragraph about the situation.

SITUATION 1: Laurence and Camille were visiting their aunt in Manila. They were in a car on their way to their aunt's house from the airport. They were excited because they were very close to their aunt and loved her very much. However, they noticed some street children selling flowers in the streets and felt a lot of pity for them. They felt very sad for the children.

Laurence : ________________ **na akong makita ang** ______________ **natin.**
Camille : **Ako rin.** ____.

Laurence : (notices the children): **Ano iyon?**
Camille : ____.

Laurence : ____.
Camille : ____.

Paragraph:

Binibisita nina Laurence at Camille ___________________________________.

____

____

____

____

____

Situation 2: Tim is proposing to Mishel. He is telling her how much he loves her and that he would like to follow tradition and go to her parents' house to ask for her hand in marriage. Mishel accepts Tim's proposal and also expresses her love for him. They plan to get married in April and honeymoon in Palawan island. (Note: Remember, use several words for "love.")

____

____

____

____

____

____

____

____

____

____

____

____

____

____

Paragraph:

SITUATION 3: Andre and Peter are in Baguio City, a popular holiday destination in northern Philippines because of its colder climate. They have been having a great time going to the parks, horseback riding, and shopping. On their third day, they saw a rally in front of the shopping mall and learned that the mall administration was planning to cut down trees to make way for a new structure. They became angry at this plan and also feared that this would lead to more floods and landslides.

Paragraph:

Gramatika Grammar

Practice/study verb affixes and aspects with words that express feeling. Note how the affix changes when the focus of the sentence changes.

Affixes "na-," and "ikina-" and Actor and Reason Focus

Review how the affix **na-** is used when the focus is on the actor and how **ikina-** is used when the focus is on the reason of the action. Note how the verb in the first sentence changes into a noun in the second sentence. Here are a few examples.

Example 1: root word **galit**

Actor Focus: **Nagalit ako kay Juan dahil nagsinungaling siya sa akin.**
I got angry at Juan because he lied to me.

Object/Goal Focus: **Ikinagalit ko ang pagsisinungaling ni Juan sa akin.**
I got angry with Juan for lying to me [=Juan's lie].

Example 2: root word **tuwa**

Actor Focus: **Lubha akong natuwa dahil nanalo ako sa contest.**
I was very happy because I won in the contest.

Object/Goal Focus: **Lubha kong ikinatuwa ang pagkapanalo ko sa contest.**
I was happy because of my winning the contest.

Study more examples of conjugation in the following charts:

Actor Focus chart:

Root	Infinitive	Completed	Incompleted	Contemplated
sindak	nasindak	nasindak	nasisindak	masisindak
lungkot	nalungkot	nalungkot	nalulungkot	malulungkot
lumbay	nalumbay	nalumbay	nalulumbay	malulumbay
suklam	nasuklam	nasuklam	nasusuklam	masusuklam
takot	natakot	natakot	natatakot	matatakot

Reason Focus chart:

Root	Infinitive	Completed	Incompleted	Contemplated
sindak	ikinasindak	ikinasindak	ikinasisindak	ikasisindak
lungkot	ikinalungkot	ikinalungkot	ikinalulungkot	ikalulungkot
lumbay	ikinalumbay	ikinalumbay	ikinalulumbay	ikalulumbay
suklam	ikinasuklam	ikinasuklam	ikinasusuklam	ikasusuklam
takot	ikinatakot	ikinatakot	ikinatatakot	ikatatakot

Affixes "um-," "mag-," "ikina-," and "ipinag-"

Although most words use the affixes **na-** and **ikina-**, some words that express feelings use **um-**, **mag-**, and **ikina-** (used for words that use **um-** affixes), and **ipinag-** affixes (used for words that use **mag-** affixes.)

Actor Focus chart:

Root	Infinitive	Completed	Incompleted	Contemplated
saya	sumaya	sumaya	sumasaya	sasaya
ligaya	lumigaya	lumigaya	lumiligaya	liligaya
damdam	nagdamdam	nagdamdam	nagdaramdam	magdaramdam
luksa	nagluksa	nagluksa	nagluluksa	magluluksa
ngitngit	nagngitngit	nagngitngit	nagngingitngit	magngingitngit

Reason Focus chart:

Root	Infinitive	Completed	Incompleted	Contemplated
saya	ikinasaya	ikinasaya	ikinasasaya	ikasasaya
ligaya	ikinaligaya	ikinaligaya	ikinaliligaya	ikaliligaya
damdam	ipinagdamdam	ipinagdamdam	ipinagdaramdam	ipagdaramdam
luksa	ipinagluksa	ipinagluksa	ipinagluluksa	ipagluluksa
ngitngit	ipinagngitngit	ipinagngitngit	ipinagngingitngit	ipagngingitngit

For the word **damdam**, note that instead of **ipinagdadamdam**, the second "**d**" is converted into "**r**," supposedly for a more pleasing sound.

"In-an" Affixes and Directional Focus

By now, you have gained a certain familiarity with sentences wherein the focus is either actors (with verbs usually using affixes **mag-**, **um-**, **na-** and **mang-**) or objects (with verbs usually using **in-** affixes)

There are some words/verbs that might cause confusion because of the pronouns (for example, **ako** and **ko**). So that you won't get confused, just ask yourself the question—where is the focus of the verb—or simply, who is the action directed towards? Many of the verbs above are not used with **in-an** affixes but a few are. What is the difference?

Let us take the word **suklam**:

Actor Focus: **Nasuklam ako kay Pedro dahil sa ginawa niya.**
I hated Pedro because of what he did.

Reason Focus: **Ikinasuklam ko ang ginawa ni Pedro.**
What I hated was what Pedro did.

Directional Focus: **Kinasuklaman ko si Pedro dahil sa ginawa niya.**
I hated Pedro because of what he did.

Do not confuse this with:
Directional Focus: **Kinasuklaman ako ni Pedro dahil sa ginawa ko.**
Pedro hated me because of what I did.

Avoiding Confusion in Directional-Focused Sentence Construction
Let us review again how one may experience confusion with verbs using **in-** affixes immediately preceding pronouns. Let us take, for example, the root word **mahal** (love).

Actor Focus: **Nagmamahal ako kay Pedro.**

However, it is more common to say:
Directional Focus: **Minamahal ko si Pedro.**
I love Pedro.
Here, we know, that the focus is the recipient, Pedro because of the marker **si**. The direction of the "love" is towards Pedro.

Do not mistake this as having the same meaning as:

Minamahal ako ni Pedro.
Pedro loves me.
The focus again, is the recipient, **ako** (I), not Pedro, because of the marker **ni**.

Here are more examples:

Nagalit ako kay Pedro.
I got angry at Pedro.
Clearly, the focus is on the actor or doer of the action, because of the word **ako** and the use of the affix **na-**.

Ginalit ko si Pedro.
I made Pedro angry.
The focus is on Pedro—to whom the action was directed.

Ginalit ako ni Pedro.
Pedro made me angry.
The focus is on **ako**—to whom Pedro's action was directed.

Umiibig ako kay Pedro.
I love Pedro. (Actor focus)

Iniibig ko si Pedro.
I love Pedro. (Direction-focus)

Iniibig ako ni Pedro.
Pedro loves me. (Direction-focus)

Pagsasanay Practice
Emotions Quiz

Practice what you have learned from the grammar section of this lesson by responding to the following questions. Note that there is more than one way of answering some questions. Some answers are provided with clues to help you along.

1. TANONG : **Bakit ka sumaya?**
   SAGOT : **Sumaya ako dahil** ______________________________.
   SAGOT : **Ikinasaya ko ang** (insert noun) ______________________.

2. TANONG : **Ano ang ikinalulungkot mo?**
   SAGOT : __________ **ako dahil** ______________________.
   SAGOT : **Ikinalungkot ko ang** ______________________________.

3. TANONG : **Ano ang ikinagalit mo?**
   SAGOT : ____.
   SAGOT : ____.

4. TANONG : **Ano ang ikinatatakot mo?**
   SAGOT : ____.
   SAGOT : ____.

5. TANONG : **Sino ang minamahal mo?**
   SAGOT : ______________ **ko si** ______________________.
   SAGOT : ______________ **ako kay** ____________________.

6. TANONG : **Sino ang nagmamahal sa iyo?**
   SAGOT : ______________ **ako ni** _____________________.

7. TANONG : **Kanino ka nagagalit?**
   SAGOT : ______________ **ako kay** ____________________.

8. TANONG : **Ano ang ikinagagalit mo?**
   SAGOT : ____.

Mga Talang Pangkultura
Mga Bugtong Riddles

Gawing-Bahay Homework/**Talakayan**
Mga Bugtong Riddles

Do some research on Tagalog/Filipino riddles. Classroom learners can come to class with a riddle to share while individual learners can write down the riddles below:

____

____

____

Now, try to translate your riddle into English:

____

____

____

If you are a classroom learner, ask and answer the following questions in class. If you are an individual learner, write down your thoughts.

1. What are the images/metaphors used in the riddle?
2. How do Tagalog/Filipino riddles compare to the riddles in your first language/culture?

Pakikinig: Regalo Gift

Pagbabasa Reading: **Salubong** Meeting

Read the following short short story. The story is set on Easter Sunday (**Pasko ng Pagkabuhay**) in Angono, Rizal. A popular theatrical performance on this day is the **Salubong** (Meeting) which reenacts the meeting of Jesus Christ and the Virgin Mary.

Here are some vocabulary words that you might want to review: **hindi matanggihan** (could not refuse); **Semana Santa** (holy week); **Biyernes Santo** (Good Friday); **magdiwang** (celebrate); **Birheng Maria** (Virgin Mary); **terno** (traditional Filipina dress); **bandera** (flag); **pamangkin** (niece/nephew); **itik** (duck); **dumulog** (appealed); **tinatanggal** (removing); **belo** (veil).

After reading the story, answer the questions that follow.

Salubong

Madaling-araw pa lang, nasa Angono na si Mrs B. Hindi niya kasi matanggihan ang imbitasyon ng kaibigan niyang si Propesor Ligaya Rubin na doon magdiwang ng Pasko ng Pagkabuhay.

"Sige na, masaya talaga sa bayan namin. Pagkatapos, kakain tayo sa bahay ko," sabi ni Ligaya sa kanya noong isang linggo. Kaya nga maagang gumising si Mrs. B. at nagmaneho papunta sa Angono.

Oo nga naman. Ang lungkot ng Semana Santa. Isang buong linggo ng hinagpis at pagluluksa. Biyernes Santo, inaalala ang pagkamatay ni Hesus. Sabado de Gloria, wala raw Diyos. Kaya, sige na nga, magdiwang na nga tayo ngayong Linggo.

Sumama sila ni Ligaya sa prusisyon, sumusunod sa estatuwa ng Birheng Maria. Sa wakas, dumating din sila sa plaza. Napakaraming tao malapit sa entablado. Mayroon ding *galilea*—may apat na poste, apat na ibon na gawa sa papel, at sa gitna nito, may malaking puso na yari sa papel. Naghihintay ang lahat sa sayaw ng dalawang magagandang babae na nakasuot ng mga terno. Tumugtog ang banda. Tumayo ang babaeng nakasuot ng asul na terno at malalaking hikaw at nagsayaw, hawak ang isang bandera. "Iyan ang tinyenta," bulong ni Ligaya. "Pamangkin ko iyan, e."

"Hindi nga pala ako magtatagal, Ligaya," bulong ni Mrs. B. "Pupunta kasi sa bahay ko ang mga anak ko. Magtatanghalian kami nang sama-sama."

"Magluluto ka pa ba? Gusto mo bang magdala ng fried itik?" tanong ni Ligaya. Fried itik kasi ang specialty sa Angono.

"Hindi na. Sila ang magluluto. Pero nag-order ako ng lechon."

Hindi niya maintindihan kung bakit nag-order siya ng lechon. Nagdidiyeta ang anak niyang si Anne; vegetarian naman ang anak niyang si JL; at isda ang paborito niyang ulam. Si Jonas lang ang paborito ang lechon.

At parang on cue, tinanong ni Ligaya ang tanong na ayaw niyang marinig. "Ano ang balita tungkol kay Jonas?"

Tapos na ang sayaw, tumutula na ang kapitana, ang babaeng nakasuot ng puti. Parang naiiyak pa at nanginginig ang boses, habang tumutula tungkol sa Birheng Maria:

"Pighati at lungkot, walang hanggang dusa
Ang iyong dinanas, noong panahong una…

"Walang balita, Ligaya."

Walang balita. Naikot na niya ang lahat ng kulungan, dumulog na siya sa lahat ng korte, kinausap na niya ang lahat ng heneral, politiko, opisyal, kahit na sinong puwedeng kausapin. Hindi raw alam ng mga militar kung sino ang dumukot at bakit dinukot si Jonas. Hindi raw ba aktibista ang anak niya? Kung hindi, e bakit tumutulong sa mga magsasaka? Organic farming expert? E bakit hindi nagtatrabaho

sa isang agricultural corporation? Sigurado ba siyang hindi rebelde ang anak niya?

Tumugtog uli ang banda. Biglang-bigla, lumipad ang mga ibong papel at binuksan ang malaking puso. Unti-unting bumaba ang anghel—isang bata na mga siyam na taong gulang, nakabihis ng puti. Umaawit ang anghel ng *Regina Coeli Laetare o Queen of Heaven, Rejoice*. Tinatanggal ng anghel ang itim na belo ng Birheng Maria, pinapawi ang kalungkutan ng Birhen.

At sa kanyang isip, kinakausap ni Mrs. B. ang anghel: Ako rin, ako rin. Nanay din ako. Tanggalin mo rin ang belo ko.

1. How is Easter Sunday celebrated in Angono, Rizal?
2. Who invited Mrs. B. to witness the celebration?
3. Who were the performers?
4. What did Mrs. B. plan to do later that day?
5. What did she order for lunch?
6. What happened to her son Jonas?
7. What did Mrs. B. ask the angel to do?

Pagsusulat Writing: Kontrapunto Counterpoint

Choose one of the following topics. Write a short essay, story or dialogue using the vocabulary words and sentence structures you have learned in this lesson:

1. An instance, wherein you, someone you know, or a fictitious character was sad during a usually happy occasion;
2. An instance, wherein you, someone you know, or a fictitious character was happy during a usually sad occasion;
3. An instance, wherein you, someone you know, or a fictitious character felt relief after a terrifying incident.

Paglalagom Summing Up

In Lesson 10, you have:

- Learned words, phrases and idiomatic expressions used to express feelings;
- Reviewed/Learned actor and reason focus;
- Studied riddles;
- Learned a song and read a short short story.

Pagsasalaysay ng Pangyayari

Narrating an Incident

In this lesson, learn the second skill you need in the effective use of a language—**pagsasalaysay** or narrating an incident or a story. Study words/phrases you can use in narrating an event or telling a story; review words for describing people, review the use of connectors, study the affix **napa-**, and review how to express past progressive action.

Diyalogo Dialogue

Nakita ko ang lahat! I saw everything!

*Read the following dialogue between a news reporter (***mamamahayag***), Atom Araullo, and a witness. In this scene, Kathleen, a waitress, narrates how she saw three men abducted two women in a restaurant within a shopping mall.*

ATOM (reporter) : **Nakita niyo po ba ang pangyayari?**
Did you see the incident?

KATHLEEN : **Opo, nakita ko po. Nakatayo po ako roon at kinukuha ko po ang order ng table na iyon nang nagkaroon ng gulo.**
Yes, I saw it. I was standing over there and I was getting the order of that table when a commotion happened [started].

Atom : **Tapos, ano po ang nangyari?**
Then, what happened?

Kathleen : **Pumasok po sa restawran ang tatlong lalaki.**
Three men entered the restaurant.

Atom : **Ano po ang mga itsura nila?**
What did they look like?

Kathleen : **Naku, malalaking tao ho. Matipuno ho ang mga pangangatawan. Matangkad iyong dalawa, at katamtaman lang ang taas noong dalawa pa. Iyong isa hong lalaki, may kulay ho ang buhok. Naka-sunglasses po ang dalawa, iyong isa namang lalaki nandidilat ho ang mata at nakasimangot. Kalbo ho iyong isang lalaki.**
They were huge people [=men]. They have huge builds. Two were tall, and the two others were of medium build. One of the men had colored hair. Two were wearing sunglasses and one man had popping eyes and was grimacing. One man was bald.

Atom : **Ano ho ang ginawa nila?**
What did they do?

Kathleen : **Lumapit sila sa dalawang babaeng nakaupo sa mesang iyon, at pagkatapos, bigla na lang hinatak ang dalawang babae palabas.**
They approached the two women sitting at that table over there, and then, they suddenly dragged the two women outside.

Atom : **Natatandaan niyo po ba ang itsura ng dalawang babae?**
Do you remember what the two women looked like?

Kathleen : **Mukha ho silang mga estudyante. Bilugan ang mukha ng isa at mahaba ang buhok. Palangiti siya. Iyong isa naman, maliit pero mukhang atleta. May suot po siyang bandana.**
They looked like students. One was round faced and had long hair. She was always smiling. The other was small [=petite] but looked like an athlete. She was wearing a bandana.

Atom : **May sinabi ba ang mga lalaki?**
Did the men say anything?

Kathleen : **Sabi po ng pinakamatangkad na lalaki, "Mga pulis kami. Nagbebenta ng droga ang mga ito."**
They said, "We are police officers. These (women) are selling drugs."

Atom : **Mga pulis nga ba sila?**
Were they really police officers?

Kathleen : **E, hindi ho sila nakauniporme. Nakasuot ho sila ng itim na mga T-shirt, at may dalawang nakasuot ng itim ding pantalon. May isang nakasuot ng camouflage na pantalon. Nakabotas ho iyong isa.**

They were not wearing uniforms. They were wearing black T-shirts, and there were two who were also wearing black pants. One was wearing camouflage pants. One was wearing boots.

Patricia : **Ano ho ang ginawa ng mga babae?**
What did the women do?

Kathleen : **Nagpupumiglas po sila at nagsisisigaw. Sabi nila, "Mga estudyante kami! Mga estudyante kami!" Nakatakbo pa nga nang kaunti iyong babaeng mas payat pero nahuli siya kaagad.**
They were trying to break free and were shouting. They said, "We are students!" The slimmer girl was [still] able to run a little but she was caught at once.

Atom : **Ano naman ho ang ginagawa ninyo sa mga sandaling nangyayari ito?**
And what were you doing at the moment [=time] that this was happening?

Kathleen : **Naku, napasigaw na rin ho ako ng "Saklolo! Saklolo!" Tapos, nagyakapan kami noong kaibigan kong waitress din dahil sa takot namin.**
Oh my [=Well], I was [suddenly prompted to] shout "Help! Help!" Then, my other waitress friend and I hugged each other because of fear.

Atom : **Ano pa ho ang nangyari?**
What else happened?

Kathleen : **Aba, sinubukan pong tulungan ng guard iyong dalawang babae pero tinulak po siya ng mga lalaki.**
Oh, the guard tried to help the two women but the men pushed him.

Atom : **Paano po kayo naapektuhan nito?**
How were you affected by this?

Kathleen : **Naging matatakutin na po kami rito. Baka kasi bumalik ang mga lalaking iyon.**
We've became easily scared. Those men might come back.

Bokabularyo at Pagsasanay

Review and study words that we can use when describing people, learn new action words, and practice how they can be conjugated. Remember that it is important to review adjectives because this will help you firm up your description skills. Also, observe how the affixes you have learned in previous lessons affect the meaning of the verb. For example, with the use of **naka-**, the verb means *able to* + verb. Finally review the connectors that you already know at this point and that can help you give a better description of the action happening.

Words/Phrases that describe people: matipuno ang pangangatawan (muscular); **matangkad** (tall); **katamtaman ang taas** (of average height); **may kulay ang buhok** (has colored hair); **nandidilat ang mata** (has popping eyes); **nakasimangot** (grimacing); **bilugan ang mukha** (round-faced); **palangiti** (always smiling)

Verbs used in the dialogue: kinukuha (getting/taking); **hinatak/hinila** (pulled); **nagpupumiglas** (trying to break free); **nagsisisigaw** (kept on shouting); **nakatakbo** (was able to run); **nahuli** (was caught); **lumapit** (approached); **napasigaw** (suddenly shouted, caused by something); **nagyakapan** (embraced each other); **sinubukan** (tried); **tinulak** (pushed); **tinulungan** (helped); **kinaladkad** (dragged)

Other verbs used to describe incidents/accidents: tinulak (pushed); **sinagasaan** (ran over; refers to a vehicle hitting a person, animal or object); **nagbanggaan** (collided); **pinaputok** (fired); **tinutukan ng baril** (was aimed at with a gun; was held at gunpoint); **binitiwan** (released); **nakialam** (intervened); **hinimatay/nawalan ng malay** (fainted)

Adverbs: bigla (suddenly); **kaagad** (at once); **nang kaunti** (a little); **palabas** (outwards); **papunta** (going towards); **pataas** (upwards); **pababa** (downwards); **palapit** (closer); **palayo** (farther); **mabilis** (quickly); **dahan-dahan** (slowly); **maingat** (carefully); **nagmamadali** (in a hurry) **pagkatapos/makalipas ang limang minuto** (after five minutes); **pagkatapos/makalipas ang ___ minuto** (after ___ minutes)

Note the use of the affix **pa-**, indicating direction, in the adverbs **paakyat**, **pababa**, **palapit**, and **palayo**.

Connectors: at (and); **nang** (when); **habang** (while); **pagkatapos**; **bago** (before)

Interjections: naku! (oh my!); **aba** (exclamation of surprise, wonder or disgust)

Other Words: mamamahayag/reporter (reporter); **gulo** (commotion); **naging matatakutin** (became easily afraid)

To ensure familiarity with the verbs or action words you have learned, practice conjugating/changing these words, as well as using the affix **naka-** (able to). The new verb form we are studying here is expressing action that is constantly repeated. In the dialogue you have just read, you saw **nagpupumiglas** (kept trying to break free). This was done using this formula: **nag-** + first syllable of completed form + root word.

Please complete the following chart:[1]

Root	Completed Aspect, Actor Focus	Completed Aspect, Object Focus	Completed with "naka-" or "nakapag-" (was able to OR had been able to)	Past Repeated Action, Actor Focus	Locative or Directional Focus ("in- -an" affixes)
Kuha	**kumuha**	**kinuha**		**nagkukukuha**	**kinunan**
Piglas		**not applicable**	**nakapiglas**	**nagpupumiglas**	**not applicable**
Sigaw	**sumigaw**	**not applicable**			**sinigawan**
Takbo	**tumakbo**	**not applicable**	**nakatakbo**		**tinakbuhan**
Subok		**sinubok**		**nagsusubok**	**sinubukan**
Tulak	**nagtulak**		**nakatulak; nakapagtulak**	**nagtututulak**	
Tulong	**tumulong**	**tinulong**	**nakatulong**	**nagtututulong**	
Kaladkad	**nagkalad-kad**		**nakapagka-ladkad**	**not applicable**	**n.a.**

Now, let us study two more new verbs constructions. One, **napasigaw**, with the affix **napa-** + the root word **sigaw** (shout). What does the affix **napa-** indicate? This shows unplanned sudden action. In the dialogue, we have the sentence, **Napasigaw na rin ho ako ng "Saklolo! Saklolo!"** (*Well, I was [suddenly prompted to] shout "Help! Help!"*)

Second, **nagyakapan**, formed with the affixes **nag- -an** + the root word **yakap** (embrace/hug). This sentence appears in the dialogue: **Tapos, nagyakapan kami noong kaibigan ko dahil sa takot namin**. (*Then, my other waitress friend and I hugged each other because of fear.*) We use the affixes **nag- -an** to show reciprocal action.

Practice the use of these verb affixes and verb constructions by completing the chart below. Here, we have three other verbs for practice: **kuwento** (tell a story); **halik** (kiss); and **suntok** (punch).

[1] What is usually used is **pinagkakakaladkad**, where the focus is on the object. For example, "**Pinagkakaladkad ko ang mga silya papunta sa classroom.**" (*I kept on dragging the chairs towards the classroom.*)

Root	Completed Aspect, Actor Focus	Completed, Object Focus	Completed Aspect, Directional	"Napa-" affix, indicating unplanned sudden action	"Nag- -an" affixes indicating reciprocal action
Sigaw	sumigaw	isinigaw	sinigawan	napasigaw	nagsigawan
Yakap	yumakap	n.a.	niyakap	napayakap	nagyakapan
Kuwento	nagkuwento	ikinuwento	kinuwentuhan		
Halik	humalik	n.a.	hinalikan		
Bigay	nagbigay	ibinigay	binigyan		

Mga Pangungusap Sentences

Following the verbs you have learned, let us now study how these verbs can be used in sentences. Focus on three things: first, how the verbs change depending on aspect, focus or usage; second, connecting words that help you give a more accurate description of an incident; and third, the use of adverbs.

Let us start with the waitress describing what she was doing at the time that the incident occurred:

1. **Nakatayo po ako roon at kinukuha ko po ang order ng table na iyon nang nagkaroon ng gulo.**
   I was standing over there and I was getting the order of that table when a commotion happened [started].

In the sentence above, note the use of connectors **at** (and) and **nang** (used here to mean "when.") Also, the verb **kinukuha** is in the incompleted aspect (while).

Here are two more examples that will help you review how to construct sentences narrating simultaneous action.

3. **Umiinom ako ng kape sa restawran nang sinigawan ng isang kostumer ang waitress.**
   I was drinking coffee at a restaurant when a customer shouted at the waitress.
4. **Tumatawid ako nang kalye nang biglang sinagasaan ng kotse ang isang lalaki.**
   I was crossing the street when a car suddenly ran over a man.

Now, let us study how the waitress narrated the incident at the restaurant:

5. **Lumapit sila sa dalawang babaeng nakaupo sa mesang iyon, at pagkatapos, bigla na lang hinatak ang dalawang babae palabas.**
   They approached the two women sitting at that table over there, and then, they suddenly dragged the two women outwards [=outside].

Note that literally, **at pagkatapos** means "and afterwards," but it is used here to mean "and then." Also, adverbs **bigla** (suddenly) and **palabas** are used for clarity and to add more color to the scene. Here are a couple more examples using the words you have just learned/reviewed in the vocabulary section.

6. **Binuksan ng manedyer ang kuwarto, at makalipas ang ilang minuto, dahan-dahan niyang tinulak ang mabigat na mesa papasok sa kuwarto.**
   The manager opened the door, and after a few minutes he/she slowly pushed the heavy table going inside [=into] the room.
7. **Sumigaw ang pulis ng "Tigil!," at pagkatapos, agad niyang pinaputok ang baril niya pataas.**
   The police officer shouted "Stop!" and then, he/she immediately fired his/her gun upwards.

Also study this sentence wherein the waitress continues to describe the incident:

8. **Nakatakbo pa nga nang kaunti iyong babaeng mas payat pero nahuli siya kaagad.**
   The slimmer woman was [still] able to run a little but she was caught at once.

Note the use of the affix **naka-**, meaning "was able to" in **nakatakbo** (was able to run), the adverbs **kaunti** and **kaagad**, and the enclitic particles **pa nga** (used here together to mean "more" or "still" or "yet") to have the full meaning of "the slimmer girl was still able to run…" In English, you wouldn't really need **pa nga**, because it would seem superfluous in this sentence, but it sounds natural in Tagalog/Filipino.

Here is a similar sentence, this time using the connectors **kahit na** (even if).

10. **Nakatakas pa nga ang dalawang suspek kahit na agad silang hinabol ng mga pulis.**
    The two suspects were [still] able to escape even if they were immediately chased by the police.

Finally, let us study the reactions of the waitress and her friend during the incident.

11. **Naku, napasigaw na rin ho ako ng "Saklolo! Saklolo!" Tapos, nagyakapan kami noong kaibigan kong waitress din dahil sa takot namin.**
    Oh my [=well], I was [suddenly prompted to] shout "Help! Help!" Then, my other waitress friend and I hugged each other because of fear.

As you have learned in the Vocabulary section, the affix **napa-** in **napasigaw** shows sudden, unplanned action while the **nag- -an** affixes in **nagyakapan** show reciprocal action. Note also the use of the interjection **naku**, which makes speech more natural. Here are two similar sentences, with the second one using the other interjection you learned, **aba**.

12. **Naku, napaiyak ako nang marinig ko ang balita.**
    Oh my [=Well], I cried when I heard the news.
13. **Aba, natakot kami nang nagsigawan ang dalawang kostumer sa restawran.**
    Oh, we felt scared when the two customers shouted at each other in the restaurant.

Pagsasanay

Read the dialogue again. Now, pretend that you were also at the restaurant, as a customer. You were having lunch with two friends when the incident occurred. The incident prompted you to immediately leave the restaurant without finishing your meal. The reporter, Atom, is also interviewing you. Practice what you have just learned in the Vocabulary and Sentence sections. If you are a classroom learner, work with a partner or your groupmates. If you are an individual learner, write down your responses below.

1. TANONG : **Ano ho ang ginagawa ninyo nang mangyari ang insidente?**
   SAGOT : ____.

2. TANONG : **Ilan po ang lalaking pumasok sa restawan?**
   SAGOT : ____.

3. TANONG : **Ano ho ang ginawa ng mga lalaki pagkatapos nilang lumapit sa dalawang babae?**
   SAGOT : ____.

4. TANONG : **Ano ho ang ginawa ng dalawang babae?**
   SAGOT : ____.

5. TANONG : **Ano ho ang ginawa niyo pagkatapos ng insidente?**
   SAGOT : ____.

Now, pretend you are the reporter Atom and you are interviewing the security guard who tried to help the two women being abducted.

6. TANONG : ____?
   SAGOT : **Nakatayo lang po ako sa labas ng restawran nang mangyari ang insidente.**

7. TANONG : ____?
   SAGOT : **Hinatak ko po iyong isang babae mula doon sa isang lalaki.**

8. TANONG : ____?
   SAGOT : **Tinutukan po ako ng baril ng isang lalaki kaya binitawan ko ang babae.**

9. TANONG : ____?
   SAGOT : **Tumawag po agad ako sa aming security agency at sa estasyon ng pulis.**

10. TANONG : ____?
    SAGOT : **Ang sabi po ng mga pulis, mag-iimbestiga raw sila pero wala namang pumunta dito.**

Role-Play: Saksi Eyewitness

Study the following situations below. Review the vocabulary words and sentences by creating dialogues between a newspaper reporter/s/manager/police officer and a witness/witnesses (you and/or your friend/s). Remember that you need to narrate what you were doing when the incident happened, what happened and your reaction to the incident. Classroom learners can form pairs or groups and read/perform role-plays. You can also adjust the given situations—for example, increase the number of reporters or witnesses so that each member of your group can have a part. Individual learners should write dialogues. Some parts of the first dialogue are provided to help you along and to serve as a guide.

SITUATION 1: You were at a park. While you (and your husband/wife/partner) and your child were playing ball with your dog, you saw two men shouting at each other. Then, suddenly the two men began hitting each other. It was good that [or luckily] a police officer saw them fighting, went to them, and intervened. Your child was so scared that he/she hugged you. You all rushed back to your car and drove away.

REPORTER (**Mamamahayag**): **Ano ho** ________________________________?
YOU : ____________________ **ho kami ng bola ng anak ko sa aso namin nang** ________________________________.
REPORTER : **Ano** ________________________________?
YOU : ________________________________.
REPORTER : **Ano ho** ________________________________?
YOU : ________________________________ **ho ang anak ko sa akin.**
REPORTER : ________________________________?
YOU : **Nagmamadali** ________________________________.

SITUATION 2: You were in a shopping mall. You were in a store trying on a pair of shoes when a woman close to the payment counter suddenly fainted. The sales clerk immediately came to her assistance. Another customer said, "I am a doctor!" and went to help the woman at once. You dialled 911. The mall manager deemed it best to investigate the incident.

MANAGER : ________________________________?
YOU : ________________________________.

MANAGER : ________________________________?
YOU : ________________________________.

MANAGER : ________________________________?
YOU : ________________________________.

MANAGER : ________________________________?
YOU : ________________________________.

SITUATION 3: You were waiting for your bus when you saw a bicycle being hit by a car that suddenly turned on the street and did not see the crossing cyclist. The cyclist fell off his/her bike and was on the ground. This caused a bystander to scream for help. Another bystander rushed to help the cyclist as the car sped away. However, you were able to take down the license plate number of the car.

POLICE OFFICER : ________________________________?
YOU : ________________________________.

POLICE OFFICER : ______________________________?
YOU : ______________________________.

POLICE OFFICER : ______________________________?
YOU : ______________________________.

POLICE OFFICER : ______________________________?
YOU : ______________________________.

Gramatika Grammar

Study the following grammar points on expressing past progressive action.

Expressing past progressive action

In English, the past progressive tense is used when we want to put an emphasis on a course of action in the past, when two actions were happening at the same time in the past, and when an action was going on at a certain time in the past.

As you know by now, Tagalog/Filipino does not have "tenses." Thus, to express past progressive action, we simply use the incompleted action, and for stress (usually in written Filipino) we can double the first syllable of the root word.

Study how this was used in the following sentence from the dialogue:

Nagpupumiglas po sila at nagsisisigaw.
They were trying to break free and shouting.

Obviously, you would need to know the context of this sentence to be able to understand that it is expressing past progressive action. Otherwise the double first syllable of the root word could also indicate plurality.

Do not be confused nor bothered by this ambiguity of meaning. Remember that such is the characteristic of the indigenous **baybayin**, and also a trait in Philippine culture.

Now, let us use the sentence above in other ways:

Nagpupumiglas sila at nagsisisigaw nang dukutin sila ng mga lalaki.
They were trying to break free and shouting when they were abducted by the men.

Nagpupumiglas sila at nagsisisigaw habang kinakaladkad palabas ng restawran.
They were trying to break free and shouting while they were being dragged outside the restaurant.

Alternatively, you can also say:

<u>Nagpumiglas</u> sila at <u>sumigaw</u> habang kinakaladkad palabas ng restawran.

In the first sentence, with the use of **nang** (used here to mean "when"), the second clause is in the completed aspect, and thus we know that the first clause expresses past progressive action. In the second and the third sentences, with the use of **habang** (while), the second clause is in the incompleted aspect.

Mga Talang Pangkultura
Pagdamay Expressing Sympathy and Compassion

Talakayan/Diskusyon: Pakikisangkot Involvement

Look up the meaning of the words **pagdamay**, **pakikilahok**, and **pakikisangkot**. If you are a classroom learner, form small groups and discuss one of the questions/topics below. If you are an individual learner, write down your thoughts.

1. Do you and and your family help your relatives in the Philippines? How do you do this?
   Tumutulong ka ba o ang iyong pamilya sa inyong mga kamag-anak sa Pilipinas? Paano ninyo ginagawa ito?

2. Are you a member of a Filipino group, or do you know of a Filipino group based in the United States or any other country? Do you/the group help Filipinos in the Philippines? How?
   Miyembro ka ba ng isang grupo ng mga Filipino o may alam ka bang grupo ng mga Filipino na naka-base sa Amerika o ibang bansa? Tumutulong ba kayo/ito sa mga Filipino na nasa Pilipinas? Paano?

Pakikinig: 43

Pagbabasa: Excerpt from an article

Read the following article published at *Pinoy Weekly* online on November 28, 2011. The full article can be accessed at http://pinoyweekly.org/new/2011/11/dinedemolis-na-residente-sa-bir-rd-pinaputukan-ng-pulisya/.

Review/study the following vocabulary words: **pinaputukan** (was fired at); **magkagirian** (had a face off); **mahigit-kumulang** (approximately; literally, more-less); **nagkabatuhan** (threw stones at each other); **magkabilang-panig** (both sides); **nagkagulo** (had a commotion); **inihagis** (was thrown); **narekober** (was recovered); **sukbit** (carried over the shoulder).

Answer the comprehension questions that follow:

Dinedemolis na Residente sa BIR Road, Pinaputukan ng Pulisiya
Resident [Homes] Being Demolished at BIR Road, Fired at by the Police
by Ilang-ilang Quijano

Pinaputukan ng mga miyembro ng Quezon City Police District (QCPD) ang mga residente ng BIR Rd., East Triangle sa tangkang demolisyon sa kanilang mga kabahayan.

Pasado alas-12 ng tanghali nitong Nob. 28 nang magkagirian ang mga residente at mahigit-kumulang 30 pulis, kasama ang isang pangkat ng demolition team mula sa lokal na gobyerno ng QC. Nagkabatuhan sa magkabilang-panig, at maya-maya pa, narinig ang sunud-sunod na mga putok ng baril.

Ayon sa mga residente, nagmula ang mga putok sa isang pulis na naka-damit sibilyan, na hindi nila matiyak ang identidad.

"Bigla silang nagpaputok ng baril. Miyembro ng pulis 'yon, naka-sibilyan. Sila ang nagpaputok, kaya nagkagulo," kuwento sa *Pinoy Weekly* ni Antonio Marinas, isang tagasuporta ng mga residente ng BIR Rd. Natamaan si Marinas sa ulo ng bato na inihagis umano ng miyembro ng demolition team.

Ipinakita ng mga residente sa *Pinoy Weekly* ang mga basyo ng M-16 na narekober sa lugar. Ilan sa mga pulis na naroroon ay may sukbit na armalayt.

1. Who fired at the residents of BIR road? Why did they fire?
2. What happened at around noon on the 28th of November?
3. What happened to Antonio Marinas?
4. What did the residents show the news reporters of *Pinoy Weekly*?
5. Try to do additional research on the situation of the urban poor in the Philippines. What did you find out? What reasons are given for driving out informal settlers?

Pagsusulat Writing
Isang Insidente An Incident

Write a paragraph about a fictitious incident. Choose one of the following prompts to start your paragraph:

1. **Nagluluto ako nang...**
2. **Nag-aabang si Ana ng dyipni nang...**
3. **Bumibili si Rico ng pantalon nang...**

Paglalagom Summing Up

In this lesson you have:

- Learned how to describe an incident;
- Studied how to construct verbs showing past repeated action and reciprocal action, as well as the use of the affix **napa-**;
- Learned about the concept of **pagdamay**;
- Reviewed/learned about the use of adverbs for more effective narratives;
- Listened and read about human rights in the Philippines.

Aralin
Lesson
12

Pagsasalaysay ng Pangyayari at Balita

Narrating an Event and the News

In this lesson, learn how to narrate an event, review/study location/direction focus, reference focus, and reciprocal verbs. Also listen to, read and write a news report.

 Diyalogo: Interbyu sa Telebisyon Television Interview

Study the following dialogue of an interview between a talk show host, Francine Mapa, and a student leader, Vencer Capulong. In this lesson, focus on navigating between the completed, incompleted, and contemplated aspects, and on specific words that make your narrative sentences seem more precise. Some of the words below will also be reviewed later in this lesson as we study noun affixes, location and reference focus, and review reciprocal verbs.

FRANCINE : **Magandang umaga po. Kasama po natin ngayon si Vencer Capulong, ang tagapangulo ng Anakbayan, isang pambansang grupo ng mga kabataan.**
Good morning. Today, we are with Vencer Capulong, the president of Anakbayan, a national youth group.

VENCER : **Magandang umaga po, mga mahal na manonood.**
Good morning, dear viewers.

FRANCINE : **Noong Biyernes, ika-30 ng Nobyembre, nagmartsa ang mga kabataan natin sa Mendiola. Paano ninyo pinaghandaan ito?**
Last Friday, November 30, our youth marched to Mendiola. How did you prepare for this?

VENCER : **Buong linggo po kaming tuloy-tuloy na naghanda. Nagkaroon po ng mga pagtitipon, diskusyon, at rali sa iba't ibang unibersidad dito sa Kamaynilaan. Sa opisina ng Anakbayan, inihanda rin namin ang mga mga plakard at streamers. Gumawa rin po kami ng mga maskara.**
We prepared for this continuously for a whole week. We had gatherings, discussions, and rallies in different universities here in Manila. We also prepared placards and streamers in the Anakbayan office. We also made masks.

FRANCINE : **Para saan ang mga maskara?**
What did you use the masks for?

VENCER : **Mga maskara po ito ni Andres Bonifacio, ang magiting na tagapagtatag ng Katipunan. Ginugunita po natin kasi ang kabayanihan niya sa araw ng kanyang kapanganakan, ika-30 ng Nobyembre. Alam po ninyo, noong walang-takot na itinatag niya at ng kanyang mga kasamahan ang Katipunan, dalawampu't siyam na taong gulang lamang siya. At marami po sa mga sumali, mga kabataan.**
These are masks that depict Andres Bonifacio, the founder of Katipunan. We commemorate his heroism every year on his birthday on November 30. You know, when he and his companions founded Katipunan, Andres Bonifacio was only twenty nine years old. Many of those who joined were young people.

FRANCINE : **Ano po ang naganap noong araw ng pagkilos ninyo?**
What happened on the day of your [protest] action?

VENCER : **Una po muna, nagmartsa kami mula sa Unibersidad ng Pilipinas sa Diliman hanggang sa Unibersidad ng Santo Tomas. Nagsalubungan po roon ang mga mag-aaral mula sa iba't ibang unibersidad. Tapos, sama-sama na po kaming nagmartsa papuntang Mendiola.**
First, we marched from the University of the Philippines, Diliman to the University of Santo Tomas. Students from different universities met with each other there. Then, we all marched to Mendiola.

FRANCINE : **Bakit kayo nagtungo sa Mendiola?**
Why did you go to Mendiola?

VENCER : **Una po, alam naman nating lahat na ito ang opisina at opisyal na tahanan ng Pangulo. Ikalawa, mahaba po ang kasaysayan ng Mendiola sa pagkilos at pakikibaka ng mga kabataan. Matatandaan natin ang pagbubuwis ng buhay ng mga kabataan sa Mendiola noong Battle of Mendiola, ika-30 ng Enero, 1970.**
First, we all know that it is the office and official house of the President. Second, Mendiola has a long history of youth action and struggle. We remember the youths who offered their lives in Mendiola during the Battle of Mendiola on January 30, 1970.

FRANCINE : **Pagdating niyo sa Mendiola, ano po ang nangyari?**
What happened after you arrived in Mendiola?

VENCER : **Hinarang po kami ng mga pulis. Wala raw kaming permit.**
The police blocked us. They told us that we did not have a permit.

FRANCINE : **Ano ang ginawa niyo?**
What did you all do?

VENCER : **Nagpumilit po kami at nakipaggitgitan. Biglang pinagpapalo po kami ng batuta, tapos, iniumang po sa amin iyong mga water cannon nila.**
We insisted and jostled with the police. The police hit us with truncheons and then aimed their water cannon at us.

FRANCINE : **Marami ba ang nasaktan?**
Were there a lot of people who got hurt?

VENCER : **Marami po ang nabugbog, kaya humangos kami sa ospital para magamot ang mga duguan. Pati po ako, hinambalos.**
Many were beaten up, so we rushed to the hospital so that the people who were bleeding can be attended to and be treated immediately. Even I was beaten.

FRANCINE : **Ano po ang balak niyo ngayon?**
What is your plan now?

VENCER : **Balak po naming bumalik sa susunod na linggo.**
We plan to go back next week.

FRANCINE : **Sa Mendiola?**
To Mendiola?

VENCER : **Opo, Mendiola uli ang pagdarausan namin ng kilos-protesta. Patuloy po ang protesta namin sa pagtaas ng matrikula at sa kakulangan ng badyet para sa edukasyon.**
Yes, we will hold the protest action in Mendiola again. We will continue to protest against the tuition fee increase and lack of budget allocated for education.

Bokabularyo Vocabulary

Study the following words and phrases. Some of them were used in the dialogue and some of them will be useful to you when describing events.

First, let us review/study nouns. Note the affixes that are used in the formation of these nouns:

NOUNS: tagapangulo (president/chair); **tagapagtatag** (founder); **kabataan** (youth); **kabayanihan** (heroism); **kapanganakan** (date of birth); **kasamahan** (companion); **kasaysayan** (history); **kakulangan** (lack of); **pagtitipon** (gathering); **pagkilos** (action); **pakikibaka** (struggle); **pagbubuwis ng buhay** (giving of life; martyrdom); **pagdating** (arrival); **pagtaas** (rise); **maskara** (mask); **batuta** (truncheon)

Next, let us review/study the action words. Why do we need to increase our verb vocabulary? Remember that in narratives, it is important to be clearer and more accurate. For example, instead of **lumakad** (walked), and **tumakbo** (ran) the word **humangos** (rushed) implies more urgency.

Here are the verbs used in this dialogue. First, try to determine the aspect used. Then, practice conjugating these verbs.

Verbs in the dialogue: nagmartsa (marched); **pinaghandaan** (prepared for); **naghanda/inihanda** (prepared); **nagkaroon** (had); **gumawa** (made); **ginugunita** (remembering); **itinatag** (formed); **sumali** (joined); **nagsalubungan** (met each other); **nakipaggitgitan** (jostled with); **nagpumilit** (insisted); **pinagpapapalo** (was repeatedly hit); **nabugbog** (were beaten up); **humangos** (rushed); **hinambalos** (hit with extreme force, usually right and left with a stick); **iniumang** (aimed); **magdaraos** (will hold)

Other verbs: binabati (congratulating); **ipinalabas** (performed); **idinaos** (held)

Finally, review/study adjectives and adverbs that will help you create more vivid narratives:

Adjectives: pambansa (national); **mahal** (dear; also used to mean "love"); **magiting** (brave; heroic)

Adverbs: tuloy-tuloy (continuously); **walang-takot** (fearlessly); **sama-sama** (together); **bigla** (suddenly); **kamakailan** (recently)

Pagsasanay

Let us practice the new words we have learned. Please provide answers to the questions below. Some of your answers may be true to life, but feel free to "make up" answers as well.

1. Tanong : **Sino ang mga nagmartsa sa Inauguration Day parade?**
   Sagot : ______________________________.

2. Tanong : **Paano mo pinaghandaan ang eksamen mo?**
   Sagot : ______________________________.

3. Tanong : **Ano ang ginawa mo para sa selebrasyon n'yo?**
   Sagot : ______________________________.

4. Tanong : **Ano ang ginugunita sa Thanksgiving Day?**
   Sagot : ______________________________.

5. TANONG : **Kailan itinatag ang unibersidad mo?**
   SAGOT : ______________________________.

Now, please provide questions to the following answers:

6. TANONG : ______________________________?
   SAGOT : **Sumali ako sa Filipino Students' Association.**

7. TANONG : ______________________________?
   SAGOT : **Binugbog ng mga nakasakay sa jeep ang snatcher.**

8. TANONG : ______________________________?
   SAGOT : **Nagpumilit silang pumasok ng auditorium dahil gusto nilang manood ng concert.**

9. TANONG : ______________________________?
   SAGOT : **Nagsalubungan ang mga estudyante sa Sproul Plaza.**

10. TANONG : ______________________________?
    SAGOT : **Iniumang ng bata sa kanyang kapatid ang water pistol.**

Role-Play: Student Activities

Study the four situations below that are typical of activities of student organizations: a cultural show; a bake sale; a rally protesting budget cuts; and a medical mission to an underprivileged community. Then, using the vocabulary words you have just learned, as well as vocabulary you have learned in past lessons, create dialogues. Remember that the role-play should have these components: the purpose of the activity; the actions involved; and plans for the next activity. There are two or more characters: the talk show host of your university radio program and an organizational spokesperson/s.

Classroom learners should form pairs or small groups while individual learners should write down the dialogue. The first dialogue uses the fill-in-the-blanks format and can be used as a guide.

SITUATION 1: The talk show host is congratulating you. Your organization successfully performed the show "Recuerdo: Kasaysayan ng Pilipinas sa Awit at Sayaw" (*Remembrance: Philippine History Through Song and Dances*) to commemorate your 25th anniversary as a student group. The show commemorated the heroism of

those who gave their lives to resist colonial rule in the Philippines. You invited the founders of the group and prepared for the event by rehearsing daily for a month. More than 1,000 people watched the show at Zellerbach Theater and you had a party after the show. Next month, you will perform excerpts of the show at a noontime program during Filipino American Day on campus.

Talk Show Host : **Magandang ______________________________?**
You : ______________________________.

Talk Show Host : ______________________________ **sa inyong palabas kamakailan. Ano na nga ho ang pamagat ng palabas ninyo?**
You : ______________________________.

Talk Show Host : **Bakit kayo nagpalabas nito?**
You : ______________________________.

Talk Show Host : **Sino-sino ang mga inimbita ninyo para manood?**
You : **Siyempre po,** ______________________________.
Talk Show Host : **Ilan** ______________________________.

You : ______________________________.
Talk Show Host : ______________________________?
You : **Sa Zellerbach Theater ho.**

Talk Show Host : ______________________________ **pagkatapos ng palabas?**
You : ______________________________.

Talk Show Host : **Kailan** ______________________________?
You : ______________________________.

Situation 2: Your organization recently held a successful bake sale. Five members prepared for this by meeting at your friend's house and baking cookies, pies, and cakes all day. Then you sold these baked goods at the Multicultural Center. You donated the money you raised to the Women's Shelter for Survivors of Domestic Abuse. You plan to go to the shelter next week for the shelter's anniversary.

SITUATION 3: Your organization joined the rally organized by several groups on campus to protest the budget cuts. You prepared for the rally by making streamers and placards and practicing a modern version of the *tinikling* which you performed at the rally. There were two marches from the north and south sides of the campus and the students met up at the Free Speech Square. However, the campus police used truncheons to break up the rally and many students were beaten. You had to rush two group members to the university health center. Students are planning to hold a protest rally tomorrow and continue the struggle for a higher budget for public education.

SITUATION 4: Your organization recently held a medical mission to help survivors of the recent typhoon in the Philippines. You decided on this activity because there was a lack of medical assistance in this particular town. You prepared for this mission by collecting donations of medicine, clothes, and cash. Four volunteer doctors and six nurses joined the medical mission. Around 100 people were hurt because of the floods and landslides. You plan to visit them again next month.

Gramatika Grammar

Review/study the following grammar points.

Noun affixes

Among the noun affixes are:

-an or **-han** – used to indicate place, time of action; or used when the noun is an article or instrument; when the root is duplicated, indicates pretense or make-believe
ka-an or **ka-han** – used for concepts or for collective action
mag- – used for relationships and occupations
mang- – used for occupations or professions
sang-, **sam-**, or **san** – used to indicate wholeness or say "one"
pag – used to form verbal nouns
tag- – used to indicate time
taga- – used to indicate where one is from or one's duty or work
tala- – used for lists

Here are some examples. The nouns using the affixes are underlined. The meanings of some words that you may not be familiar are in parenthesis.

Tuwing pasukan (start of the school year), **marami sa mga mag-aaral ang nasa aklatan**.
Katarungan (justice) at **pagkakapantay-pantay** (equality) **ang nais ng mga manggagawa at magsasaka.**
Abala tuwing tag-ani ang mga taga-gapas (those who harvest using a scythe) **ng palay**.
Naglalaro ng bahay-bahayan (playing house) **ang mga magkakapatid**.
Santaong malungkot ang sangkapuluan (whole archipelago) **dahil sa trahedya**.

Location/Direction focus—"Pag- -an" affixes

By now, you are familiar, with actor focus and object focus but need more practice with location/direction focus. In the dialogue, you learned the following sentence:

Opo, Mendiola uli ang pagdarausan namin ng kilos-protesta.
Yes, we will hold the protest action in Mendiola.

Notice the word **pagdarausan**—with the affixes **pag-** and **-an**. Now see how the sentence above differs from the following sentences, which have the same meaning, but where the focus differs.

Magdaraos kami ng kilos-protesta sa Mendiola. (actor focus – **kami**)
Idadaos namin ang kilos-protesta sa Mendiola. (object focus – **kilos-protesta**).

Now, let us study more verbs and sentences:

Baul ang pinagtaguan ko ng mga sulat.
I hid my letters in a chest.
St. Joseph's Church ang pinagsisimbahan ko tuwing Linggo.
I go to church at St. Joseph's.

Thus, locative or location/direction focus refers to where the action is located or directed at. Three affixes are used. Also review both **in- -an** and **-an** affixes which you may have studied in *Tagalog for Beginners*. This is best illustrated by comparing actor, object and location focus.

English: *I threw the papers at him/her.*
Nagtapon ako ng mga papel sa kanya. (actor focus)
Itinapon ko ang mga papel sa kanya. (object focus)
Tinapunan ko siya ng mga papel. (location focus)

English: *I will put plates on the table.*
Maglalagay ako ng mga plato sa mesa. (actor focus)
Ilalagay ko ang mga plato sa mesa. (object focus)
Lalagyan ko ng mga plato ang mesa. (location focus)

Reference Focus

Study the following sentence, also from the dialogue:

Paano niyo pinaghandaan ito?
How did you prepare for this?

Again, we used the affixes **pag-**, **-in** and **-an**. Now, compare the following sentences.

English: *How did you prepare banners for the rally?*
Paano kayo naghanda ng mga bandera para sa rally? (actor focus)
Paano ninyo inihanda ang mga bandera para sa rally? (object focus)
Paano ninyo pinaghandaan ang rally? (reference focus)

When do we use the affixes **pag- -an**? What do we mean by the word "reference?" This means "we do something about something." Let us look at a few more examples:

Pinag-awayan namin ang oras ng party.
We fought about the time of the party.
Pinapag-usapan namin ang tungkol sa balita araw-araw.
We talk about the news everyday.
Pag-aaralan ko ang sinabi mo.
I will study [=think about] what you just said.

Reciprocal verbs, "nag- an" affixes

In previous lessons, you have studied reciprocal verbs (or verbs wherein the doers perform a reciprocal action) using the **nag-** affix, such as **nag-usap** (talked), **nagkita** (saw each other) or **nag-away** (fought with each other.)

Let us review reciprocal verbs using the **nag- an** affixes. Study the following sentence from the dialogue:

> **Nagsalubungan po roon ang mga mag-aaral mula sa iba't ibang unibersidad.**
> *Students from various universities met each other there.*

Here are other examples:

> **Naghalikan ang magkasintahan.**
> *The lovers kissed each other.*
> **Nagbigayan kami ng mga regalo noong Pasko.**
> *We gave each other gifts last Christmas.*
> **Nagyakapan ang magkapatid.**
> *The siblings embraced each other.*

Pagsasanay

Let us practice the following: location/direction focus, reference focus, and reciprocal verbs. Study the following situations and create role-plays or have conversation practice with a partner. Possible words that can be used are provided. Most of these words are familiar to you, having been introduced in earlier lessons. It would also be good to practice the new words you are studying in this lesson. Although you are familiar with many of the vocabulary words, less frequently used words are provided meanings to help you recall them.

Ask and answer questions. A few starting questions are provided. Then, you need to provide your own.

SITUATION 1: Landslide (**Pagguho ng Lupa**)

A landslide or **pagguho ng lupa** occurred in Bukidnon in Mindanao, southern Philippines. Many homes were destroyed and five people were injured because of falling rocks. One girl showed heroism when she rescued her younger brother. Citizens' Disaster Response Center, a non-profit organization working with the United Nations, rushed to give assistance to the residents but also criticized the government for allowing loggers to exploit the forests.

WORDS: **pinangyarihan** (where the accident happened); **nawasak** (destroyed); **nagtulungan** (helped each other); **pagtotroso** (logging); **nahulugan** (was hit by something falling); **iniligtas** (saved); **pinaghandaan** (prepared for); **kabayanihan** (heroism); **humangos** (rushed); **pagdating** (arrival); **nasaktan** (hurt); **pinagsamantalahan** (exploited); **kagubatan** (forest); **binatikos** (criticized)

1. **Anong lugar ang pinangyarihan ng insidente?**
2. **Ano ang nangyari sa mga bahay?**
3. **Ilang tao ang nahulugan ng bato?**
4. **Sino ang iniligtas ng batang babae?**
5. **Sino ang tinulungan ng Citizens' Disaster Response Center?**
6. **Bakit binatikos ng Citizens' Disaster Response Center ang gobyerno?**

SITUATION **2: Prusisyon ng Poong Nazareno** *Procession of the Black Nazarene*

Around two million devotees joined the procession of the Black Nazarene in Quiapo last Friday. Emergency volunteers estimate that around 900 people got hurt because of the shoving and pushing by the people who wanted to get close to the statue of the Black Nazarene. The procession was delayed when the carriage carrying the image broke down. Several people also tried to overturn the van the police officers were using to address the crowd. Devotees got angry when the police tried to change the route of the procession upon orders of the rector of the Minor Basilica of the Black Nazarene. The monsignor wanted to bring the statue directly to Quiapo church. According to Pulse Asia, there is a correlation with increasing poverty and increasing religious faith.

WORDS: **prusisyon** (procession); **tinataya** (estimated); **nagtutulakan**, **estatwa**, **binaligtad**, **pinalitan**, **rutang pinagdaraanan**, **pananampalataya** (faith)

1. **Ilan ang sumali sa prusisyon?**
2. **Bakit nasaktan ang mga deboto?**
3. **Bakit nagalit ang mga deboto?**
4. **Ano ang gustong palitan ng Monsignor?**

Online PDF

Mga Talang Pangkultura
Mga Pahayagan sa Panahon ng Kolonyalismo

Newspapers During Colonial Rule

Talakayan: Ang Editoryal The Editorial

The editorial in the culture notes talked about three birds of prey: the eagle (**agila**); the owl (**kuwago**) and the vulture (**buwitre**). Here are some possible questions/topics that you can discuss in groups if you are a classroom learner. Individual learners should write down their thoughts. Please use Tagalog/Filipino in your discussion. If you find you need words you don't know, do not hesitate to use a dictionary. This is all part of the learning process, and will help you build your own glossary based on "learner need."

1. Why did the author compare an academic to these birds of prey? **Bakit hinambing ng awtor ang isang akademiko sa mga ibong mandaragit?**
2. What was the role of several academics in the imperialist project of the United States? **Ano ang naging papel ng mga akademiko sa proyektong imperyalista ng Estados Unidos?**
3. In your opinion, why does the writer end with "MANE, TECEL, PHARES?" **Sa inyong opinyon, bakit nagtatapos ang manunulat sa "MANE, TECEL, PHARES?"**

Pakikinig: 13 Killed in Quezon Shoot-out

Pagbabasa Reading
Balita News Report

Read the following news report, then answer the comprehension questions below.

REVIEW/STUDY THE FOLLOWING VOCABULARY WORDS: **tangkain** (attempted); **pagtatayo** (putting up); **binubungkal** (being cultivated); **mapasakanila** (to be theirs); **hanay** (ranks); **pinakawalan** (released); **sinampahan** (charged); **binalaan** (warned)

7 magsasakang dumedepensa sa lupa, inaresto sa Pangasinan[1]

7 farmers defending their land, arrested in Pangasinan

by Pinoy Weekly Staff

Pitong lider-magsasaka ang inaresto matapos nila tangkaing pigilan ang pagbabakod ng pulisya sa kanilang lupain sa Camp Gregg Military Reservation, Bayambang, Pangasinan.

[1] http://pinoyweekly.org/new/2012/01/7-magsasakang-dumedepensa-sa-lupa-inaresto-sa-pangasinan/

Ayon sa ulat ng Alyansa ng mga Magbubukid sa Gitnang Luson (AMGL) at Kilusang Magbubukid ng Pilipinas-Pangasinan, noong nakaraang linggo pa pinipigilan ng mga magsasaka ang pagtatayo ng kongkretong mga bakod. Iniutos umano ang pagbabakod ni Pangasinan Gob. Amado Espino, na napapabalitang nais magtayo ng pribadong resort sa bahaging iyon ng reserbasyon.

Deklarado ng Department of Environment and Natural Resources (DENR) na pampublikong lupain ang 289.54-ektaryang Camp Gregg Military Reservation. Ilang dekada na itong binubungkal ng mga magsasaka, at ipinaglalabang mapasakanila.

Bandang alas-onse ng umaga noong Enero 13 sa Brgy. Bical Sur, nakikipagnegosasyon sa pulisya ang mga magsasaka nang biglang sabihin ng pulisya na may armadong kalalakihan umano sa hanay ng mga magsasaka. Hindi nahuli ang sinasabi nitong "armado." Sa halip, inaresto ang mga magsasaka na sina Rodolfo Natividad, Emeterio Paningbatan, Felipe Caron, Bernardito Dizon, Rudy Peralta, Rodrigo Asuncion at Ludivico Mejia, mga lider ng lokal na organisasyong Ulopan Na Umbaley Ed Camp Gregg Military Reservation.

Bandang alas-sais ng gabi, pinakawalan ng pulisya ang apat na magsasaka, pero patuloy na ikinulong sa lokal na istasyon sina Paningbatan, Dizon, Mejia at sinampahan ng kasong attempted murder. Naninindigan ang mga magsasaka na mapayapa nilang hinaharang ang pagbabakod at walang dalang anumang armas.

"Nananawagan kami ng kagyat na pagpapalaya sa inosenteng mga magsasaka. Binabalaan namin si Gobernador Espino: kapag itinuloy niya ang kanyang pangangamkam sa lupa, sisiguruhin ng mga magsasaka na magtatapos ang kanyang pampulitikang ambisyon sa 2013," ayon kay Joseph Canlas, tagapangulo ng AMGL.

Dagdag pa ni Canlas, ilegal na claimant ang sinumang nagnanais angkinin ang Camp Gregg Military Reservation, na isang pampublikong lupaing ibinalik ng gobyerno ng Amerikano sa Bureau of Lands noong 1949.

Inaangkin din umano ang reserbasyon ng Central Azucarera de Tarlac Realty Corp., na pagmamay-ari ng pamilya Cojuangco-Aquino. Pinaghihinalaan ng mga magsasaka na mga ispekulador para sa pamilya Cojuangco-Aquino ang iba pang pribadong mga indibidwal na umaangkin sa lupa.

1. Why were the farmers arrested?
2. What do the farmers want?
3. Who owns the land in dispute?
4. What is Canlas calling for?
5. What do the farmers suspect?

Pagsusulat Writing: **Balita** News

Write any of the following, using the vocabulary words you have learned in this lesson. Pay attention to three things: what happened before the event; the event itself; and plans after the event.

1. Campus news;
2. Fictitious news item about a particular group, for example, youth, peasants, workers, an alleged syndicate;
3. Fictitious news item about the Philippines.

Paglalagom Summing Up

In this lesson you have:

- Learned how to use more action words;
- Practiced verbs using location/directional focus;
- Practiced reciprocal verbs;
- Read an authentic news report;
- Written a news item.

Aralin 13
Lesson

Ang Kuwento ng Kuwento
The Story of the Story

This is our second lesson in the study of **pagsasalaysay** or narrations. In this lesson, we will look at two conflicting accounts of an incident. Study: how to quote someone; how to use affixes to show intentional and unintentional action; and verbs as nouns.

 Diyalogo: Ang Sabi ng Saksi What the Witness Said

Study the following dialogue between a police officer and the account of the sister of the suspect.

PULIS : **Asawa ninyo ho ang nakapatay, hindi ho ba?**
Your husband was the one who killed the victim, right?

BABAE: **Oho, pero ipinagtanggol lang ho niya kami.**
Yes, but he was just defending us.

Pulis : **Ano ho ba ang nangyari?**
What exactly happened?

Babae : **Kumakain ho kami ng hapunan nang dumating ang biktima. Parang lasing ho siya at medyo galit.**
We were eating dinner when the victim arrived. He seemed drunk and a little angry.

Pulis : **Alam niyo ba kung bakit?**
Do you know why?

Babae : **Nakipaghiwalay ho kasi sa kanya ang nanay ko. Limang taon na ho silang magnobyo.**
My mother broke up with him. They were together for five years.

Pulis : **Ano ho ang gusto niya?**
What did he want?

Babae : **Gusto niya hong magbalikan sila ng nanay ko, pero ang sabi ng nanay ko, dapat daw ay umalis na siya sa bahay namin.**
He wanted to get back together with my mother, but my mother said she wanted him out of our house.

Pulis : **Ano ho ang ginawa niya?**
What did he do?

Babae : **Inilabas po niya ang baril niya at gusto niya kaming i-hostage. Nakipag-agawan po ng baril ang asawa ko at nabaril niya ang biktima.**
He took his gun out and attempted to make us his hostages. My husband struggled for the possession of the gun and accidentally shot the victim.

Bokabularyo Vocabulary

Study the following words. Some of these words may have been introduced in earlier lessons but are here for your review:

Words from the dialogue: ang nakapatay (the person who killed [the victim]); **ipinagtanggol** (defended); **parang** (seems to be); **lasing** (drunk); **nakipaghiwalay** (broke up with/separated from); **magbalikan** (to get together with); **nakipag-agawan** (struggled for the possession of); **nabaril** (was shot unintentionally)

Mga Tanong At Sagot

Answer the following questions about the dialogue and then write/ask your own questions. At this point, you need to practice writing your own questions. Classroom learners should form pairs to come up with questions, while individual learners should write down their questions.

1. Tanong : **Kaano-ano ng babae ang bumaril sa biktima?**
   Sagot : ________________________________.

2. Tanong : **Ano ang ginagawa ng babae nang dumating ang biktima?**
   Sagot : ________________________________.

3. Tanong : **Bakit nagalit ang biktima?**
   Sagot : ________________________________.

4. Tanong : **Ano ang inilabas ng biktima?**
   Sagot : ________________________________.

5. Tanong : ________________________________?
   Sagot : ________________________________.

Diyalogo
Ang Sabi ng Ikalawang Saksi What the Second Witness Said

Study this other version of the same incident.

Pulis : **Kapatid niyo ho ang napatay, hindi ho ba?**
Your brother was the one who was killed, right?

Lalaki : **Ganoon nga po.**
Yes, actually.

Pulis : **Alam niyo bang may balak ang kapatid niyong i-hostage ang pamilya ng dati niyang nobya?**
Did you know if he had planned on making his former girlfriend's family his hostages?

Lalaki : **Wala ho siyang ganoong balak.**
He did not have that plan.

Pulis : **Gusto raw niyang makipagbalikan sa dati niyang nobya.**
He wanted to get back together with his former girlfriend.

Lalaki : **Hindi ho. Ang nobya ho niya ang ayaw makipaghiwalay sa kanya.**
No, his girlfriend was the one who did not want to break up with him.

Pulis : **Bakit ho siya pumunta sa bahay na iyon?**
Why did he go to that house?

Lalaki : **Gusto niya hong isauli ang mga gamit ng dati niyang nobya.**
He wanted to return his former girlfriend's belongings.

Pulis : **Naniniwala ho ba kayong nagtanggol lang sa sarili ang bumaril?**
Do you believe that the man who shot him just wanted to defend himself and his family?

Lalaki : **Hindi ho. Tatlong beses hong binaril sa dibdib ang kapatid ko.**
No, he shot my brother on the chest thrice.

Bokabularyo Vocabulary

Study/review the following words used in the dialogue

Words used in the dialogue: napatay (the person who was killed); **balak** (plan/intention); **dati** (former); **naniniwala** (believe)

Mga Tanong at Sagot

Answer the questions, then make up questions for the provided answers:

1. Tanong : **Bakit pumunta ang biktima sa bahay ng dati niyang nobya?**
   Sagot : ______________________________.

2. Tanong : **Ilang beses binaril sa dibdib ang biktima?**
   Sagot : ______________________________.

3. Tanong : ______________________________?
   Sagot : **Kapatid niya ang biktima.**

4. Tanong : ______________________________?
   Sagot : **Hinostage daw ang pamilya ng bumaril.**

Pagsasanay

Study the following news items (**mga balita**). If you are a classroom learner, work with a partner. One of you should play an investigating officer and the other should play the role of a witness/witnesses. If you are an individual learner, write six-line dialogues. In some instances, there are two witnesses with conflicting accounts.

An English translation is provided after each news item. Please try not to read this translation as you make up the dialogue and only refer to it to check accuracy.

Study/review the following words/phrases that might be useful in your dialogues:

Nasagasaan	Got run over
Nakasagasa	The person who was responsible for hitting/running over [the victim]
Sa halip	Instead
Tumakas	Escaped
Nasunog	Burned down
Barong-barong	Shanties
Ninakawan	Was robbed
Nakagapos	Tied wrists
Kasambahay	Domestic worker

BALITA 1: Nasagasaan ang isang tatlumpong taong gulang na lalaki habang tumatawid sa Katipunan Avenue. Ang sabi ng dalawang saksi, nagmamaneho raw ng isang kulay asul na Honda Civic ang nakasagasa sa biktima. Hindi ito huminto, at sa halip ay tumakas. *A thirty-year-old male got run over while crossing the street of Katipunan Avenue. Two witnesses said that the person responsible for running over the victim was driving a blue Honda Civic. That person did not stop but escaped instead.*

PULIS : ____?
LALAKI : ____.
PULIS : ____?
LALAKI : ____.
PULIS : ____?
LALAKI : ____.

BALITA 2: Nasunog ang limampung bahay sa Barangay West Triangle kagabi, alas-dos ng madaling-araw. Ang sabi ng mga bumbero, nagkasunog daw dahil may sumabog na kalan sa isang bahay. Ang sabi ng mga residente, intensiyonal daw ang sunog para umalis sila sa komunidad. Noong isang linggo, sinubukang i-demolish ng mga pulis ang kanilang mga barong barong. *Fifty houses in the West Triangle district burned down last night at twelve midnight. The firefighters said that a stove in one of the houses exploded. On the other hand, the residents said that the fire was a set up or was intentional so that the people will be forced to leave the community. Last week, the police tried to demolish the shanties where these people lived.*

SAKSI 1 : ____.
PULIS : ____?
SAKSI 1 : ____.
PULIS : ____?
SAKSI 2 : ____.

BALITA 3: Ninakawan ang bahay nina Mr. at Mrs. Juan at Roselie Ildefonso kagabi, bandang alas-onse. Wala sa bahay ang mga biktima dahil dumalo sila ng party. Nakuha ang kanilang cash at mga alahas na nagkakahalaga nang dalawang daang libong piso. Nang dumating sila sa bahay, nakagapos ang kanilang dalawang kasambahay. Ang sabi ng mga kasambahay, nakamaskara ang mga magnanakaw. *Mr. and Mrs. Juan and Roselle Ildefonso's house was robbed last night at around eleven. The victims were not at home because they were at a party. They lost cash and jewelry worth two hundred thousand pesos. When they got home, the two domestic workers who work for them were tied up. They said that the robbers were wearing masks.*

PULIS : ____?
SAKSI 1 : ____.
PULIS : ____?
SAKSI 1 : ____.
PULIS : ____?
SAKSI 2 : ____.

Gramatika Grammar

Study the following grammar points: verbs and adjectives used as nouns; review of **naka-**; use of **in-** affix vs. **na-** affix; tag questions; and reported speech.

Verbs and adjectives used as nouns

Combined with markers such as **ang** and **ng**, as well as the preposition **sa**, verbs and adjectives may be used as nouns. Usually, the meaning that can be given is "the person who...."

Study the following examples from the dialogues you have learned:

Asawa n'yo ho ang nakapatay, hindi ho ba?
Your husband was the one who killed [the victim], isn't it?
Kapatid n'yo ho ang napatay, hindi ho ba?
Your brother was the one who was killed, isn't it?

Here are a few other examples:

Siya ang bumaril sa biktima.
He/she [is the person who] shot the victim.
Mataas ang mga grado ng mga masipag sa klase.
The grades of [those who are] hard-working are high.

"Naka-" as participle and/or affix to form adjectives, verbs, and nouns

Sometimes, using **naka-** as an affix and as a participle is confusing. Let us look at the various uses of **naka-**.

First, you have learned in earlier lessons that **naka-** participles express state, condition, and appearance. For example, **nakatayo** (standing), **nakasuot** (wearing [clothes]), and **nakasapatos** (wearing shoes).

Second, in some instances, **naka-** is also used to indicate ability or say "was able to..." For example:

Nakabili ako ng murang gulay sa farmers' market.
I was able to buy inexpensive vegetables at the farmers' market.

In this lesson, let us study a third use on how **naka-** was used to form a noun. Let us go back to our earlier example.

Asawa n'yo ho ang nakapatay, hindi ho ba?
Your husband was [the one] who killed [the victim], isn't it?

The sentence above is best studied "in context." Remember that the police is asking the wife of the suspect about the shooting. At this point, the police has not verified whether or not the shooting was unintentional or intentional. Thus, the word choice is **nakapatay** instead of **pumatay**. In English, only one word can be used—"killed." However, in Tagalog/Filipino the use of **nakapatay** provides the extra nuance of ambiguity—in favor of the suspect—recognizing that he/she may or may not have killed the victim intentionally.

Affix "in-" vs. affix "na-" reflecting intent

Similarly, the choice of affix between **in-** and **na-** used to show intent or to show ambiguity of intent. For example:

Sinagasaan niya ang kaaway niya.
He/she hit/ran over his/her enemy.
Nasagasaan niya ang pusa.
He/she accidentally hit/ran over a cat.

With the use of the affix **in-** the act is clearly intentional, while with the affix **na-**, lack of intent is implied.

To avoid confusion among the words **nakapatay**, **pumatay**, **napatay**, **pinatay**, here are these words in sentences:

Si Juan ang nakapatay sa biktima.
Juan killed the victim. (ambiguous if intentional or not)
Si Juan ang pumatay sa biktima.
Juan killed the victim. (Juan murdered the victim.)
Napatay ang biktima ni Juan.
The victim was killed by Juan. (ambiguous if intentional or not)
Pinatay ang biktima ni Juan.
The victim was killed by Juan. (Juan murdered the victim.)

Tag questions

Review the use of tag questions. At the end of the sentence, simply attach **hindi ba** (isn't it) (literally, "no" + question marker). For example:

TANONG : **Kayo ho ang kapatid ng biktima, hindi ba?**
You are the sister/brother of the victim, isn't it?
SAGOT : **Oho.**

Reported Speech

Review reported speech. Use **daw** or **raw**, in place of quotes. Remember to use **raw** after words ending in a vowel, and **daw** after words ending in a consonant. Insert **raw/daw** after the verb.

Look at these two ways by which you can quote someone:

> **Ang sabi ng saksi, "Kumakain kami ng hapunan nang dumating ang biktima."**
> *The witness said, "We were eating [=having] lunch when the victim arrived."*
> **Ang sabi ng saksi, kumakain daw sila ng hapunan nang dumating ang biktima."**
> *The victim said they were were eating [=having] lunch when the victim arrived.*

Pagsasanay

Go back to the three news items in the earlier exercise. Answer the following questions to practice reported speech.

1. TANONG : **Ano ang sabi ng saksi sa Katipunan Avenue?**
   SAGOT : ____.

2. TANONG : **Ano ang sabi ng saksi sa sunog?**
   SAGOT : ____.

3. TANONG : **Ano ang sabi ng saksi sa nakawan?**
   SAGOT : ____.

Mga Talang Pangkultura
Mga Kuwentong Bayan Folk Narratives

Talakayan
Ang Paborito Kong Kuwento My Favorite Story

What is your favorite story? For some, it can be a fairytale that your mother/father/carer narrated to you when you were a child. For others, it can be a favorite childhood book.

Try to recall this story and do the following:

1. Write an outline of the story in Filipino. If you don't know the words that will enable you to tell the story, look them up. Remember, you want to increase your learner-need vocabulary.
2. Tell the story to your partner/group if you are a classroom learner. If you are an individual learner, try to write one or two paragraphs about the story.
3. If you are a classroom learner, think of a question you can ask your classmate about the story he/she had just told.

Pakikinig: Pagkamatay ni Leonard Co, Kilalang Botanist Death of Leonard Co, Renowned Botanist

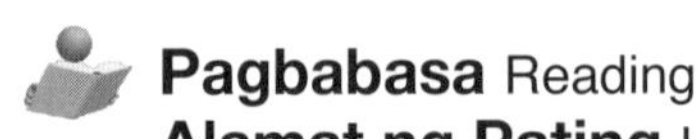

Pagbabasa Reading
Alamat ng Pating Legend of the Shark

Read the following short story for children by Rene O. Villanueva (1954–2007). Villanueva was a playwright, chldren's book author and Professor of Filipino and Philippine Literature at the University of the Philippines. He was the recipient of numerous literary awards, including the Gawad CCP para sa Sining (Panitikan) (CCP Award for the Arts [Literature]).

In this story, Villanueva uses the indigenous **alamat** genre to write a story informed by contemporary issues.

To prepare yourself, study/review the following words: **pinakatuso** (most deceitful, most cunning); **napaka-agap** (very prompt); **sunod sa layaw** (pampered; living in comfort); **tumaob** (tipped over); **umahon** (surfaced from the water); **sumisid** (dived); **nalunod** (drowned); **bakas** (traces).

Alamat ng Pating
ni Rene O. Villanueva

Si Don Paking ang pinakamayaman sa buong Palawan. Pinakamalaki ang bahay niya. Pinakamalawak ang kanyang bukirin. Pinakamarami ang kanyang bangkang-pangisda. Pinakamalaki ang kanyang tindahan sa buong lalawigan. Lahat ng tagaroon ay sa kanya namimili.

Si Don Paking din ang pinakatuso at pinakamabangis magpatubo sa utang. Halos lahat ng mangingisda ay sa kanya umuutang ng bigas, sardinas, lahat-lahat.

Napakaagap niyang maningil. Nasa baybay na siya, maagang-maaga pa. Sinasalubong niya ang bawat may utang sa kanya. Hindi siya nakikinig sa kahit anong pakiusap. "Kumpiskahin ang huli niya!" utos niya sa kanyang mga tauhan.

Malupit sa kahit sino si Don Paking, maliban sa kanyang tanging anak na si Rosa. Mahal na mahal ni Don Paking ang anak. Sunod ang lahat ng layaw ni Rosa sa ama. Laruan, damit, pagkain, lahat-lahat para kay Rosa.

Mabait at maawaing bata si Rosa, hindi tulad ng kanyang ama. Mahilig din siyang magsuot ng damit na kulay-pula.

Minsan, isang mangingisda ang hindi makabayad sa utang kay Don Paking. Malubha

Minsan, isang mangingisda ang hindi makabayad sa utang kay Don Paking. Malubha ang sakit ng kanyang apo noon. "Maraming huli, kapalit ng panibagong utang!" matigas na sabi ni Don Paking sa mangingisda.

Mabilis na naghanda papunta sa laot ang matanda kahit umuulan. Laking gulat niya nang makita sa kanyang bangka si Rosa. "Ano ang ginagawa mo rito?"

"Tutulong po ako sa inyong mangisda," anang bata, "upang kahit paano'y mapatawad ninyo ang aking ama!" At ganoon nga ang ginawa ni Rosa.

Huli na nang malaman ni Don Paking ang pagtakas ni Rosa. Mabilis siyang pumalaot kahit palakas ang ulan. "Rosaaa! Rosaaa!"

Sa lakas ng alon, tumaob ang bangka ng mangingisda. Hindi na umahon mula sa tubig si Rosa.

Nang malaman iyon ni Don Paking, mabilis siyang lumundag sa tubig para hanapin ang kaisa-isang anak.

Matagal na sumisid sa ilalim ng dagat si Don Paking para hanapin ang anak. Ngunit hindi niya makita si Rosa.

Hindi na rin muling nakita ng mga tagaroon si Don Paking. May nagpapalagay na nalunod siya. May nagsasabing nagpakalayu-layo siya dahil sa lungkot na sinapit ng anak.

Isang araw, nagkagulo sa tabing-dagat dahil sa balita ng mga mangingisda. May mabangis na hayop na noon lamang nakita sa gitna ng dagat! Matulis ang nguso at matatalim ang ngipin. Sinisila nito ang maliliit na isda—pati tao!

Napansin din nilang mabilis nitong sinusundan ang anumang bakas ng dugo. Parang si Don Paking na patuloy na naghahanap sa nawala niyang anak na si Rosa.

1. How can you describe Don Paking?
2. Why did Rosa help the fisherman?
3. What happened to Don Paking?
4. What happened to Rosa?
5. Who is Don Paking in contemporary Philippine society?

Pagsusulat Writing

Write your own legend. You can:

1. Write a legend about any animal, flower, or plant;
2. Start with a character. Think of how that character can be compared to an animal, flower or plant.

Paglalagom Summing Up

In this lesson, you have:

- Continued to learn strategies in telling stories;
- Practiced reported speech;
- Studied the difference between expressing intention and ambiguous intent;
- Learned more about legends and folk narratives.

Aralin
Lesson
14

Pagbibigay ng Instruksiyon
Giving Instructions

In this lesson, we are developing skills in **paglalahad** (explanations), one of the four skills we need to master in the use of Tagalog/Filipino. We will also study/review the use of affixes **pa-**, **naki-** and **pinaki-** and plurality, as well as common expressions. Read, listen and write about receiving and giving instructions and on the topic of festivals.

 Diyalogo: Pag-aayos ng Kotse Fixing a Car

Read the following dialogue. In this interview, neighbors Armael and Jack are fixing a car. Continue your study about natural speech, the use of idiomatic expressions, and social affixes.

ARMAEL : **Pareng Jack, may problema ba?**
Pareng *Jack, is there a problem?*

JACK : **Ayaw umandar ng kotse ko, e. Patay yata ang baterya.**
My car would not start. I think the battery is dead.

Armael : **Ano bang nangyari?**
What happened?

Jack : **Magdamag ko kasing naiwang bukas ang mga ilaw ko.**
It's because I left my headlights on all night.

Armael : **Halika, i-recharge natin ang baterya mo.**
Come, let us recharge your battery.

Jack : **Naku, maaabala ka pa.**
Oh no, it's too bothersome for you.

Armael : **Naku! Ikaw naman, parang hindi tayo magkapitbahay. Noong isang araw nga, nakiluto kami sa inyo nang maubusan ng gas ang aming kalan.**
Of course not! You speak like we're not neighbors. Do you remember the other day, we had to ask you the favor of cooking in your house when our stove ran out of gas.

Jack : **Nakakahiya naman. Papasok ka na yata sa trabaho nang makita mo ako.**
I feel ashamed to ask such a favor. It seems you were about to go to work when you saw me.

Armael : **Gawin na natin habang maaga. Kailangang maayos ito nang makapasok ka. Paano nga pala pumasok sa eskuwelahan ang mga anak mo?**
Let's do this while it is still early. We need to fix this so that you can go to work. How did your children go to school?

Jack : **Pinakisakay ko na lamang sila kay Pareng Kawal.**
I asked Pareng *Kawal to let them hitch a ride with him.*

Bokabularyo Vocabulary

Review/study the following vocabulary words and expressions. Some of them were used in the dialogue above but others will be used in the practice exercises later.

Adjectives: ayaw umandar (will not work/start—here referring to a car that would not work/start); **patay** (dead, used here metaphorically)

Adverbs: magdamag (all night); **maghapon** (all afternoon); **buong araw** (all day); **buong umaga** (all morning)

Verbs: naiwan (left); **maabala** (bothered); **nakiluto** (asked someone the favor of cooking in his/her house); **nakisakay** (asked someone the favor of hitching a ride)

Expressions: Maaabala ka pa. (You will be bothered.); **Nakakahiya naman.** (I feel ashamed [to ask this favor].); **Parang hindi tayo magkapitbahay.** ([You speak like] we are not neighbors.); **Naku!** (Interjection equivalent to "Oh no!"); **Diyos ko po!**

(Interjection equivalent to "My god!"); **Ano ka ba naman....** (Expression to show exasperation; equivalent to something like "you're such a ...")

OTHER WORDS: Pareng (short form of **Kumpadre**, originally referring to the relationship between the parent and godfather of a child baptized in Catholic rites; also used to indicate perceived closeness between friends or acquaintances)

Mga Pangungusap Sentences

First, study the use of time expressions in the following sentences:

1. **Magdamag ko kasing naiwang bukas ang mga ilaw ko.**
   It's because I left my headlights on all night.
   (Literally, All night I because left on MARKER lights my.)

Alternatively, you can also say: **Naiwan ko kasing bukas ang mga ilaw ko nang magdamag.** (Literally, Left on because MARKER lights my all night.)

2. **Gawin na natin habang maaga.**
   Let's do this while it is still early. (Literally, Do already us while early.)

Alternatively, you can say: **Habang maaga, gawin na natin.** (Literally, While early, do already us.)

In the examples above, note that you can change the word order without changing the meaning. Also, we use **nang** before adverbs of time (in example no. 1, **magdamag** or alternatively, **habang** to mean "while").

Now let us study sentences that express action that is about to happen. Note the verbs that start with the affix **pa-**:

3. **Papasok ka na yata sa trabaho nang makita mo ako.**
   It seems you were about to go to work when you saw me.
   (Literally, About to go [it] seems] to work when saw you me.)

Let us also study sentences with verbs indicating social performance. Unique to the Tagalog/Filipino language is the use of prefixes (**maki-** and **pinaki-**) which indicates that one is asking a favor to do something with another person. Here are the examples in the dialogue:

3. **Noong isang araw nga, nakiluto kami sa inyo nang maubusan ng gas ang aming kalan.**
   Do you remember the other day, we had to ask you the favor of cooking in your house when our stove ran out of gas?

(Literally, The other day PARTICLE, asked favor to cook [in your house] when ran out of MARKER gas MARKER our stove.)

4. **Pinakisakay ko na lamang sila kay Pareng Kawal.**
   I asked Pareng *Kawal to let them hitch a ride with him.*
   (Literally, Asked favor to hitch a ride I just to *Pareng* Kawal.)

We use the affix **naki-** when the focus is on the actor or doer of the action, while we use **pinaki-** for directional focus. More examples are provided in the grammar section of this lesson.

Finally, study these expressions that one can use in the banter between seemingly refusing/accepting a favor. As you know by now, in Philippine culture, one initially refuses a favor and then the giver of the favor insists on doing the favor, and only then does one accept the favor. Note also that interjections have flexible meanings. Sentence no. 5 is one expression one can use to "insist." In example no. 6, the first sentence is a common expression you have learned and which points to the value placed on **hiya** (shame). This is then followed by an explanation on why "it is too much" to impose on the giver of the favor.

5. **Naku! Ikaw naman, parang hindi tayo magkapitbahay.**
   Of course not! [You speak like] we're not neighbors.
   (Literally, Oh no! You PARTICLE, it's like not we neighbors.)

6. **Nakakahiya naman. Papasok ka na yata sa trabaho nang makita mo ako.**
   I feel ashamed to ask such a favor. It seems you were about to go to work when you saw me.

Pagsasanay

Let us review and practice some common expressions you have learned. In the following brief dialogues, what expressions can you use? Classroom learners should work with their partners while individual learners should write down the expressions:

SITUATION **1:** You went to your friend's house to study. After learning that you have not eaten, your friend's mother (**nanay**) wanted to heat up (**mag-iinit**) dinner for you. Remember to use honorifics (**po**, **opo** or **ho**, **oho**).

NANAY : **Kumain ka na ba?**
IKAW (YOU) : ______________________________.

NANAY : **Mag-iinit ako ng hapunan. Makikain ka na rito.**
IKAW : ______________________________?

NANAY : **Naku, sandali lang ito.**
IKAW : ______________________________________.

SITUATION **2:** You saw your classmate standing by the bus stop. You would like to give him/her a ride to her home. She declines but you insist that her house is along the way. Please use the word **makisakay**.

IKAW : ______________________________________?
KAKLASE : **Pauwi na ako sa bahay ko.**

IKAW : ______________________________________?
KAKLASE : **Nakakahiya naman sa iyo.**

IKAW : ______________________________________?
KAKLASE : **Sige. Salamat.**

SITUATION **3:** This is a telephone conversation. You have a problem with your computer. Your friend knows a lot about computers and offers to let you come to his/her house so he/she can fix your computer. You can also print out your report in his/her house.

IKAW : **Hello? Puwede ko bang** ______________________________?
KAIBIGAN : **Si** ______________________________ **nga ito.**

IKAW : **Naku,** ______________________________________?
KAIBIGAN : **Talaga? Ano ang nangyari?**

IKAW : ______________________________________?
KAIBIGAN : **Puwede ka bang pumunta sa bahay ko? Puwede kong ayusin ang kompyuter mo.**

IKAW : ______________________________________?
KAIBIGAN : **Okay lang. Puwede ka ring maki-print sa printer ko.**

IKAW : ______________________________________.

Gramatika Grammar

Review/study the use of **na** as a relative pronoun, expressions of time, use of **ayaw** and **yata**, and the affix **pa**.

Practicing "na" (contracted as "-ng at -g") as a relative pronoun

In previous lessons, you have learned that **na** can be used as a relative pronoun. Here are a few more examples that will enable you to see how **na** can be used in the same manner as we use relative pronouns (in English, *who*, *what*, *where*, *when*, *that*).

Ang ilaw <u>na</u> naiwang bukas ang dahilan ng pagkakasira ng baterya. *The light [=headlights] that was left on was the reason why the battery got destroyed [=went dead].*

Note that in the example above, you can alternately say "**ang ilaw na naiwang bukas** (literally, MARKER light that on left LINKER on) or "**ang naiwang bukas na ilaw**" (literally, MARKER left **na** open LINKER light). Both mean the light that was left on.

Why can this sentence be confusing? First, notice how **na** is used both as a relative pronoun and as a linker. In "**naiwang bukas**," **na** is used as a linker between **naiwan** (was left) and **bukas** (on). In "**ilaw <u>na</u> naiwang bukas**," (light that was left on), **na** is used as a relative pronoun. Second, **bukas** (accent on the second syllable) means "open," but it is used here to mean "on." You may have noticed that some Filipinos say "Open the lights" instead of "Turn on the lights." This is because of the word **bukas**.

Here are two more examples:

Ang kotseng nasira ay kotse ni Jack.
The car that broke down is Jack's car.

Kapitbahay ni Armael si Juang malilimutin.
Forgetful Juan is Armael's neighbor.
(literally, Neighbor of Armael MARKER Juan who is forgetful.)

In this last sentence, note how a proper noun with **na** as relative pronoun and the adjective **malilimutin** (forgetful) can be used as a nickname. In your field research or in reading authentic texts, you may encounter names such as **si Mariang madasalin** (Maria who is fond of praying) or **si Clarang matulungin** (Clara who is helpful).

Practicing expressions of time ("mga ekspresyon ng panahon")

In *Tagalog for Beginners*, you became familiar with words such as **umaga** (morning), **hapon** (afternoon), **gabi** (evening), **linggo** (week) and **buwan** (month). But how do you say "all day," or "all night"? There are two ways, although these are not interchangeable. In some instances you notice the use of the affix **mag-** such as in **magdamag** and **maghapon**—however, note that **magdamag** does not have a root word. Another is simply to attach the word **buong** before the adverb of time.

Here are a few examples:

<u>Magdamag</u> kong naiwang bukas ang ilaw.
I left the light on all night. (literally, All night I left open MARKER light.)

<u>Maghapon</u> akong nagpahinga.
I rested all afternoon. (All afternoon I rested.)

Buong araw akong nasa opisina.
I was in the office all day. (literally, All day I in office.)

Buong linggo akong nasa Tokyo.
I was in Tokyo all week. (literally, All week I in Tokyo.)

You might wonder: why are the translations for the last two sentences in the past tense when the word **nasa** can simply be translated into "in"? This brings us again to the assertion of Tagalog grammar experts that there are no tenses in Tagalog, but rather "aspects." In Tagalog/Filipino, this ambivalence whether the action has been completed or not, is fine.

Practicing the use of "ayaw" and "yata"

The ambivalence in the previous grammar point continues with the changing meanings and use of the words **ayaw** and **yata**.

In *Tagalog for Beginners*, you learned that **ayaw** means "don't/doesn't like." For example, we can say "**Ayaw ko ng maanghang na pagkain.**" (I don't like spicy food.) Or "**Ayaw kong kumain.**" (I don't want to eat.)

However, look at how **ayaw** is used in the following sentences. Note that **na** here has a different use—it is used to mean "already."

Ayaw tumunog ng radyo. Ubos na yata ang baterya.
The radio does not have a sound. It seems like it has run out of batteries.
(literally, Doesn't like to sound MARKER radio. Run out already perhaps MARKER battery.)

Ayaw sumindi ng ilaw. Pundido na yata.
The light is not turning on. Perhaps it is broken.
(literally, Doesn't like to light up MARKER light. Broken already perhaps.)

Thus, **ayaw** here seems to imbue in the object the capacity to have feelings—to like or dislike. One can say that this is a metaphorical way of talking about something that is broken.

Can one say "**Walang tunog ang radyo**." (The radio doesn't have a sound.)? Of course. However, this other use of **ayaw** is common and should be learned.

What about **yata**? It means "perhaps." What one needs to remember, though, is to put it either after the adjective or verb or when using **na** to mean "already," after **na**.

Using the affix "pa-" to indicate something one is about to do

In *Tagalog for Beginners*, you learned the difference between **papunta** (going to) and **pupunta** (will go to). Practice using the affix **pa-** with other verbs to indicate an action that is about to happen.

Paalis siya papuntang Cebu.
He/she is about to leave for Cebu.
(literally, About to leave he/she going to Cebu.)

Papunta siya ng Maynila.
He/she is about to go/going to Manila.
(literally, About to go/Going to go he/she to Manila.)

Patulog na ako nang ginising mo ako.
I was about to sleep when you woke me up.
(literally, About to sleep already I when woke up you me.)

Pakain na ako nang may dumating na bisita.
I was about to eat when a visitor [=guest] arrived.)
(About to sleep already I when there was arrived LINKER visitor.)

Using social affixes "naki-" and "pinaki-"

In the dialogue, you reviewed/learned about the use of the affixes **naki-** and **pinaki-**.

Noong isang araw nga, nakiluto kami sa inyo nang maubusan ng gas ang aming kalan.
Do you remember the other day, we had to ask you the favor of cooking in your house when our stove ran out of gas?
(Literally, The other day PARTICLE, asked favor to cook [in your house] when ran out of MARKER gas MARKER our stove.)

Pinakisakay ko na lamang sila kay Pareng Kawal.
I asked Pareng *Kawal to let them hitch a ride with him.*
(Literally, Asked favor to hitch a ride I just to *Pareng* Kawal).

You also learned that we use the affix **naki-** when the focus is on the actor or doer of the action while we use **pinaki-** for directional focus. Now let us look at more examples:

Nakikain ako sa bahay ng kaibigan ko nang ginagawa namin ang project namin.
I was given the favor of eating at my friend's house when we were doing our project.

Nakitulog ang mga kapitbahay ko sa bahay namin dahil nasunog ang bahay nila.
Our neighbors were given the favor of sleeping in our house because their house got burned.

Using other aspects, we can say:

Nakikikain sina Silay at Vencer sa bahay ng mga magulang ni Silay araw-araw dahil magkapitbahay sila.
Silay and Vencer eat [as a favor] at the house of Silay's parents every day because they are neighbors.

Makikitulog ako sa bahay ni Guia kapag pumunta ako sa Los Angeles para sa kumperensiya ko.
I will sleep [as a favor] at Guia's house when I go to Los Angeles for a conference.

Also, remember that when using **paki-**, the situation is that you are asking a favor from someone to do something for/about someone/something. For example:

Pinakibigay ko kay Marma ang regalo ko para sa kaibigan ko dahil hindi ako makakapunta sa birthday party niya.
I asked Marma to give my gift [as a favor] to my friend because I cannot come to his/her birthday party.

Pinakidala ko ang mga libro kay Robyn sa Pilipinas dahil magbibiyahe siya sa susunod na linggo.
I asked Robyn to bring the books [as a favor] to the Philippines because she will travel next week.

Now, in what situation can you, for example, convert the verbs **nakitulog** and **nakikain** into **pinakitulog** and **pinakikain**? Let's pretend that you are helping your friends whose homes have been submerged in the flood. Since you no longer have space in your house, you asked your sister, who lives a few blocks away, to accommodate them—give them food and shelter. You can thus say:

Pinakitulog ko ang mga kaibigan ko sa bahay ng kapatid ko.
Pinakikain ko ang mga kaibigan ko sa bahay ng kapatid ko.

Pagsasanay

Let us practice adverbs of time such as **magdamag**, **maghapon**, **buong umaga**, **buong araw**, **buong linggo**, **buong buwan**, and **buong taon**.

Ask and answer questions. Please answer in complete sentences. Classroom learners should work in pairs while independent learners should fill out the blanks.

1. TANONG : **Gaano katagal kang nasa Department of Motor Vehicles sa Maynila?**
   SAGOT : ______________________________.

2. TANONG : **Gaano katagal mong niluto ang** ____________________?
   SAGOT : ____________________.

3. TANONG : **Gaano katagal kang nagbakasyon sa** ____________________?
   SAGOT : ____________________.

4. TANONG : **Gaano katagal kang** ____________________?
   SAGOT : ____________________.

Now, let us practice the use of the affix **pa-**. "What were you about to do when…." Study the example, and then ask and answer the questions.

5. TANONG : **Ano ang ginagawa mo nang dumating ang kaibigan mo?**
   What were you about to do when your friend arrived?
   SAGOT : **Pakain na ako nang dumating ang kaibigan ko.**

6. TANONG : **Ano ang ginagawa mo nang tumunog ang telepono?**
   SAGOT : ____________________.

7. TANONG : **Ano ang ginagawa mo nang lumindol?**
   SAGOT : ____________________.

8. TANONG : **Ano ang ginagawa mo nang nagkasunog?**
   SAGOT : ____________________.

9. TANONG : ____________________?
   SAGOT : ____________________.

10. TANONG : ____________________?
    SAGOT : ____________________.

Finally, let us practice the use **naki-** and **pinaki-** affixes in asking for favors:

11. TANONG : **Saan ka nakikain?**
    SAGOT : ____________________.

12. TANONG : **Bakit ka nakitulog sa bahay ng kaibigan mo?**
    SAGOT : ____________________.

13. TANONG : **Ano ang pinakidala mo kay Sarita sa Maynila?**
    SAGOT : ____________________.

14. TANONG : ____________________?
    SAGOT : **Nakisakay ako kay Rob papunta sa airport.**

15. TANONG : ____?
    SAGOT : **Pinakibili ko ang mga libro na iyan kay David.**

 Diyalogo: Pag-iimbita sa Kaibigan Inviting a Friend

Armael had fixed Jack's car. Jack now wants to invite Armael to his son's birthday party. In this lesson, we are studying the affix **nagsi-**, *used for the plural form of the verb affix* **nag-**. **Nagsi-** *is no longer used often in colloquial speech, but remains important to know should you read it older texts or hear in films and television.*

JACK : **Salamat, Pareng Armael. Ang husay mo palang magmekaniko.**
Thank you **Pareng** *Armael. I didn't know you were such a good mechanic.*

ARMAEL : **Hindi naman. Ang lagay ay mahilig lang talaga akong magkutingting ng kotse. Pinagpapraktisan ko nga ang mga lumang kotse ng mga kaibigan ko.** *Not really. The thing is... I am just fond of tinkering with cars. I practice with the old cars of my friends.*

JACK : **Oo nga pala, bago tayo magsilakad, iimbitahin sana kita. Kaarawan na ng inaanak mo sa Linggo.**
By the way, before we go, I would like to invite you. It is your godson's birthday on Sunday.

ARMAEL : **Saan ba ang party?**
Where is the party?

JACK : **Dito lang sa bahay. Maliit na salosalo lang. Pakisabi na lamang sa asawa mo at mga anak.**
Just here at home. It is just a small party. Please tell your wife and your children.

Armael : **Anong oras?**
What time?

Jack : **Tanghali. Magsisikain siguro tayo ng mga alas-dose.**
Noon. Perhaps we will eat at around twelve o'clock.

Armael : **Sige. Dadalo kami.**
Okay. We will attend.

Bokabularyo Vocabulary

Review/study the following vocabulary words and expressions. Some of them were used in the dialogue above but others will be used in the practice exercises later.

Words: magmekaniko (to be a mechanic); **mahilig** (fond of); **magkutingting** (tinker); **inaanak** (godchild), **salosalo** (gathering).

Expressions: Ang lagay ay mahilig lang akong magmekaniko. (The situation is [=thing is]... I am just fond of being a mechanic.) Note that the expression "**ang lagay**" is used to explain a situation. Related to this is the word "**kalagayan**" which means "situation"; **Dito lang.** (*Just here.*)

Mga Pangungusap Sentences

Review/study plurality. Here are the sentences used in the dialogue above. The plural forms are underlined.

1. **<u>Pinagpapraktisan</u> ko nga ang mga lumang kotse ng mga kaibigan ko.**
   I practice with the old cars of my friends.

2. **Oo nga pala, bago tayo <u>magsilakad</u>, iimbitahin sana kita.**
   By the way, before we go, I would like to invite you.

3. **<u>Magsisikain</u> siguro tayo ng mga alas-dose.**
   Perhaps we will eat at around twelve o'clock.

Gramatika Grammar

Review plural action words and plural question words.

Using plural action words: We use the affixes: **magsi-** (plural affix for **um-** verbs); **magsipag-** (plural affix for **mag-** verbs); **pag-in** (plural form for **in-** verbs) and **pag-an** (plural affix for **–an** verbs). Let us look at a few examples:

Kumain ang bata ng tinapay.
The child ate bread.
Nagsikain ang mga bata ng tinapay.
The children ate bread.
Nagsisikain ang mga bata ng tinapay.
The children are eating bread.
Magsisikain ang mga bata ng tinapay.
The children will eat bread.

Nag-aral ng kasaysayan ang estudyante.
The student studied history.
Nagsipag-aral ng kasaysayan ang mga estudyante.
The students studied history.
Nagsisipag-aral ng kasaysayan ang mga estudyante.
The students are studying history.
Magsisipag-aral ng kasaysayan ang mga estudyante.
The students will study history.

Hiniwa ko ang kamatis.
I sliced the tomato.
Pinaghihiwa ko ang mga kamatis.
I sliced the tomatoes.
Pinaghihihiwa ko ang mga kamatis.
I am slicing the tomatoes.
Paghihiwain ko ang mga kamatis.
I will slice the tomatoes.

Binuksan ko ang bintana.
I opened the window.
Pinagbubuksan ko ang mga bintana.
I opened the windows.
Pinagbububuksan ko ang mga bintana.
I am opening the windows.
Pagbububuksan ko ang mga bintana.
I will open the windows.

How useful is knowing how to use the plural form of these verbs? Truthfully, in everyday spoken Filipino (which here in particular, we distinguish from Tagalog, the language of the Tagalog ethnolinguistic group), people seldom use the plural form of the verb. However, it is also not accurate to say that they are NEVER used. Moreover, you will probably encounter these forms in literature as well as in film or television. Thus, although you may not use these affixes yourself, they are important for listening/reading comprehension.

Using plural question words: For plural question words, simply double the word. We can do this for **sino** (who), **ano** (what), and **saan** (where). Literally, the word **sino-sino** means "who were/are" and **ano-ano** means "what were/are." We cannot double the question words **ilan** (how many), **kailan** (when), and **bakit** (why). For example:

Sino ang mga pumunta sa party mo?
Who went to your party?
Sino-sino ang mga pumunta sa party mo?
Who were the people who went to your party?

Ano ang binili mo?
What did you buy?
Ano-ano ang mga binili mo?
What were the things that you bought?

Saan ka namasyal?
Where did you go around?
Saan-saan ka namasyal?
Where did you go around?

Pagsasanay

Here are a few questions and answers using common verbs in their plural forms. Try to practice.

1. TANONG : **Ilang tao ang nagsidalo sa graduation mo?**
   SAGOT : **Isang daang tao ang nagsidalo sa graduation ko.**

2. TANONG : **Ano-ano ang mga pinagluluto ninyo para sa party?**
   SAGOT : ______________________________.

3. TANONG : **Sino-sino ang mga nagsibili ng mga libro?**
   SAGOT : ______________________________.

4. TANONG : **Kailan nagsisulat ng mga tula ang mga estudyante?**
   SAGOT : ______________________________.

5. TANONG : ______________________________?
   SAGOT : **Pagbububuksan ko ang mga regalo galing sa pamilya ko bukas.**

6. TANONG : ______________________________?
   SAGOT : **Mga prutas ang paghihiwain ko mamaya para sa ensalada.**

7. TANONG : ____?
   SAGOT : ____.

8. TANONG : ____?
   SAGOT : ____.

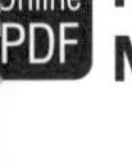

Mga Talang Pangkultura
Mga Mito sa Kasaysayan Historical Myths

Pakikinig: Mga Tsekpoint sa Panahon ng Eleksiyon
Checkpoints During Election Season

Pagbabasa Reading
Penitensiya sa Kuwaresma Penitence during the Holy Week

Read the following short essay by National Artist for Literature Professor Virgilio Almario. In the essay, Almario talks about the Lenten season in the Philippines.

To prepare for this reading exercise, review/study the following vocabulary words: **Kuwaresma** (Lent); **banal** (sacred), **pag-aayuno** (sacrifice); **paghuhugas ng kasalanan** (washing of sins); **sagradong sagisag** (sacred symbols); **pananampalataya** (faith); **pangkaluluwa** (for the soul); **taimtim na panata** (solemn vow); **dinudumog** (flocked to); **pangingilin** (repentance); **iling** (shaking of the head); **tinangkas** (brought)

Penitensiya sa Kuwaresma[1]
ni Virgilio Almario

May panahong ang Kuwaresma ay araw na banal. Mga araw ito ng pamamahinga, pag-aayuno at paghuhugas ng kasalanan. Ang palaspas, pabasa, bisita iglesya, penitensiya, o senakulo ay mga sagradong sagisag ng pananampalataya.

May panahong ang pabasa o pagbasa ng Pasyon ay isang debosyon. Ang pagganap o pagtulong sa pagtatanghal ng dulang senakulo (na mula sa pangalan ng lugar na pinangyarihan ng Huling Hapunan) ay isang taimtim na panata. Ang bakasyon sa Huwebes Santo at Biyernes Santo ay kailangan upang magkaroon ng pagkakataon ang lahat na iwan ang karaniwang gawain, mapag-isa at makapag-alay ng sarili sa mga bagay na espiritwal.

Ngayo'y higit na panturista kaysa pangkaluluwa ang Kuwaresma. Matatanda na lamang ang marunong umawit ng Pasyon. Dinudumog ng kamera ang pagpapako

---

[1] *Mula sa F_l_p_no ng mga F_l_p_no: Mga Problema sa Ispeling, Retorika, at Pagpapayaman ng Wikang Pambansa.* Virgilio Almario, awtor. Pasig: Anvil Publishing, 2009.

sa krus at halos matuksong mag-meyk-ap ang mga Hudas at Longino para sa Fuji at Kodak. Isang kakaibang joyride ang pagdalaw sa mga kapilya para sa maraming tinedyer. Ang bakasyon, siyempre, ay isang pag-iisip sa malayong dalampasigan, palakbayan, piknik, madyungan, handaan, at iba pang mapag-aaliwan.

Mabuti't kahit paano'y may artikulo ang mga peryodiko tungkol sa Kuwaresma (mula sa Espanyol na cuaresma at tumutukoy sa buong panahon ng pangingilin katumbas ng Lent sa Ingles). Kung sakali, baka ni walang makapansin sa Miyerkules de Senisa. Lalo ngayong sa halip na Pasyon ay jinggel at panawagan ng mga kandidato ang nasa himpapawid.

Ang salita mismong Kuwaresma ay wala sa bokabularyo ng mga kabataan. Sabihin mong galing sa cuaresma ng mga Espanyol at sasagutin ka ng iling o blangkong titig. "E ano?" Mas mainam pang sabihin mong Lent at baka medyo maintindihan ka.

"Penitensiya" naman nilang itinuturing ang pananatili sa bahay. Ibig sabihin, wala silang kabarkada o kamag-anak sa probinsiya na puwedeng pagbakasyunan. Ibig ding sabihin, lalo't Semana Santa, walang mapaglibangan sa siyudad. Sarado ang mga disco at puwede lamang nilang pagtiyagaan ang mga kupas na pelikulang Ten Commandments, The Bible, Samson and Delilah at Ben Hur. (Paningit: Hindi na ito totoo ngayong laganap ang cable TV at maaari kang pumili sa mahigit 50 estasyon ng imported na palabas kahit Mahal na Araw.)

Anupa't weird ka kapag boluntaryo kang namalagi sa lungsod sa Semana Santa. Ibig sabihin, ayaw mong mag-enjoy ng bakasyon. May sakit ka siguro? Alerdyik sa araw o alikabok? Takot sa tubig?

Sinubok ko ngang sumunod sa uso noong Linggo. Maaga pa, tinangkas ko ang aking mag-anak patungo sa isang resort. Kumpleto kami sa baong pagkain at gamit pampaligo. Pero pagdating namin sa resort ay sinalubong kami ng tanawing lungsod. Nilalanggam sa tagalungsod ang buong dalampasigan. Tinutulig ng paligsahang istereo ang mga puno ng niyog. Kailangang makipagsiksikan ang salbabida ng aking mga anak para mabasa ng alon.

Ako nga'y nagpilit maghanap ng isang bakanteng lilim. Nakakita naman ako at nagpuwesto na para magbasa. Pero saglit lamang. Isang nakangiting anino ang biglang lumapit. Kinamayan ako at inabutan ng polyeto ni kung sinong kongresman.

The Observer, 1987

1. According to Virgilio Almario, what is given more attention during Lent?
2. What are the kinds of devotions during Lent?
3. What are the forms of penitensiya described?
4. What did the author do with his family one Lenten season?
5. Describe the experience of Almario's family at a resort.

Pagsusulat Writing

Remember that in this lesson, we are studying "explanations." You can write about any of the following:

1. A festival you are familiar with;
2. Instructions on how to fix something;
3. Your own thoughts and/or experiences about changing customs.

Paglalagom Summing Up

In this lesson, you have:

- Learned how to explain things and give instructions;
- Practiced the use of more colloquial language;
- Studied the affixes **pa-**, **naki-** and **ipinaki-** and the plural form of verbs;
- Read more about festivals, customs, and history.

Aralin
Lesson **15**

Pagpapaliwanag
Explaining

This is our second lesson in improving our explanation skills.

 **Diyalogo: Pagbibigay ng Direksiyon 2** Giving Directions 2

In this dialogue, a tourist is asking directions from a passerby. Review how to give directions as well as descriptions of landmarks.

TURISTA : **Mawalang-galang na ho, maaari ho bang magtanong?**
Excuse me, may I ask a question?

DUMARAAN : **Aba, oho. Ano ho ba ang maitutulong ko sa inyo?**
Of course. How can I help you?

TURISTA : **Saan ho ba ang papuntang Manila Hotel? Nawala ho kasi ako, e.**
Where is the way going to Manila Hotel? [=How do I get to Manila Hotel])? I got lost.

DUMARAAN : **Diretsuhin niyo lang ho itong Roxas Boulevard. Maglakad ho kayo papuntang Luneta Park.**
Just go straight Roxas Boulevard. Walk towards Luneta Park.

TURISTA : **Pagkatapos ho?**
And then?

DUMARAAN : **Pagkalampas ng mga dalawang kanto, makikita n'yo na ho sa kanan ang monumento ni Rizal.**
After you go past two corners [=blocks], you can see Rizal's monument on your right.

TURISTA : **Lalampasan ko ba ho?**
Will I go past it?

DUMARAAN : **Oho, lampasan niyo pagkatapos, makikita niyo na ho sa bandang kaliwa niyo ang Manila Hotel.**
Yes, go past it, and then, you will see Manila Hotel on your left.

TURISTA : **Ano ho ba ang itsura ng gusali?**
What does the building look like?

DUMARAAN : **Puti at berde. May dalawang magkakabit na gusali. May gusaling mas luma ang estilo ng arkitektura at may gusali na mas mataas at mas bago.**
White and green. There are two adjoining buildings. There is a building that has a more traditional architectural style, and a taller building that is newer.

TURISTA : **Mayroon pa ho sana akong gustong itanong.**
I hope to ask one more thing [=I want to ask one more thing].

DUMARAAN : **Ano iyon?**
What is it?

TURISTA : **Pagkatapos ho kasi ay pupunta ako sa Unibersidad ng Pilipinas sa Diliman. Ano ho ba ang sasakyan?**
It's because after this, I will go to the University of the Philippines in Diliman. What will (shall/should) I ride [=take]?

DUMARAAN : **Ganoon ba? Sumakay ka lang ng jeep na may nakasulat o karatulang UP Diliman.**
Is that so? Ride [=Take] a jeepney with the sign UP Diliman.

Turista : **Saan ho ako sasakay?**
Where will (shall/should) I ride [=take the jeepney]?
Dumaraan : **Sa jeepney stop sa Luneta.**
At the jeepney stop in Luneta.

Turista : **Anong oras ho ang dating ng jeep?**
What time will the jeep arrive?
Dumaraan : **Wala hong oras ang jeep dito. Maghintay na lang kayo.**
Jeepneys have no time [=Jeepneys do not operate on a time schedule]. Just wait.

Turista : **Magkano ho ang pamasahe?**
How much is the fare?
Dumaraan : **Kinse pesos ho.**
Fifteen pesos.

Turista : **Salamat ho sa tulong n'yo.**
Thank you for your help.
Dumaraan : **Walang anuman ho.**
You are welcome.

Bokabularyo Vocabulary

There are very few new words in this lesson because the focus is on the nuances of the language and flexibility of meaning. However, it is important to practice the following groups of words which you have learned in past lessons both in *Tagalog for Beginners* and the earlier lessons of this textbook.

Review the following:

Words used to give directions including use of the imperative or command form: kumanan ka (turn right); **kumaliwa ka** (turn left); **dumiretso ka** (go straight); **lumampas ka** (go past); **sumakay ka** (ride; get on); **bumaba ka** (get off)

Words used to describe buildings and houses: arkitektura (architecture); **disenyo** (design); **luma** (old); **tradisyonal** (traditional); **makabago/moderno** (modern); **mga kulay** (colors); **harap/harapan** (in front of); **yari sa/gawa sa** (made of); **taas** (height); **lapad** (width); **malaki** (huge); **maliit** (small)

Words used for financial transactions: magkano (how much); **pamasahe** (fare); **sukli** (change)

Study the following new words and expressions: **nawala** (got lost); **pagkalampas** (after you go past); **itsura** (looks like); **magkakabit** (adjoining); **Aba**, **oho**. (why, yes/ of course); **ganoon ba?** (is that so?)

Mga Pangungusap Sentences

Focus on vocabulary and word order and how you can say one thing in different ways. Here are a few examples from the dialogue:

1. **Mawalang-galang na ho, maaari ho bang magtanong?**
   Excuse me, may I ask a question?

This is a formal way of speaking, which you need to know because the phrase **mawalang galang na ho** and the word **maaari** should be in your vocabulary. However, on the street, you can also say:

2. **<u>Excuse me, puwede</u> ho bang magtanong?**

You can also change question words. Look at the following examples, the first one from the dialogue, and the second, an alternative way.

3. **Saan ho ba ang papuntang Manila Hotel?**
   Where is the way going to Manila Hotel? [=How do I get to Manila Hotel?]

4. **Paano ho pumunta sa Manila Hotel?**
   How do I go to Manila Hotel? (literally, How HONORIFIC go to Manila Hotel?)

You can also change the word order. Note the placement of the words **kasi** (because) and **pagkatapos** (after/afterwards) in the sentence from the dialogue (no. 5) and in the example.

5. **Pagkatapos ho kasi ay pupunta ako sa Unibersidad ng Pilipinas sa Diliman.**
   It's because after this, I will go to the University of the Philippines in Diliman.
   (Literally, <u>After</u> HONORIFIC <u>because</u> **ay** MARKER will go I to University of Philippines in Diliman.)

6. **Kasi, pupunta ho ako sa Unibersidad ng Pilipinas sa Diliman pagkatapos.**
   (Literally, <u>Because</u> will go HONORIFIC I to University of Philippines in Diliman <u>after</u>.)

Note also the word **ay**—as you know, it has no exact equivalent for it in Tagalog/ Filipino but it is used as an equivalent of the verb *to be*. Because the more common sentence structure is predicate-subject (**Mataas ang gusali** [The building is tall]) rather than subject–predicate (**Ang gusali ay mataas.**), **ay** does not appear often in conversations.

Finally, you can choose to drop some words in conversations. You can say:

7. **Ano ho ba ang sasakyan?**
   What will (shall/should) [I] ride [=take]?
   (Literally, What HONORIFIC **ba** MARKER ride)

instead of:

8. **Ano ho ba ang dapat na sakyan ko?**
   (Literally, What HONORIFIC **ba** MARKER should LINKER ride I?)

Pagsasanay

See below two maps, as well as a fare schedule.[1] If you are a classroom learner, exchange dialogues with your partner based on the situations given below. If you are an individual learner, write dialogues. Some sentences, phrases or words are given to help you along.

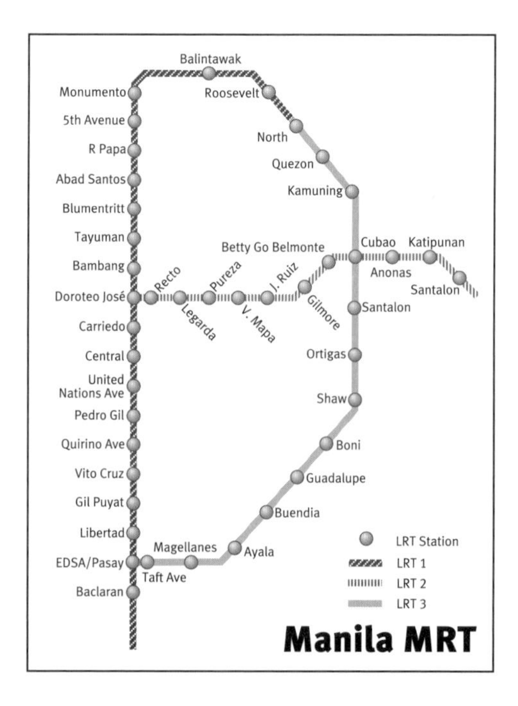

[1] Please note that in real life U.N. station is at the corner of United Nations Avenue and Taft Avenue. However, for the purpose only of language practice, pretend that for this exercise, U.N. station is at the corner of U.N. Avenue and Bocobo Street.

Note that for learning purposes, we will pretend that U.N. station is at the corner of United Nations Avenue and Bocob street.

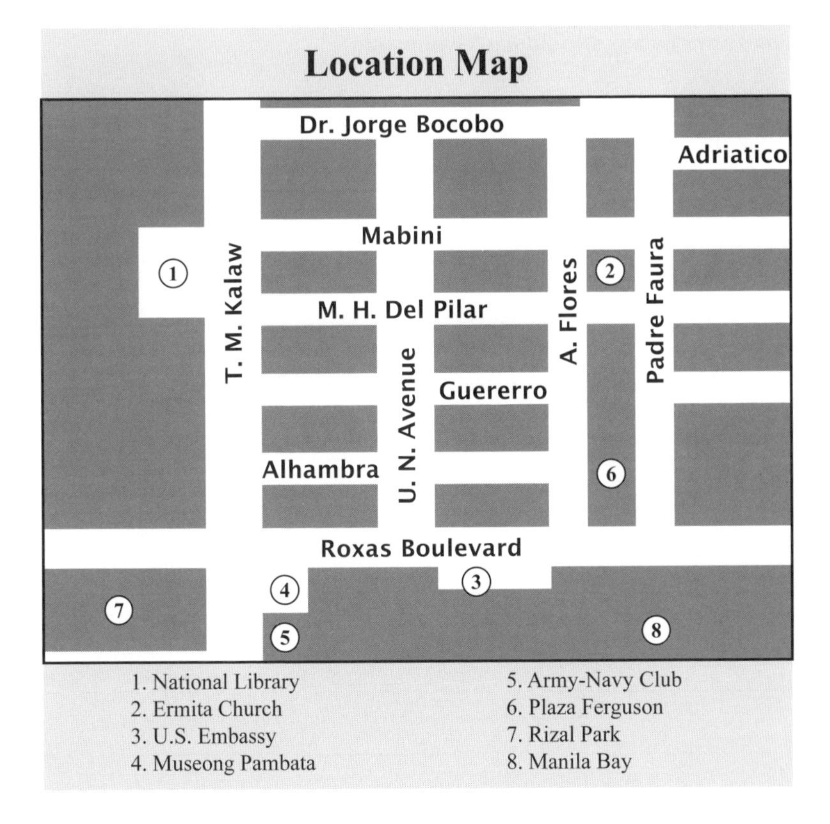

A distance-related fare structure is currently being used for Line 2. Passengers will be charged Php12.00 for the first three (3) stations, Php 13.00 for four to six (4-6) stations, Php14.00 for seven to nine (7-9) stations and Php15.00 for ten (10) stations.

LRT LINE 2	Stations / Fare			
Distance (no. of inter-stations)	1-3	4-6	7-9	10
Single Journey or Stored Value Ticket Fare (PhP)	12	13	14	15

SITUATION 1: You are at the US Embassy. You want to go to the National Library. Then, you want to take the train to Monumento.

A : **Mawalang-galang na ho, saan ho ang papunta sa National Library?**
B : ____.

A : **Puwede pa ho bang magtanong?**
B : ____.

A : **Saan ho ako sasakay ng tren?**
B : ____.

A : **Anong linya ho ang papuntang Monumento?**
B : ____.

A : **Saan ho ako bababa?**
B : ____.

A : **Magkano ho ang pamasahe?**
B : ____.

SITUATION 2: You are at Museong Pambata (Children's Museum). You want to go to Ermita Church. Then, you need to go to Ayala Avenue in Makati.

A : ____?
B : ____.

A : ____?
B : ____.

A : ____?
B : ____.

A : ____?
B : ____.

A : ____?
B : ____.

A : ____?
B : ____.

SITUATION 3: You are in Rizal Park. You want to go Plaza Ferguson. Then, your next appointment is in Cubao, Quezon City.

A : ____?
B : ____.

A : ____?
B : ____.

A : ____?
B : ____.

A : ____?
B : ____.

A : ____?
B : ____.

A : ____?
B : ____.

Gramatika Grammar

For this lesson, let us study how we can explore several ways of saying the same thing. This includes changing question words, the use of **may** or **mayroon** (have), and using the words **sana** (hope) and **kasi/dahil** (because).

Asking the question: "How do I go to...?"

There are many ways by which you can ask the question: *How do I get from Point A to Point B.* Let us study our options:

Paano ho pumunta mula sa Point A hanggang sa Point B? *How do I go from Point A to Point B?* (literally, How HONORIFIC to go from Point A to Point B?)—This is the most complete way of asking the question. It includes the words **mula** (from) and **hanggang** (to). Also note the use of the word **pumunta** which means "to go," and the verb is in the infinitive form.

Paano ho ako pupunta sa Point B? (literally, How HONORIFIC I go to Point B?)—Here you have an actor (**ako** or I) and the verb is in the incompleted form **pupunta** (will go).

Saan ho ang papunta sa Point B? *Where is the way going to Point B?* (literally, Where HONORIFIC MARKER going to Point B?)—Here, the question word **paano** (how) is replaced by the word **saan** (where). Also, note that **papunta sa Point B** is used as a noun phrase meaning "the way to Point B."

The use of "sana" (hope)

In previous lessons, you have learned that **sana** means "hope". The most simple way of using **sana** can be illustrated through these sentences starting with the word **sana**.

Sana, pumasa ako sa eksamen.
I hope I pass the exam. (literally, Hope pass I in exam.)
Sana, manalo ako sa raffle.
I hope I win in the raffle. (literally, Hope win I in raffle.)

You can, however, change the word order of these sentences and say:

Pumasa sana ako sa eksamen.
Manalo sana ako sa raffle.

In the dialogue for this lesson, **sana** is found in the middle of the sentence:

Mayroon pa ho sana akong gustong itanong.
I hope to ask one more thing [=I want to ask one more thing].
(literally Have another HONORIFIC hope I want to ask.)

Simply put **sana** either after **pa**, which indicated "one more" or "another" or after **ho**, in case you are using an honorific.

Here are a few more examples. In these sentences **sana na** is contracted into **sanang**. Note that the English words "want" and "hope" are collapsed into a single Tagalog/Filipino word—**sana**.

Gusto ko sanang bumili ng bahay.
I hope to buy a house. (literally, Want I hope buy MARKER house.)
Gusto ko sanang makabili ng bahay.
I hope to be able to buy a house. (literally, Want I hope able to buy MARKER.)

Giving reasons: Using "kasi" and "dahil"

When do we use **kasi** and when do we use **dahil**? In conversational Tagalog/Filipino, we hear **kasi** more often. The more formal-sounding **dahil**, however, is often used in written Tagalog/Filipino.

In the previous lesson, we studied:

Pagkatapos ho kasi ay pupunta ako sa Unibersidad ng Pilipinas sa Diliman.
It's because after this, I will go to the University of the Philippines in Diliman.
(literally, After HONORIFIC, because LINKER go to University of the Philippines in Diliman.)

You can put **kasi** in other positions in this sentence and also use **dahil** instead of **kasi**. However, note that when using **dahil**, you should put it just before the reason given, although you can put **pagkatapos** immediately after **dahil**. Its position is not flexible unlike **kasi**.

Kasi, pagkatapos ho, pupunta ako sa Unibersidad ng Pilipinas.
(Literally, Because, after HONORIFIC, go I to University of the Philippines.)
Kasi pupunta ako sa Unibersidad ng Pilipinas pagkatapos.
(Literally, Because go I to University of the Philippines after.)

Dahil pagkatapos, pupunta ako sa Unibersidad ng Pilipinas.
(Literally, Because after, go I to University of the Philippines.)
Dahil pupunta ako sa Unibersidad ng Pilipinas pagkatapos.
(Literally, Because, go I to University of the Philippines after.)

Note, however, that the above sentences are "conversational sentences." What does this mean? In English, it is fine to say "Because I am going to UP afterwards." However, we know that the meaning is incomplete and thus if we were to write this in an essay, we would need to complete the meaning. Thus, we can say for example: "Because I am going to UP afterwards, I want to ask you how to get there." The same is true for Tagalog/Filipino.

Navigating meaning

Although the first step in learning a language is to keep thinking of equivalent meanings, the second step is to learn how to navigate our way through meanings in order to come up with natural-sounding translations.

For example, in the dialogue, we learned:

Sentence: **Wala hong oras ang jeep dito.**
Literal Translation: **No** HONORIFIC LINKER **time** MARKER jeepney here.
Basic Translation: *Jeepneys* ***have no time*** *here.*
Meaning: *Jeepneys* ***do not operate on a time schedule*** *here.*

Pagsasanay sa Pagsasalin Translation Practice

Let us try to practice our translation skills. Here are three paragraphs from three news items from the website of *Pinoy Weekly*, an online newspaper. Classroom learners should work in pairs while individual learners should write down the translation. Remember, before looking up the meaning of an unknown word in a dictionary, try to guess the meaning first using the context in which the word was used. The third news item is longer, but it is also an easier passage.

1. Labor News[2]

Inireklamo ng mga manggagawa ng isang pabrika ng kilalang kapeng herbal na hindi umano sila pinasasahod ng manedsment ng kompanya.

Inirereklamo nila ang Glomar Herbal Philippines sa Taytay, Rizal, na hindi umano nagpasahod sa 46 manggagawa mula Enero ngayong taon at hindi rin nagpapapasok sa kanilang mga trabaho.

[2] Excerpt from "Obrero sa Kompanya ng Kapeng Herbal, Di Pinasasahod?" ni Macky Macaspac, *Pinoy Weekly*. http://pinoyweekly.org/new/2012/02/obrero-sa-kompanya-ng-kapeng-herbal-di-pinasasahod/

____
____
____
____
____
____
____
____.

2. News on Women[3]

Isang milyong pirma ang target na malikom ng militanteng grupong pangkababaihan na Gabriela sa kanilang petisyon kontra sa pagtaas ng presyo ng batayang mga produkto, kabilang ang langis.

Tinaguriang "Altapresyo(n)," o Alerto sa Taas-Presyo Network, pinakikilos umano ng Gabriela ang iba't ibang miyembro at tsapter nito sa Kamaynilaan at sa mga probinsiya para makalikom ng mga pirma sa petisyon. Layon nilang isumite ito sa Kongreso at administrasyong Aquino sa Marso 8, pandaigdigang araw ng kababaihan.

____
____
____
____
____
____
____
____.

3. Cultural News[4]

Sa pamamagitan ng Pandayang Lino Brocka Political Film and New Media Festival, laging buhay si Lino Brocka bagamat marami pang mga organisasyon at kilusan na nagbibigay-pugay hanggang ngayon sa Pambansang Alagad ng Sining sa Pelikula.

Kamakailan nga ay ipinagpaliban ang palugit ng pagsusumite ng mga lahok sa PLB, pinaikling patungkol sa pandayan, upang makahabol pa ang mga intresado, lalo na mula sa hanay ng mga estudyante at mga tagapaglikha ng pelikula sa mga lalawigan, malayo man o malapit.

Sa Miyerkules, ika-22 ng Hunyo, 2011 ang huling araw ng pagtanggap ng mga lahok sa pestibal na ito, na progresibo at naghahandog ng kamalayan sa publiko

---

[3] Excerpt from "1M pirma vs taas presyo, target malikom ng Gabriela" by the *Pinoy Weekly* staff. http://pinoyweekly.org/new/2012/02/news-1m-pirma-vs-taas-presyo-target-malikom-ng-gabriela/.

[4] Excerpt from "Laging Buhay si Lino Brocka" by Boy Villasanta, *Pinoy Weekly*, http://pinoyweekly.org/new/2011/07/laging-buhay-si-lino-brocka-2/

sa pamamagitan ng pelikula, anuman ang porma nito—maikli, may sapat na haba o full feature film, dokyumentaryo at iba pang genre na puwedeng paglimliman at pagsilangan ng isang malayang akda.

____

____

____

____

____

____

____

____.

Mga Talang Pangkultura: Mga Lungsod Cities

Pakikinig: Sa Araw ng Kordilyera On Cordillera Day

Pagbabasa Reading
Walang Kamatayang Undas Never-ending All Souls' Day

In the Philippines, the first day of November is the day that people troop to cemeteries to honor the dead. Read this short essay explaining Undas.

To prepare for this reading exercise, review/study the following vocabulary words: **namaalam** (had said goodbye; had passed away); **naninibago** (feels strange); **nasisindak** (shocked); **anghitin** (stinky); **hihimatayin** (will faint); **puntod** (cemetery grave); **paniniwala** (belief); **alalahanin** (remember); **malas** (bad luck); **pamahiin** (superstition); **malupit** (cruel; used here metaphorically to mean "extreme"); **sulok-sulok** (corners)

Kumusta ang Undas ninyo?
by Pinoy Weekly Staff

Noong hapon ng Nobyembre 1, tila buong Kamaynilaan ang dumaan sa mga kalsadang patungong North Cemetery. Bata, matanda, babae, lalaki, kulot, tuwid, pangit, pogi, naglakad sila para mabisita ang mga namaalam nilang mahal sa buhay. Taun-taong ritwal ito, pero tila, taun-taon ding naninibago ang bawat isa. Nagugulat sa kapal ng tao. Nasisindak sa putikang daan, sa usok, alikabok, ulan, sa katawan ng dalawang anghiting mama na nakasuksok sa magkabilang braso mo. Nagugulat ka't di ka pala nakapagdala ng sapat na pagkain, aabutin ka pala ng gabi sa daan. Mababasa ka sa pawis at ulan. Halos hihimatayin ka bago makarating sa puntod ng kaanak mo sa looban ng sementeryo.

Ito ang naabutan namin sa North Cemetery. Ang mistulang pistang taun-taon ipinagdiriwang, at di pinagsasawaan. Hindi na dapat nakapagtataka, labis pa rin ang pagpapahalaga natin sa ating namatay na mga mahal sa buhay. Labis pa rin ang paniniwala nating kailangan silang alalahanin sa araw na ito, kung ayaw nating multuhin nila tayo, abutin ng malas, o konsensiyahin. Pagdadalhan natin ng pagkain. May nag-alay ng pansit, ispageti. May *full meal*, isang beses sa isang taon lang kasi sila siguro makakakain. May nag-alay din ng softdrink, at ng mineral water. Baka kasi masama ang tubig sa sementeryo.

Sabi nila, "great equalizer" daw ang kamatayan. Ibig sabihin, mayaman o mahirap, pantay-pantay pagdating ni Kamatayan. Pero sa sementeryo, may mayaman at mahirap pa rin. Hayun nga, sa bungad ng North Cementery, nakahanay ang mga musoleo na tila wala nang bumibisita. May malalaking istruktura, tulad ng bubong at bahay, ang ilan. Malalaki ang mga lote, maganda ang landscape design, pero iisa lang ang nakalibing. Makikita, halimbawa, sa bungad ng sementeryong ito ang libingan nina dating presidente Sergio Osmeña. Malawak ang lote. Sa labas nito, siksikan ang mga tao, halos magkapalitan na ng mukha.

Kung sana nabuksan ang mga musoleo, kahit para man lang makadaan ang mga tao. Pero bawal, kasi may bantay. Sa una-unahan, nandun ang mga mala-apartment na mga puntod. Kasinlaki na siguro ng buong lote ni Osmeña ang sumunod na lote, na daan-daan ang nakalibing.

Hindi naman bago sa atin ang pagdiriwang na ito, ang mga pamahiing ito. Hindi rin ito kakaiba sa atin. Sa Latin America, lalo, buhay na buhay din ang pagdiriwang ng Dia delos Muertos, o araw ng mga patay. Hindi katoliko, kundi paganong praktika ang pag-alay ng mga pagkain sa patay. Pamahiin ito, na sabi ng marami'y wala naman mawawala sa atin kung susundin. Pero sa totoo lang, mayroon. Mawawalan tayo ng pagkain.

Sa mga probinsiya, mas malupit ang Undas. May mga nagbibidyoke, may nagmamahjong, nagbabaraha. Pero sa maraming malalaking sementeryo, ipinagbawal na raw ito. Gayunman, parang pista pa rin ang Undas sa North Cemetery. Pagsapit ng hapon, namamaho na ang napapanis na pagkain na itinapon sa mga suluk-sulok ng sementeryo. Pagdating ng gabi, uwian na sila. Sa susunod na taon uli, gugunitain ang mga yumao. Sa ngayon, abala muli sa mga buhay. Abala muli sa hanapbuhay. Abala muli sa pakikibaka ng buhay.

1. What surprises people about Undas?
2. How is Undas celebrated by Filipinos?
3. What are the superstitions regarding Undas?
4. What do the authors mean when they refer to Undas as a "great equalizer"?
5. How is class a factor in Undas?
6. Describe how Undas is celebrated in the countryside.

Pagsusulat Writing
Pagbibigay-Impormasyon Giving Information

Try writing a short paragraph,or a short short story on:

1. A village or a town;
2. An urban myth;
3. A travel experience in an unfamiliar place.

Paglalagom Summing Up

In this lesson, you have:

- Reviewed giving directions;
- Practiced the use of **sana**, **kasi**, and **dahil**;
- Practiced translation work;
- Read and written about geographical spaces.

Aralin 16
Lesson

Pagluluto
Cooking

In this lesson, we continue to practice the third skill we want to master—**pagpapaliwanag** or giving explanations. Review/study vocabulary for preparing dishes, constructing causative sentences, modals, and verbal nouns.

 Diyalogo: Ano ang lulutuin mo? What will you cook?

In this dialogue, Katie and Armael, the two characters you had met in earlier lessons, are talking about what they plan to cook for Rhonda's birthday. In the next part of the dialogue, birthday celebrant Rhonda and party guest Raquel are talking about the dishes.

KATIE : **Ano ang balak mong lutuin para sa kaarawan ni Rhonda?**
What do you plan to cook for Rhonda's birthday?

ARMAEL : **Balak kong magluto ng kare-kare.**
I plan to cook kare-kare.

KATIE : **Ano ang gagamitin mong hiwa ng baka?**
What part of the beef will you use?
ARMAEL : **Tuwalya at buntot ng baka.**
Tripe and the tail of the cow.

KATIE : **Paano mo palalambutin?**
How will you make it tender?
ARMAEL : **Pakukuluan ko nang apat na oras. Ikaw?**
I will boil it for four hours, and you?

KATIE : **Pinasingaw na tilapia.**
Steamed tilapia.
ARMAEL : **Paano mo pasisingawan ang tilapia mo?**
How will you steam your tilapia?

KATIE : **Lalagyan ko ng maraming kamatis at sibuyas, at babalutin ko ng dahon ng saging.**
I will put a lot of garlic and tomatoes and will wrap it with banana leaves.

At the party, Rhonda and Raquel are complimenting Armael and Katie for their dishes.

RHONDA : **Armael, ang sarap ng pagkakaluto mo ng kare-kare na ito.**
Armael, the way you cooked this kare-kare *is so delicious.*
RAQUEL : **Gaano katagal mong pinakuluan itong tuwalya at buntot ng baka?**
How long did you boil the tripe and cow's tail?
ARMAEL : **Naku, apat na oras.**
Oh, four hours.

ARMAEL : **Ang tagal pala!**
So long!
RHONDA : **Katie, ang ganda ng pagkakahanda mo sa mga putahe. Salamat.**
Katie, the way you served the dishes was beautiful.
KATIE : **Salamat, Rhonda.**
Thanks, Rhonda.

Bokabularyo Vocabulary

Review/study the following words and phrases you can use in describing cooking processes. If you need to review words about food, please refer to Lessons 3 and 4.

VERBS: balak mong lutuin (plan to cook); **palalambutin** (to make tender/soft); **pakukuluan** (boil/simmer); **sangkutsahin** (parboil); **pinasingaw** (steamed); **babalutin** (wrap); **iprito** (fry); **ihawin** (grill/broil); **igisa** (saute); **hanguin mula sa kawali** (remove from the pan); **magsaing** (cook rice); **mag-init** (heat); **masahin** (knead); **palamigin** (cool); **balatan/talupan** (peel); **hiwain** (cut/slice); **tadtarin** (chop); **gayatin** (dice/shred); **hiwain nang pahaba** (slice lengthwise); **haluin** (mix); **batihin** (beat); **dagdagan** (add); **budburan** (sprinkle); **pagsamahin** (combine); **ibuhos** (pour); **ilagay** (put); **ibabad** (marinate); **kudkurin/kayurin** (grate); **dikdikin** (pound); **hanguin** (remove from water/liquid); **ihain** (serve); **takpan** (cover); **bumula** (become frothy); **ilubog** (immerse)

Note that there is no difference in Filipino between the English words "boil" and "simmer." The word **pakuluan** is used to mean both "boil" and "simmer," although you might use a qualifier such as **pakuluan sa mahinang apoy** (cook in weak [=low] heat). Also, it is more natural to just use **i-bake mo** to mean "bake" and the English word "oven" instead of **hurno**.

VERBAL NOUNS: **pagkulo** (boiling); **pagpapakulo** (having something boil); **sangkutsado** (parboiled); **paglambot** (tenderizing); **pagpapalambot** (having something tenderized); **pagsingaw** (steaming); **pagpapasingaw** (having something steam); **pagbalot** (wrapping); **pagkakabalot** (your way of wrapping); **pagprito** (frying); **pagkakaprito** (way of frying); **pag-ihaw/pag-iihaw** (grilling/broiling); **pagkakaihaw** (way of grilling); **pag-init/pag-iinit** (heating); **pagsaing/pagsasaing** (cooking rice); **pagmasa/pagmamasa** (kneading); **paglamig** (cooling); **pagpapalamig** (having something cooled); **pagbalat/pagbabalat** (peeling); **paghiwa** (cutting/slicing); **pagkakahiwa** (way of slicing); **paghalo** (mixing); **pagkakahalo** (way of mixing); **pagbati/pagbabati** (beating); **pagdagdag** (adding); **pagkakadagdag** (way of adding); **pagbudbod/pagbubudbod** (sprinkling); **pagsama/pagsasama** (combining); **pagbuhos** (pour); **pagkakabuhos** (way of pouring); **paglagay/paglalagay** (putting); **pagkakalagay** (way of putting); **pinagbalatan** (shell coverings)

ADVERBS: **pahalang** (horizontally); **pahaba** (vertically); **pahiwas/pa-dayagonal** (diagonally); **panatilihin** (let something remain, for example: **panatilihing nakababad** means "let it remain marinated")

KITCHEN UTENSILS/EQUIPMENT: **hurno** (oven); **stove** (kalan); **kawali** (pan); **kaldero** (soup pot); **palayok** (pot); **siyanse** (cooking utensil)

INGREDIENTS: **rekado/sangkap** (ingredients); **sahog** (other ingredients apart from the main ingredient); **mantika** (oil); **asin** (salt); **paminta** (pepper); **bawang** (garlic); **sibuyas** (onion); **kamatis** (tomato); **luya** (garlic); **dahon ng saging** (banana leaves); **giniling na karne** (ground meat); **atay** (liver); **toyo** (soy sauce); **suka** (vinegar); **patis** (fish sauce); **bagoong** (fermented fish or shrimp); **kintsay** (celery)

OTHER NOUNS: **putahe** (dishes); **ulam** (anything eaten with rice; viand); **sopas** (soup); **sabaw** (broth); **ensalada** (salad); **panghimagas** (dessert); **de-lata** (canned); **caramelo** (caramel); **katas** (juice); **torta/tortilya** (omelette)

Mga Pangungusap Sentences

Review/study the following causative sentences with object focus that we find in the dialogue:

1. **Paano mo palalambutin?**
   How will you make it tender?

2. **Pakukuluan ko nang apat na oras. Ikaw?**
   I will boil [it] for four hours, and you?

As you may notice, the verbs are formed using the affixes **pa-** and **-in/-an**. Remember that in causative sentences, the affixes also differ depending on the focus, which may be on the following: causer, actor, object, location, instrument, and goal. For this part of the lesson, we are concentrating first on object focus, and will review the others in the grammar section.

Now, let us look at two more examples, using the completed and incompleted aspects. The completed aspect, object focus is formed using the affix **pina-** + root word while the incompleted aspect is formed using **pina-** + first syllable for root word + root word.

3. **Pinasingaw ni Katie ang tilapia niya na may kasamang kamatis at sibuyas.**
   Katie steamed her tilapia with tomatoes and onions.

4. **Pinakukuluan ko ang tuwalya nang dalawang oras kapag nagluluto ako ng kare-kare.**
   I boil tripe for two hours when I cook kare-kare.

5. **Pinalambot ko ang tuwalya sa pamamagitan ng pagpapakulo nito nang dalawang oras.**
   I made the tripe tender by boiling/simmering it for two hours.

In sentence number 5, note the use of the verbal noun **pagpapakulo** (boiling/ simmering). Now, let us review the use of modals with verbs in the infinitive form. In the dialogue above, we find the following sentences:

6. **Ano ang balak mong lutuin para sa kaarawan ni Rhonda?**
   What do you plan to cook for Rhonda's birthday?

7. **Balak kong magluto ng kare-kare.**
   I plan to cook kare-kare.

As you know, these verb phrases are formed with the structure modal + actor + verb in the infinitive form (either actor or object focus). Note that the verb changes when the focus changes from the object (**lutuin**, using the affix **-in**) to the actor (**magluto**, using the affix **mag-**).

Other examples of modals that you have learned are: **gusto/nais** (want); **ayaw** (don't like); **puwede/maaari** (can/may); **dapat** (should); and **kailangan** (need). Here are more examples:

8. **Ano ang dapat mong ihanda para magluto ng tilapia?**
   What should you prepare to cook tilapia?

9. **Dapat akong maghanda ng kamatis, sibuyas at dahon ng saging.**
   I should prepare tomatoes, onions, and banana leaves.

10. **Sino ang kailangan mong tawagan para sa party?**
    Who do you need to call for the party?

11. **Kailangan akong tumawag kay Raquel dahil siya ang magdadala ng panghimagas.**
    I need to call Raquel because she will bring the dessert.

Finally, do not be confused with the use of verbal nouns. Remember that meaning changes depending on the affix used. Study the following examples.

12. **Ang tagal ng pagkulo ng tubig.**
    The boiling of the water is [too] long [=takes a long time].
    (Literally, MARKER long MARKER boiling of water.)

13. **Kailangang matagal ang pagpapakulo mo ng tubig.**
    [Your] boiling [of] the water should be long.
    (Literally, Need long the boiling your of water.)

14. **Matagal ang pagluluto ng kare-kare.**
    Cooking kare-kare *[takes a] long [time].*
    (Literally, Long MARKER cooking MARKER *kare-kare*.)

15. **Masarap ang pagkakaluto mo ng kare-kare.**
    The way you cooked kare-kare *was delicious.*
    (Literally, Delicious MARKER way cooked you MARKER *kare-kare*.)

 Pagsasanay: Mga Tanong at Sagot

Review the vocabulary words and sentence structures you have just learned. Practice asking and answering questions.

In this particular situation, you are planning a surprise birthday party for your friend Kuusela. You have just cooked Filipino style spaghetti which uses spaghetti noodles, ground meat, hotdogs, banana ketchup, canned (**de-lata**) tomato sauce, onions and tomatoes. You made your ground meat tender by simmering it for 20 minutes. Your friend Jasen is in your kitchen and would like to know more about your recipe. Also, he is planning to make leche flan by first making a caramel on the stove, using it to line the baking pan, then steaming a combined batter of six eggs, a can of condensed milk and a can of evaporated milk, and a teaspoon of vanilla for around an hour.

1. TANONG : **Ano-ano ang mga sangkap ng iyong spaghetti?**
   SAGOT : ______________________________.

2. TANONG : **Gaano katagal mong pinakuluan ang spaghetti noodles?**
   SAGOT : ______________________________.

3. TANONG : **Anong klaseng karne ang ginamit mo?**
   SAGOT : ______________________________.

4. TANONG : **Paano mo pinalambot ang giniling na karne?**
   SAGOT : ______________________________.

5. TANONG : **Paano lulutuin ni Jasen ang leche flan?**
   SAGOT : ______________________________.

6. TANONG : **Matamis ba o maalat ang pagkakaluto ng spaghetti na Filipino-style?**
   SAGOT : ______________________________.

7. TANONG : ______________________________?.
   SAGOT : **Pa-dayagonal ang pagkakahiwa ko ng hotdog.**

8. TANONG : ______________________________?
   SAGOT : **Hotdog ang espesyal na sahog ng Filipino-style spaghetti.**

9. TANONG : ______________________________?
   SAGOT : **Caramelo ang lulutuin ni Jasen sa ibabaw ng kalan.**

10. TANONG : ______________________________?
    SAGOT : **Pasisingawin ni Jasen ang leche flan nang mga isang oras.**

 Pagsasanay: Mga Resipi Recipes

Navigate your way by conjugating the vocabulary words you have learned and see if you can use the root words as nouns, adjectives and verbs. Also, use your dictionary to find out the Tagalog/English equivalents of ingredients.

Complete the following simple instructions:

RECIPE 1 **Omelette:** You are making a tomato, onion, and mushroom omelette.

__________ ang kamatis ________________ at mga kabute. Maglagay ng kaunting ____________ sa _________________. _____________ ang mga rekado. Kapag naluto na, hanguin _____________________________.
_________________ ng apat na itlog. _________________ ang binating itlog sa _______________. Tiklupin ang ___________ kapag natutuyo-tuyo na ito. _______ _________________________________ at ilagay sa plato.

RECIPE 2 **Apple Tart:** You are making an apple tart. Here are your ingredients: **isa at kalahating tasang harina, dalawang kutsarang asukal, isang stick na mantekilya, kaunting asin, dalawang kutsarang tubig, tatlong mansanas, isang kutsarang katas ng limon, isang kutsaritang cinnamon.**

Paghaluin ang ____. Kailangang malamig ang _________________________. Ilagay ang crust na ito sa tart pan. ___________________ang crust sa refrigerator.
________________ ang mansanas. Ihalo sa mansanas ang __________________ __________.
__________________ ang crust mula sa refrigerator. __________________ ang ________________________. Mag-brush ng pinatunaw na mantekilya sa ibabaw ng ________________. ___________________________________.

RECIPE 3 **Chicken Afritada:** You are making a Filipino dish derived from a Spanish recipe. It is called chicken afritada. Your ingredients are: **hiniwang manok, bawang, sibuyas, patatas,** carrots, bell pepper, **guisantes,** laurel, **sabaw ng manok,** tomato sauce, **patis.**

Ihanda ang mga sangkap. _________________________ ang sibuyas at bawang. _______________ ang bell peppers. ________________ ang patatas.
Sa isang kawali, _______________ ng mantika. ___________ ang bawang at sibuyas. Ilagay ang _______________ at lutuin hanggang sa maging brown. _____________ ang tomato sauce at sabaw ng manok. ____________ at ibaba ang apoy. Lutuin nang mga 20 minuto.

__________ ang patatas at lutuin nang mga 10 minuto. _______ ang _______ at guisantes at lutuin nang mga isa o dalawang minuto. Lagyan ng patis, asin at paminta, ayon sa panlasa.

Gramatika At Pagsasanay

Review/study the formation of causative sentences and forming verbal nouns.

Causative sentences

In past lessons, you have studied causative sentences but in a different context. Let us try to briefly recall these sentences so you can contextualize this lesson. In Lesson 6, you learned:

Actor/Causer Focus:
Si Rose ang nagpapakain kay Mrs. Marchant ng almusal.
It is Rose who feeds Mrs Marchant breakfast.

Directional Focus:
Pinakain ni Rose si Mrs. Marchant ng almusal.
Rose fed Mrs. Marchant breakfast.

Object Focus:
Almusal ang ipinakain/pinakain ni Rose kay Mrs. Marchant.
Breakfast is what Rose fed Mrs. Marchant.

In another context, in the same lesson we studied the sentences below. Note that in this case the situation is different. The "causer" of the action is asking the "actor" or doer of the action to "act."

Causer Focus:
Nagpaluto si Maristelle ng sopas sa kusinera para sa kapatid niya.
Maristelle asked the cook to make soup for her sister/brother.

Actor Focus:
Pinaluto ni Maristelle ang kusinera ng sopas para sa kapatid niya.
Maristelle asked the cook to make soup for her sister/brother.

Object Focus:
Sopas ang ipinaluto/pinaluto ni Maristelle sa kusinera para sa kapatid niya.
Soup is what Maristelle asked the cook to make for her sister/brother.

Directional/Receiver Focus:
Pinalutuan ni Maristelle ng sopas sa kusinera ang kapatid niya.
The cook was asked by Maristelle to cook soup for her sister/brother.

Now, do not be confused. There are several grammar books that discuss causative sentences and these books sometimes vary in their terms—some will use the term "receiver," others will use "directional." I think it is better to focus on what term will help you remember how to use the affixes you are learning.

Notice how different the situations are in Sets 1 and 2. In set 1, the situation is that Rose is doing something for Mrs. Marchant. Rose is both the causer of the action and the actor, while Mrs. Marchant is the recipient of the action, and one can say that the action is directed towards Mrs. Marchant. The object here is breakfast. In Set 2, the context is different. Maristelle causes the action to be done, the action is done by the cook, the object is the soup, while the receiver (sometimes called beneficiary) of the action is the sister/brother.

Now, let us go back to the examples in this lesson. We constructed causative sentences with object focus by using the affixes **pa-**, **pa-in**, and **pa-an**. In the dialogue, you learned the following sentences:

Paano mo palalambutin?
How will you make it tender?
Pakukuluan ko nang apat na oras.
I will boil it for four hours.
Paano mo pasisingawan ang tilapia mo?
How will you steam your tilapia?

The situation here is again different from Sets 1 and 2 above. But let us take things slowly by starting with the root word **lambot** (tender/soft). Study the following sentences:

Lumambot ang karne.
The meat became tender.
Pinalambot ko ang karne.
I made the meat tender.

In the first sentence, the verb **lumambot** was conjugated using the affix **um**. It can be conjugated into **lumambot**, **lumalambot**, **lalambot**. In the second sentence, emphasis is given to the doer of the action—**ako**/I—the person who enabled the meat to become tender.

Please do not say: **Pinalambot ako ng karne.**
The meat made me tender.

See how the words **lambot**, **kulo**, and **singaw** can be conjugated and then try to fill-out the boxes for the other verbs: **tuyo** (dry); **lamig** (cool); **init** (heat).

Verb	Infinitive/ imperative	Completed	Incompleted	Contemplated
Lambot – um	lumambot	lumambot	lumalambot	lalambot
Lambot – pa-in	palambutin	pinalambot	pinalalambot	palalambutin
Kulo – um	kumulo	kumulo	kumukulo	kukulo
Kulo – pa-an	pakuluan	pinakuluan	pinakukuluan	pakukuluan
Singaw – um	sumingaw	sumingaw	sumisingaw	sisingaw
Singaw – pa	pasingawin	pinasingaw	pinasisingaw	pasisingawin
Tuyo – na	matuyo	natuyo		matutuyo
Tuyo – pa-in	patuyuin		pinatutuyo	
Lamig – um		lumamig		lalamig
Lamig – pa-in	palamigin	pinalamig	pinalalamig	
Init – um	uminit		umiinit	iinit
Init – pa-in	painitin	pina-init		paiinitin

Let us now look at ways by which we can change the focus of the verb **lambot**.

Causer/Actor Focus:
Nagpalambot ako ng karne gamit ang pressure cooker.
I made the meat tender using a pressure cooker.

Object/Directional Focus:
Pinalambot ko ang karne gamit ang pressure cooker.
I made the meat tender using a pressure cooker.

Instrumental Focus:
Pressure cooker ang ipinampalambot ko sa karne.
I used the pressure cooker to make the meat tender.

It is possible that some grammarians will identify **nagpalambot** as having causer focus; others as having actor focus. I am using both terms here simply to emphasize that the action is done and/or caused by **ako**. The **karne** here can be referred to as both the object (what is being made tender) and that to which the action is directed.

Now, you may notice that in the chart above, the verbs **pinasingaw** (was steamed) and **pinalambot** (was made tender) were formed by **pina** + root word, while **pinakuluan** (was boiled) was formed by **pina-** + root word + **an**. Briefly go back to Set 2 discussed earlier. Formula 1 (**pina** + root word) was used for object focus (the **sopas**) while Formula 2 was used for receiver/directional focus (Maristelle's sister/brother).

In my study of the Tagalog/Filipino language, the best explanation I can come up with is that in verbs wherein the action is caused in a particular location, Formula 2 can be used. This is best explained through the following examples:

Kumulo ang tubig.
The water boiled.
Nagpakulo ako ng tubig.
I boiled water OR *I caused the water to boil.*
Pinakuluan ko ang karne sa tubig.
I boiled the meat in water.

Therefore, what we are trying to say in **pinakuluan** is that we are boiling "something"—in this case, meat, in water. Here are a few more examples to clarify when to use **-an**.

Pinasingaw ko ang tilapia.
I steamed the tilapia.
Pinasingawan ko ang tilapia sa bamboo steamer.
I steamed the tilapia in the bamboo steamer.
Pinasingawan ko ang tilapia.
I steamed the tilapia [somewhere].

It is the third sentence that confuses us. Why? Because the use of the location—the bamboo steamer—is just implied. You don't really have to say it.

Forming Verbal Nouns

In Lesson 12, you studied noun affixes, among them **-an/-han**, **ka-an**, **mag**, **mang**, **sang/sam/san**, **pag-**, **tag-**, **taga-**, and **tala-**.

Let us continue studying how to form nouns in the context of this lesson. Here we are just studying the difference between using **pag-**, **pagpapa-** and **pagkaka-** in forming noun forms. Let us review the sentences we have learned.

Ang tagal ng pagkulo ng tubig.
The boiling of the water is [too] long [=takes a long time].
(literally, MARKER long MARKER boiling of water.)
Kailangang matagal ang pagpapakulo mo ng tubig.
[Your] boiling [of] the water should be long.
(Literally, Need long MARKER the boiling your MARKER water.)
Matagal ang pagluluto ng kare-kare.
Cooking kare-kare *[takes a] long [time].*
(Literally, Long MARKER cooking MARKER *kare-kare*.)
Masarap ang pagkakaluto mo ng kare-kare.
The way you cooked kare-kare *was delicious.*
(Literally, Delicious MARKER way cooked you MARKER *kare-kare*.)

There are only two things you should remember here. First, use **pagpapa-** to indicate that you are causing the water to boil, or doing something so that the water will boil. Second, use **pagkaka-** to mean "the way you did something."

Let us practice by filling in the blanks with the appropriate form of the verb. The root word is at the end of the sentence. First, let us practice the **pagpapa-** affix. Remember, the formula is very simple: **pagpapa** + root word.

1. **Mabagal ang __________________ ng tuwalya. (lambot)**
2. **Madali lang ang ________________________sa tilapia. (singaw)**
3. **Si Katie ang may responsibilidad ng ________________________ sa mesa. (ganda)**

Now, let us practice the use of the affix **pagkaka-**. Use the formula **pagkaka-** + root word.

4. **Ang sarap ng ____________________ mo ng spaghetti. (luto)**
5. **Napakatamis ng ______________________ ng leche flan. (gawa)**
6. **Simple ang gusto kong ________________ ng mga dekorasyon. (ayos)**

Online PDF Mga Talang Pangkultura: Pagkain Food

Pagsasalin: Mga Resipi Recipes

Translate one or more recipes below. The first one is my own recipe for **adobo**, and the two others are from the *Liwayway* magazines discussed earlier. For the first recipe, fill in the blanks. Some words have been translated to help you along. It will help you to reread all of the vocabulary section and the culture notes before doing this exercise instead of simply referring to these sections.

1. *Adobong Manok At Baboy*

Isang tasang suka
Isang tasang tubig
Kalahating tasang toyo o ayon sa panlasa
Kalahating kilong manok
Kalahating kilong baboy
Kalahating kilong atay ng manok
Paminta
Dalawang kutsarang bawang
Dalawang pirasong laurel
Mantika

Ibabad ang manok, baboy, at atay sa isang tasang suka at kalahating tasang toyo o ayon sa panlasa. Lagyan rin ng bawang at laurel. Panatilihing nakababad nang buong magdamag.

Isalang sa kalan ang lahat ng sangkap sa itaas. Dagdagan ng isang tasang tubig. Huwag haluin. Pakuluan ito at pagkatapos ay ibaba ang apoy. Kapag naluto na ang baboy, manok at atay, hanguin mula sa kalan.

Ihiwalay ang ilang pirasong atay. Dikdikin ito. Ihiwalay rin ang bawang.

Sa ibang lutuan, magpainit ng mantika at igisa ang bawang. Iprito ang naluto nang manok at baboy. Pagkatapos, ibuhos ang pinaglutuang suka at toyo. Ihalo sa sabaw na ito ang dinikdik na atay. Hayaang lumapot ang sarsa ng adobo.

Para sa ayaw ng atay, puwede ring tanggalin ito sa resipi.

Translation: Chicken and Pork *Adobo*
One cup of ____________
_______________ of water
Half _________ of _______ or by taste
Half a kilogram of _____________
_______________ of pork
_______________ chicken liver
Pepper
Two tablespoons of ___________
___________ laurel leaves
Mantika

Marinate the __________, ___________, and liver in ____________ vinegar, half a cup of ______________ or according to your _________. Also put ________ and the laurel leaves in the marinade. Marinate _____________.

Put all the ________________ over the ________. ________ one cup of ________. Do not mix. Let it _____________ and ____________ the fire. When the pork, chicken and liver are __________, _____________ them from the pan.

Separate a few pieces of ________ and ________. Also ___________ the garlic.

In a different pan, heat the ___________ and ___________ the garlic. __________ the cooked ______________. After this, ____________ the vinegar and soy sauce marinade. Mix the _____________ into the mixture. Let the adobo sauce get thick.

Those who do not like liver can just __________ it from the recipe.

2. *Sopas na Mais*
Sampung puso ng mais
Kalahating tasang hipon na pinirito
Isa at kalahating kutsarang bagoong
Isang dakot na dahon ng ampalaya at dahon ng sili
Mantika, bawang, sibuyas, pinagdikdikan ng ulo ng hipon at pinaghugasan ng sinaing

Piliin ninyo ang murang puso ng mais. Gayatin ninyo ang laman nito. Talupan ang hipon at biyakin sa gitna ng likod at ang ulo at pinagbalatan ay dikdikin at kunan ng katas.

Papulahin ninyo sa kawaling may mantika ang bawang, isunod ang sibuyas at hipon. Kapag mapula na ang hipon, ilagay ninyo ang bagoong at saka takpan. Idagdag ninyo pagkaraan ang mais na ginayat bago ihulog ang hipon at takpang muli. Kung sangkutsado na, ay ibuhos ang tubig sa bigas. Bago hanguin at ihain, ihulog ang dahon ng sili o dahon ng ampalaya.

TRANSLATION:

____

____

____

____

____

____

____

____

____

____

____

3. *Tortilyang Talong*
Limang talong
Sampung sentimos na baboy na giniling
Dalawang kamatis, isang malaking sibuyas na pinaghiwa-hiwa nang maliliit, isang kutsarang arina, bawang, mantika, dalawang itlog, at suka

Ihawin ang talong, pagkatapos ay alisan ng balat. Papulahin ang bawang sa kawaling may mantika, ihulog ang sibuyas na hiwa-hiwa, kamatis, at sa huli ay ang tinadtad na baboy. Timplahan ng patis at takpan. Batihin ang pula ng itlog, saka isunod ang puti hanggang sa bumula nang bumula. Lagyan ng palaman ang talong. Ilubog sa binating itlog, budburan ng arina. Prituhin sa maraming mantika.

TRANSLATION:

____

____

____

____

____

____

____

____

____

____

____

Talakayan: Noong bata pa ako.... When I was a child...

Classroom learners can form small groups or discuss with their partners one or more of the questions below. Think of a favorite dish or some kind of comfort food you had when you were a child. Individual learners should write down their thoughts.

1. What was your favorite food when you were a child and why?
   Ano ang paborito ninyong pagkain noong bata pa kayo at bakit?

2. Who cooked this dish for you then?
   Sino ang nagluluto para sa inyo ng pagkaing ito noon?

3. How was this dish made?
   Paano ginagawa ang putaheng ito?

4. How can you eat this dish now?
   Paano kayo nakakakain nito ngayon?

Remember to give reaction shots to what your partner or groupmates are saying. Here are are few expressions that may be useful:

1. **Talaga?** or **Ganoon ba?**
   Really?
2. **Nakakain na rin ako niyan!**
   I have eaten that too!
3. **Ang sarap talaga niyan!**
   That's really so delicious!
4. **Naku, ang sarap niyan!**
   Oh, that's so delicious!
5. **Nakakagutom naman.**
   I feel hungry [because of what you said].
6. **Ang hirap palang gawin iyan!**
   That's so difficult to do/make!

Pakikinig: Lumpiang Galunggong Fish Spring Rolls

Pagbabasa Reading
Pagluluto sa Kulungan Cooking in Prison

Read the following essay entitled "*Buhay Kulungan*" (Life in Prison) in the regular column *Jailhouse Blog* by Ericson Acosta for the online newspaper *Pinoy Weekly*. You have read about Ericson earlier in Lesson 7. Acosta, you will remember, is the only political prisoner in the Calbayog sub-provincial jail in Samar.

In this particular entry, Acosta translates and reflects on a poem from Vietnamese leader Ho Chi Minh's *Prison Diary*. Ericson similarly talks about prison life, focusing on how prisoners cook their own food.

Review/study the following vocabulary words: **preso** (prisoner); **sentralisado** (centralized); **mainam** (good); **inirarasyon** (is rationed); **tuyo** (dried fish); **hindi kaaya-aya** (unpleasant); **tinipid** (was stingy in spending); **bara-bara** (made without care); **panggatong** (fire wood); **de-uling** (uses charcoal); **dumiskarte** (devise a way); **magasgas** (scratched); **kantidad** (quantity); **batayan** (basis); **usok** (smoke); **pambugaw** (used to drive something away); **lamok** (mosquito); **siste** (jest/joke/quip); **nagliyab** (blazed); **nakakasulasok** (makes one want to vomit); **nakasalang** (used here to mean "put on the stove"; also means "on the line").

After reading this passage, please answer the comprehension questions below.

Buhay Kulungan[1]
By Ericson Acosta

> ***Isang kalan para sa bawat bilanggo, At mga palayok na sari-sari ang laki,***
> ***Para sa paggawa ng tsaa, paglalaga ng gulay at pagsasaing. Maghapon***
> ***ang buong paligid ay balot sa usok.***
> ***—Salin mula sa "PRISON LIFE" ni Ho Chi Minh***

Gaya ng inilalarawan ni Ho, KKL dito sa CSPJ*. Kanya-kanyang luto ang mga preso (o pwede ring grupo ng mga preso) sa bawat selda. May tinatawag na kitchen room pero ang pagkain lang ng mga gwardiya at ilang piling trustee ang niluluto dito; o di kaya ay mga packed meal na dinadala sa kung saan man sa labas ng jail sa tuwing may raket sa catering ang ilang empleyado. Walang mess hall.

Sa unang tingin ay hindi problema sa mga inmate ang kawalan ng sentralisadong feeding system. Ang opinyon ng marami ay mainam na ngang KKL para ikaw na ang bahala kung anong oras mo gustong magluto, at kung paano mo lulutuin ang araw-araw na inirarasyong bigas at sariwang isda; o ang dinadalang gulay at isda ng mga dalaw; o ang binibili sa tindahan dito gaya ng itlog, noodles at tuyo. Sa ganito, sabi

---

[1] Published in *Pinoy Weekly*, Sep 18, 2012. http://pinoyweekly.org/new/2012/09/buhay-kulungan/. Accessed January 2013.

nila, maiiwasan ang hindi kaaya-aya, tinipid at bara-barang luto na karaniwan daw na nangyayari kung isahan at bultuhan.

Sa kabilang banda naman, ang karaniwang inaalala ng mga kosa sa ganito ay ang panggatong. De-uling ang tipo ng kalan na meron ang mga inmate (1-2 sa kada selda) pero dahil mahal ang uling ay kahoy ang mas ginagamit. Kung ubos na ang kahoy na dala ng dalaw mo ay kailangan mong dumiskarte para magpabili sa labas, kung meron kang pambili. Ang ilan ay may rice cooker pero pangsaing nga lang. Kung gagamitin sa iba pang pagluluto gaya ng pagpiprito ay mabilis namang nasisira kaya kakailanganin pa rin gumamit ng de-uling/ de-kahoy na kalan para hindi ito maabuso o magasgas.

Bukod sa panggatong, lumalabas na bagamat ayos lang ang bigas, ang rasyong isda ay hindi sapat sa tatlong beses na pangkain sa bawat araw. Kaya kailangan mo pa rin umasa sa mga padala ng mga dalaw o bumili sa tindahan na presyong-laya ang umiiral.

Kung sa kalakhan ay hindi paborable sa mga kosa ang sentralisadong sistema ng pagluluto, kakailanganing magawan pa rin ng paraan na maging sapat ang kantidad ng niluluto. Kailangan ng dagdag na rasyon ng uulamin. Kailangan din na maging presyong-bilanggo ang bentahan sa tindahan. Maaari ngang patakbuhin sa tindahan sa batayang kooperatiba na hindi lang magpapababa sa presyo ng mga bilihin kundi siya na ring pagmumulan ng solusyon para sa mura at regular na suplay ng panggatong.

Gaya ng inilalarawan ni Ho, nababalot din sa usok ang buo-buong mga selda lalo na sa bandang alas-siyete ng umaga, at alas-sais ng gabi. Walang problema sa amin ang usok. Bukod sa epektibong pambugaw sa lamok, araw-araw din itong hudyat ng di-pinagsasawang siste:

"Hoy kayo dyan sa selda dos, bilis-bilisan na ninyo ang pagluluto nyo ng kopra..."

Ang problema ay kung dahil sa kawalan ng panggatong ay mga lumang damit ang tirahin o kung ano pang materyal na kapag nagliyab ay nakakasulasok at masama sa kalusugan ang usok:

"Hoy selda tres, bakit nyo kami tini-teargas?!"

Ang problema ay kung sa buong araw na pag-usok ng mga kalan ay tubig lang pala ang nakasalang.

***Calbayog** sub-provincial jail

1. In Ho Chi Minh's poem, what did they use the cooking pot for?
2. Why do the inmates of the Calbayog jail think it is better for them to cook their own food?
3. What kind of cooking equipment do they use in the jail?
4. What kind of ingredients do they have and how do they get these ingredients?
5. According to Acosta, what are the needs of the prisoners?
6. What was the joke shared by Acosta towards the end of the passage?

Pagsusulat Writing
Pagkain Food

Write one of the following:

1. A recipe of your own version or your family's version of adobo;
2. Your favorite recipe;
3. A short essay on a dish or food you cannot forget;
4. A short essay on a cooking show you had watched.

Paglalagom Summing Up

In this lesson you have:

- Reviewed and studied terms related to cooking;
- Reviewed and studied causative sentences;
- Read, listened to, and discussed food and written recipes.

Aralin
Lesson **17**

Mga Liham at Pakete

Letters and Packages

So far, we have practiced three essential skills in learning a language: **paglalarawan ng tao, lugar at damdamin** (describing people, places and feelings); **pagsasalaysay ng pangyayari, insidente at kuwento** (narrating an event, incident and story); and **paglalahad** (exposition), which includes **pagpapaliwanag** (explaining) and **pagbibigay ng direksiyon o instruksiyon** (giving directions or instructions). In this lesson, review these skills through a real-life situation. Also, practice describing objects, continue your review/study of causative and abilitative sentences, using images and metaphors. Learn more about 19th-century orthography and read two letters.

Diyalogo: Sa Post Office At the Post Office

In this dialogue, Katie is at the post office. She is mailing a small package and is also trying to find out what had happened to a package her sister had sent her. Please remember that in the Philippines, weight is usually measured using kilograms instead of pounds.

KATIE : **Puwede po ba akong magpadala ng maliit na pakete?**
Can I send a small package?
CLERK : **Saan ito papunta?**
Where is this going?

KATIE : **Sa Boston po.**
To Boston.
CLERK : **Timbangin natin ang pakete mo.**
Let us weigh your package.

KATIE : **Gaano kabigat po?**
How heavy is it?
CLERK : **Halos isang kilo ang pakete mo.**
Your package is almost a kilo.

KATIE : **Magkano po aabutin?**
How much will it reach [=cost]?
CLERK : **Isang libo, anim na raan at siyamnapu't limang piso. Pero mas mura kung barko.**
One thousand six hundred and ninety-five pesos. But it is cheaper when [sent by] ship.

KATIE : **Express mail na lang po. Iyon hong ipinadala ko noong isang buwan, inabot nang mahigit isang buwan.**
I will just do an express mail. The package that I sent last month [through a ship] reached [=arrived after] more than one month.
CLERK : **Ganoon ba? Kung express mail, darating ang pakete sa loob ng sampung araw.**
Is that so? If [you send it by] express mail, the package will arrive in ten days.

KATIE : **Meron pala ho akong tanong.**
[I realized] I have a question.
CLERK : **Ano iyon?**
What is it?

KATIE : **May ipinadala po sa aking pakete ang ate ko galing ng Massachusetts. Pero ang sabi po niya, nang tingnan daw niya ang website ng United States Post Office, nasa Bureau of Customs daw.**
My elder sister sent me a package from Massachusetts. But she said, when she looked at the United States Post Office website, it said that it was at the Bureau of Customs.

Clerk : **Nakatanggap po ba kayo ng abiso hinggil sa pakete ninyo? Ang patakaran po kasi, kapag kukunin n'yo na ang pakete ninyo, magbabayad muna kayo ng buwis.**
Did you receive a notice about your package? It [=This] is because our procedure states that when you claim your package, you should pay taxes first.

Katie : **Wala pa ho akong natatanggap.**
I have not rec eived anything yet.

Clerk : **Baka nasa Customs pa nga po. Kailan po ba ipinadala?**
It might still be at the Customs. When was it sent?

Katie : **Noon pa hong isang buwan. Express mail po. Naireklamo ko na ho ito pero wala hong sagot.**
It was last month. Through express mail. I had already complained about this, but there was no answer.

Clerk : **Ano ho ang laman ng pakete?**
What are the contents of the package?

Katie : **Dalawang blusa ho na nagkakahalaga ng tig-iisang daang dolyar.**
Two blouses that are worth a hundred dollars each.

Clerk : **Talaga? Pasensiya na kayo. Wala ho akong nalalaman tungkol sa pakete ninyo.**
Really? I am sorry. I have no knowledge [=information] about your package.

Bokabularyo Vocabulary

Review/study the following words. Some of them were used in the dialogue above and some of them are for the other parts of this lesson.

Nouns: pakete (package); **liham/sulat** (letter); **abiso** (notice); **patakaran** (procedure); **buwis** (tax); **laman** (contents; also used to mean "flesh" or "meat"); **nalalaman** (knowledge/information); **pagpapadala** (sending)

Words used to describe: kapal (thickness); **bigat** (heaviness); **bilis** (speed; fast); **bagal** (slowness); **haba** (length); **lapad** (width); **taas** (height); **tangkad** (height only for people); **baba** (low); **tagal** (length of time); **pahalang** (crosswise); **pahaba** (lengthwise)

Words used for measurement: pulgada (inch); **talampakan/piye** (foot); **gramo** (gram); **kilo** (kilogram); **sa loob ng sampung araw** (in ten days)

Words/phrases meaning each: tig-iisang/tig-isang daang dolyar (one hundred dollars each); **tig-dadalawang/tig-dalawang piraso** (two pieces each); **bawat** (each)

Particles: pa (still); **nga** (really; truly)

Mga Pangungusap Sentences

Review/study how to ask about descriptions, word choices, how to say "each," and abilitative sentences.

First, let us review/study how to ask a question about a package's description. Here are two examples:

1. **Gaano kaliit?**
   How small?
2. **Gaano kabigat po?**
   How heavy is it?

Note the use of the words **kaliit** and **kabigat**. This comes from the root words **liit** meaning "smallness," and **bigat** meaning "heaviness." Now, this might be confusing to some learners who know that the Tagalog/Filipino word for "small" is the adjective **maliit** while the word for "heavy" is **mabigat**. For example, we say:

3. **Maliit ang pakete ko.**
   My package is small.
4. **Mabigat ang pakete ko.**
   My package is heavy.

So you see, we have the same word for English—"small." However, in Tagalog/Filipino, we use **maliit** as an adjective, and use **kaliit** when we want to ask a question about the "smallness" of the package. Also, note that the question word **gaano** is used with a modifier, for example, **gaano** + **kaliit** and **gaano** + **kabigat**.

Similarly, we can say:

5. **Gaano kabilis darating ang pakete ko?**
   How fast can my package arrive?
   (Literally, How fast will arrive MARKER package my?)
6. **Gaano katagal niyang hinintay ang pakete?**
   How long did he/she wait for the package?

Now, let us study how words choices are made in sentences. For example, in the dialogue we find the sentences:

7. **Magkano po aabutin?**
   How much will it reach [=cost]?
8. **Ano ho ang laman ng pakete?**
   What are the contents of the package?

As you can see in the example above, the word **aabutin** (reached) is used to mean **halaga** (cost)—this means that the speaker is concerned about the possible "ceiling amount" that the package may cost. In sentence 8, one can alternatively say **nilalaman ng pakete** (also meaning "contents of the passage") or:

9. **Ano ang nasa loob ng pakete?**
   What is inside the package?

Also, study how the affix **tig-** (used to mean "each") is used to form words in sentences that describe.

10. **Dalawang blusa ho na nagkakahalaga ng tig-iisang daang dolyar.**
    Two blouses that are worth a hundred dollars each.

Simply attach the affix **tig-** to the number; some native speakers duplicate the first syllable of the numbers, others don't, especially in conversational Filipino. The only exception is the word **tatlo**, where it is sometimes contracted from **tig-tatlo** to **tigatlo** in spoken Filipino. Thus: **tig-iisa/tig-isa**; **tig-dadalawa**, **tig-dalawa**; **tig-tatatlo/tigatlo**; **tig-aapat**; **tig-apat**; **tig-lilima**; **tig-lima**; **tig-aanim/tig-anim**; **tig-pipito/tigpito**; **tig-wawalo/tigwalo**; **tig-sisiyam/tig-siyam**; **tig-sasampu/tigsampu**.

Of course, another way of saying sentence 10 is:

11. **Nagkakahalaga ng isang daang dolyar ang bawat blusa.**

Note the use of the word **bawat** meaning "each." Finally, review/study the use of abilitative sentences with an object focus. For example:

12. **Nareklamo ko na ho ito pero wala hong sagot.**
    I was able to complain [=have already complained] about this, but there was no answer.

To change the focus to the actor, we can use the affixes **naka/nakapag-** and say:

13. **Nakapagreklamo na ako tungkol dito pero wala hong sagot.**
    I was able to complain [have already complained] about this, but there was no answer.

Pagsasanay: Mga Tanong at Sagot

First, answer a few questions about the dialogue:

1. Tanong : **Paano mo mailalarawan ang pakete?**
   Sagot : ______________________________.

2. TANONG : **Paano puwedeng magpadala ng pakete?**
   SAGOT : ______________________________.

3. TANONG : **Magkano magpadala ng pakete sa pamamagitan ng express mail?**
   SAGOT : ______________________________.

4. TANONG : **Ano ang problema ni Katie tungkol sa ipinadalang pakete sa kanya?**
   SAGOT : ______________________________.

5. TANONG : **Ano ang paliwanag ng clerk?**
   SAGOT : ______________________________.

6. TANONG : **Ano ang nangyari sa pakete?**
   SAGOT : ______________________________.

Now, let us practice the sentence constructions we have learned. Please provide the questions to the following answers, and then the answers to some questions.

7. TANONG : ______________________________?
   SAGOT : **Kalahating pulgada ang kapal ng pakete.**

8. TANONG : ______________________________?
   SAGOT : **Darating ang pakete sa Los Angeles sa loob ng tatlong araw.**

9. TANONG : ______________________________?
   SAGOT : **Aabutin ng dalawang libro ang bayad sa pagpapadala ng pakete.**

10. TANONG : ______________________________?
    SAGOT : **Mga libro ang laman ng pakete.**

11. TANONG : **Magkano ang halaga ng bawat isang blusa?**
    SAGOT : ______________________________.

12. TANONG : **Ilan ang libro ng bawat isang estudyante sa klase?**
    SAGOT : ______________________________.

13. TANONG : **Ano ang mapadadala ko sa pamamagitan ng post office?**
    SAGOT : ______________________________.

14. TANONG : **Hanggang anong oras ako makapagpapadala ng pakete sa post office?**
    SAGOT : ______________________________.

15. TANONG : **Paano ako makapagpapadala ng pera sa post office?**
    SAGOT : ______________________________.

Role-Play

Study the following situations. Then create/write a dialogue between you and a postal clerk. Here are some postal rates you can use:

PHILPOST

Revised Postage Rates for Parcel Posts Services

Destination	Weight limit (kg)	Air parcel		Surface mail	
		Rate for weight not over 1 kg (peso)	Each additional 1 kg or part thereof (peso)	Rate for weight not over 1 kg (peso)	Each additional 1 kg or part thereof (peso)
Australia	20	200	335	457	158
Cambodia	30	416	174	408	188
Canada	30	742	512	391	222
Costa Rica	30	768	560	336	261
Croatia	31.5	792	422	533	267

Situation 1: You want to send some books weighing 3 kilos to Costa Rica. The box is 5 inches wide, 7 inches long and 2 inches thick.

Situation 2: You want to send some documents by airmail to Australia. Your parcel weighs less than 1 kilo. You have a problem. Your brother based in New York sent you his old computer but the Bureau of Customs is holding it and would like you to pay 10,000 pesos in taxes.

____
____
____
____
____

SITUATION 3: You want to send a big box to Canada. It weighs 10 kilos so you would like to send it by ship. You have a problem. Your parents sent you some gifts but they seem to have been lost in the mail.

____
____
____
____
____
____
____
____
____

Gramatika At Pagsasanay

Review/study causative sentences and abilitative sentences.

"Nagpa-" and "Pina-" Affixes for Causative Sentences

In earlier lessons, you have studied about **nagpa-** and **pina-** affixes used in causative sentences. Here are a few sentences in the dialogue you just learned:

Puwede po ba akong magpadala ng maliit na pakete?
Can I send a small package? (actor focus)

May ipinadala pong pakete sa akin ang ate ko.
My elder sister sent me a package. (object focus)

Practice causative sentences by answering some questions:

1. TANONG : **Saan ka magpapadala ng pakete?**
   SAGOT : ______________________________.

2. TANONG : **Kanino mo ipadadala ang liham?**
   SAGOT : ______________________________.

3. TANONG : **Saan ka nagpatimbang?**
   SAGOT : ______________________________.

Please provide the questions to the following answers.

4. Tanong : ____?
   Sagot : **Nagpasuri ako ng mata para malaman kung kailangan ko nang magsalamin.**

5. Tanong : ____?
   Sagot : **Nagpasukat ako ng katawan dahil magpapagawa ako ng damit.**

6. Tanong : ____?
   Sagot : **Ipinakopya ko ang mga dokumento sa Manila Copy Center.**

7. Tanong : ____?
   Sagot : **Ipinabalot ko ang pakete sa kapatid ko.**

Abilitative Affix "Na- + i"

In the dialogue, you studied the sentence:

<u>Naireklamo</u> ko na ho ito pero wala hong sagot. *I was able to [-have complained] about this but there was no answer.*

You may ask: what is the difference between using **nag-**, **nakapag-** and **nai-**?

Study the following sentences:

Nagreklamo ako tungkol sa pakete ko.
I complained about my package. (actor focus)
Nakapagreklamo na ako sa pakete ko.
I have complained about my package./I was able to complain about my package. (actor focus)
Naireklamo/nareklamo ko na ang tungkol sa pakete ko.
I have complained about my package./I was able to complain about my package.

As you can see, the use of both affixes **nakapag-** and **na-** along with the word **na** shows either the present perfect tense or the past perfect tense. Here, however, is where it gets tricky. In English, there IS a difference between the present perfect tense and the past perfect tense. For example, we say:

<u>I have complained</u> *about lost mail many times.* (present perfect tense)
Tagalog/Filipino translation: **Ilang beses <u>na</u> akong <u>nakapagreklamo</u> tungkol sa nawawalang mga sulat.**
OR
Ilang beses ko nang <u>naireklamo/nareklamo</u> ang tungkol sa mga nawawalang sulat.

I told the clerk that I ***had complained*** *about lost mail many times.* (past perfect tense)
Tagalog/Filipino translation: Sinabi ko sa clerk na nakapagreklamo na ako nang ilang beses tungkol sa nawawalang mga sulat.
OR
Sinabi ko sa clerk na ilang beses ko nang naireklamo ang tungkol sa nawawalang mga sulat.

What do we notice here? In Tagalog/Filipino there is no difference between the past and present perfect tenses. In fact there are no "tenses."

Let's look at how we can conjugate the verbs **padala** (send) and **reklamo** (complain). Please fill out the blank boxes:

Verb	Completed	Incompleted	Contemplated
Padala – nagpa	nagpadala		magpapadala
Padala – pina	ipinadala	ipinapadala	
Padala – nakapagpa		nakapagpapadala	makapagpapadala
Padala – napa	napadala		mapadadala
Reklamo – nag	nagreklamo	nagrereklamo	
Reklamo – ini		inirereklamo	irereklamo
Reklamo – nakapag	nakapagreklamo		makapagrereklamo
Reklamo – na-i- *or* na	naireklamo/ nareklamo	nairereklamo/ narereklamo	

When do things become confusing? This happens when native speakers use the affix **nai-** which is used for the benefactive or indirect object focus. For example, we can also say:

Naipadala ko na ang pakete. *I was able to send the package already.*
Naireklamo ko na ang tungkol sa pakete. *I was able to complain about the package already.*

Is there a difference in meaning between **napadala** and **naipadala**? No. That is why it is confusing.

However, the grammar rules become clearer when we are able to study sentences that really have a lot of possible focus. Let us, consider for example, the verb **bili** (to buy).

Actor Focus: **Nakabili na ako ng blusa para kay Mabelle sa tindahan gamit ang credit card ko.** *I was able to buy a blouse for Mabelle at the store.*

Object Focus: **Nabili ko na ang blusa para kay Mabelle sa tindahan.**

Benefactive or **Indirect Object** Focus: **Naibili ko na si Mabelle ng blusa sa tindahan.**

Locative/Directional Focus: **Nabilhan ko na ng blusa ang tindahan gamit ang credit card ko para kay Mabelle.**

Instrumental Focus: **Naipambili ko na ang credit card ko ng blusa para kay Mabelle sa tindahan.**

Now, let us go back to **naipadala** and **naireklamo**, which are commonly used by native speakers—what is happening here? For me, the simple explanation is flexibility. One can argue that both **na-** and **nai-** can be used for "objects" direct or indirect.

Similarly, one can use both **nai-** and **na-an** for the benefactive and locative focus, since the question we are asking here is where the action is either located or directed towards. Thus, we can also say. "**Nabilhan ko na ng blusa si Mabelle sa tindahan gamit ang credit card ko.**"

Mga Talang Pangkultura at Pagsasanay Liham na Jose Rizal sa mga Kababaihan ng Malolos Jose Rizal's Letter to the Women of Malolos

Mga Tanong/Talakayan

Classroom learners can either work in pairs or form groups while individual learners can write down their responses. Discuss the letter.

1. Who did Rizal write the letter for?
   Sino ang sinulatan ni Dr. Jose Rizal sa liham na ito?
2. What was the desire or the objective of the recipients of the letter?
   Ano ang pagnanasa o adhikain ng mga sinulatan ni Rizal?
3. According to Dr. Jose Rizal, what is **kabanalan**?
   Ayon kay Dr. Jose Rizal, ano ang kabanalan?
4. What were the changes in the lives or viewpoints of the women described by Rizal in the letter?
   Ano ang mga pagbabago sa buhay o pananaw ng mga kababaihan na inilarawan ni Rizal sa liham?
5. How are women of today in similar or different situations?
   Paano kapareho o kaiba nito ang sitwasyon ng kababaihan ngayon?

Pakikinig: Liham mula sa dayuhang piitan
Letter from a Foreign Prison

Pagbabasa Reading
Sulat sa Ina Letter to My Mother

Read this excerpt from the letter that Lorena Barros wrote to her mother on July 23, 1973. Barros was a poet, an Anthropology professor at the University of the Philippines and chair of Makibaka, a women's group she co-founded in 1971.[1] During Martial Law and the Marcos dictatorship (1972–1986), Barros went underground and subsequently joined the New People's Army. Her poems have been anthologized in several publications, among them, *Kamao: Mga Tula ng Protesta*, 1987, edited by Salanga, et.al. and published by the Cultural Center of the Philippines.

In this letter that Barros (using the pen name Cita Tagumpay) had written to her mother, she talks about how their relationship had changed from being parent-child to that of comrades who are fighting together for the same cause. Being a poet, Barros uses metaphors and images—can you find these? Please study below how they are used effectively.

In our review/study of vocabulary words, let us first look at words that you already know, but are perhaps rendered differently through the use of affixes. Encircle or in same cases, write down beside them, the root words of these words and study how the affixes contribute to constructing the meaning of the words: **ikinalulungkot** (made me sad); **nakapagpaalam** (was able to say goodbye); **pag-uusapan** (topic of conversation); **kinagisnan** (grew up with; literally, woke up to); **pangungumusta** (saying hello).

Now, let us study some metaphors and images, as well as words used metaphorically: **lamang-tiyan** (literally, stomach contents; means "one only has enough food to get by"); **anino ng pagkalunos** (literally, shadow of despair; a little bit of desperation); **malamig na tubig sa naghahapding sugat** (literally, cold water on a painful wound; comfort to assuage pain); **mayamang hapag** (rich dining table); **uyayi** (lullaby); **tanglaw** (light); **liwayway** (daybreak); **sandigang bato** (literally, stone that props you up; something that you can lean on); **bukal ng lakas** (literally, wellspring of strength; source of strength).

Here are other words you need to review/study: **makasapat** (will be able to suffice); **ipaabot** (tell; literally, reach); **pahina** (pages); **kasama** (used here to mean "comrade"; literally, companion); **masigla** (lively); **mapalad** (fortunate); **pagsumikapan** (try to

---

[1] Makibaka went underground when Martial Law was declared in 1972. It is one of the organizations comprising the National Democratic Front of the Philippines.

achieve); **panunumbat** (reproach); **masustansiya** (has a lot of nutrients); **tuwiran** (directly); **hukbo** (army); **digmaang bayan** (people's war); **milagro** (miracle); **pagsubaybay** (guidance).

Sulat sa Ina[2]
ni Lorena Barros

Mahal kong ina at kasama,

Labis kong ikinalulungkot na hindi tayo nakapagpaalam nang harapan. Kay rami pa nating pag-uusapan! Subalit kailangang makasapat ang sulat na ito. Nais kong ipaabot sa iyo ang nilalaman ng ilang pahina mula sa aking notebook.

Ang una ay may petsang Mayo 21. Katatanggap ko pa lang ng isa mong liham:

"Pagkat ikaw lang ang magulang na kinagisnan ko, labis-labis ang pagmamahal ko sa iyo mula pa sa aking pagkabata. Subalit ang lahat ng taong minahal kita bilang magulang ay katumbas lang ng isang taong minahal kita bilang kasama. Kahit iilang pagkakataon lang tayo nagkita sa loob ng taong ito ay kay lapit ng ating kalooban sa isa't isa. Totoong maraming sandaling nais kong makapiling ka, ihinga sa iyo ang lahat ng kalungkutang di ko maaaring ipakita sa mga kasama pagkat dapat ay lagi tayong masigla. Subalit isipin ko lang na mauunawaan mo ako nang lubos ay gumagaan na ang aking loob. Mapalad ako sa pagkakaroon ng isang komunistang ina!"

"Lagi kong naaalala ang iyong huling sulat. Nabanggit mo ang inyong paghihirap kung paano halos lamang-tiyan na lang ang kinakain ng aking mga maliliit na kapatid. Subalit wala ni anino ng pagkalunos sa iyong mga salita—parang malamig na tubig sa naghahapding sugat ang iyong sinabi: "ang pagsumikapan nating dalawa ay ang parating manatiling matatag at masigla lalo na sa harap ng ibang kasama." Kay palad ko sa iyo, ina! Kahit minsan ay di ako nakarinig sa iyo ng panunumbat, gayong kung di ko inilaan ang aking buong buhay sa rebolusyon ay marahil di kayo maghihirap nang ganito. Naghahapdi ang aking kalooban tuwing maiisip kong nagugutom kayo ng aking mga kapatid. Lumalaki sila at kailangan nila ng masustansiyang pagkain. Masakit sa aking isiping wala akong tuwirang maitulong sa inyo. Inip na inip na akong makalabas at sumapi sa ating magiting na hukbo! Isulong ang digmaang bayan upang lalong mapabilis ang pagbagsak ng bulok na lipunan!"

---

[2] This letter was published in the book *Muog: Ang naratibo ng kanayunan sa matagalang digmang bayan sa Pilipinas: kalipunan ng mga liham, talakayangbuhay, talaarawan, reportahe, pahayag, kwento at bahagi ng nobela, 1972–1987 (Fortress: Countryside narratives during the protracted people's war in the Philippines: a collection of stories, life narratives, diaries, reportage, statements, short stories and novel excerpts 1972–1987).* Quezon City: University of the Philippines Press, 1998.

"Bago ko matanggap ang iyong sulat, kung anu-anong "multo't halimaw" ang nasa isipan ko. Lagi akong malungkot, nangingibabaw sa akin ang dalamhati para sa mga kasamang nadakip o nasawi at sa kanilang mga naiwang mahal sa buhay. Ngayon masigla ko na muling nahaharap ang bawat araw. Sino ang makaiisip na ikaw, ang awtoridad na pinaghimagsikan ko nuong aking kabataan, ay siyang magandang halimbawa sa akin ngayon! Anong mga milagro ang di nagagawa ng pakikibakang dakila tulad ng sa atin!"

Ang tulang ito ay may petsang 11 Hulyo 1973.
Ina

Ano ang isang ina?
Mayamang hapag ng
gutom na sanggol
Kumot sa gabing maginaw
Matamis na uyayi
Tubig
sa naghahapding sugat

Ngunit ano ang isang
komunistang Ina?

Maapoy na tanglaw
tungo sa liwayway
Sandigang bato
Lupang bukal ng lakas
sa digma.
Katabi sa labanan at
alalay sa tagumpay
Ang ina ko

—Cita Tagumpay

Hindi ko na kailangang sabihin pa na umaasa ako sa iyong pagsubaybay sa aming anak. Ibuhos mo sa kanya ang damdaming-ina na di ko maipadama—hanggang sa panahong makukuha ko na siya, na sana'y di hihigit sa isang taon.

Hanggang sa muli. Huwag kang mag-alala sa akin. Ipaaabot ko ang iyong pangungumusta sa ama ni Lengleng.

Sa rebolusyon,
ang iyong anak

Please answer the following comprehension questions.

1. What made the writer sad?
2. What makes the writer feel better?
3. How did the author describe her mother's words when she was talking about poverty and strength?
4. Why did the author feel bad when she learned about the poverty of her family?
5. Please list the metaphors that the poet used to describe her mother.
6. When does she plan to get her children from the care of her mother?

Pagsusulat Writing

Choose among the following prompts:

1. Write a letter to a parent;
2. Choose a historical or literary character and write a letter assuming his/her persona;
3. Write about a recent experience sending/receiving a package.

Paglalagom Summing Up

In this lesson, you have:

- Reviewed measurements;
- Studied and practiced verbs with abilitative affixes and verbs used in causative sentences;
- Read a 19th-century Tagalog text and a contemporary letter.

Aralin
Lesson **18**

Pagrereklamo

Complaining

We now start our study of the fourth and last skill necessary in using a language – **pangangatuwiran** (reasoning). Remember that you have, by now, practiced three skills: **paglalarawan** (describing); **pagsasalaysay** (narrating); and **paglalahad** (explaining). For this lesson, practice/review/study how to give arguments in everyday situations.

 Diyalogo: 13: Pagrereklamo sa Hotel Complaining at a Hotel

HOTEL CLERK : **Front desk, magandang gabi po.**
This is the front desk, good evening.

ARMAEL : **Magandang gabi naman. May problema ho dito sa kuwarto ko.**
Good evening. I have a problem here in my room.

HOTEL CLERK : **Ano po ang problema?**
What is the problem?

ARMAEL : **Hindi ako makatulog dahil maingay ang mga bata sa kabilang kuwarto.**
I cannot sleep because the children next door are loud.

Hotel Clerk : **Gusto po ba ninyong lumipat sa ibang kuwarto?**
Do you want to transfer to a different room?
Armael : **Kung maaari ho sana.**
If possible.

Hotel Clerk : **May bakante ho sa ikawalong palapag.**
There is a vacant room on the eight floor.
Armael : **Mayroon ho ba kayong dalawang double beds sa kuwartong iyon?**
Do you have two double beds in that room.

Hotel Clerk : **Naku, king-sized bed lang ho.**
Oh, we only have a king-sized bed.
Armael : **Ang gusto sana namin ay dalawang double beds.**
What we hope [=want] are two double beds.

Hotel Clerk : **Kung ganoon ho, mas mainam sa tenth floor. Pero ang bakanteng kuwarto ho roon ay mas mahal dahil mas maganda ang tanawin.**
If that is so, tenth floor is better. But the vacant room [there] is more expensive, because the view is much better.
ArmaelL : **Doon na nga lamang ho siguro. Pero kailangan ba naman magbigay ng dagdag na bayad?**
Then, I will just transfer there. But do I need to pay the extra amount?

Hotel Clerk : **Oho.**
Yes.
Armael : **Aba, hindi ho yata tama iyan. Hindi naman namin kasalanang may problema sa kuwarto namin.**
Oh, that is not right. It is not our fault that our room has a problem.

Hotel Clerk : **Hindi rin ho namin kasalanan na maingay ang kakapit-kuwarto ninyo.**
It is also not our fault that your neigboring room is loud.
Armael : **E paano ho natin malulutas ang problemang ito?**
Then how can we solve this problem?

Hotel Clerk : **Kakausapin ko ho ang manager. (Matapos ang ilang sandali.) Pumayag na ho ang manager.**
I will talk to the manager. [After a few moments] The manager agreed.
Armael : **Salamat naman. Kami naman ho ay laging tumitira dito.**
Thank goodness. We always stay here.

HOTEL CLERK : **Kailan ko ho ba maaaring paakyatin ang bell man para sa mga gamit ninyo?**
When is it possible to call the bellman to go up for your belongings?

ARMAEL : **Pagkatapos ho ng labinlimang minuto. Mag-aayos lang ako.**
After fifteen minutes. I will just prepare.

HOTEL CLERK : **Ipahahanda ko na rin ho ang bagong kuwarto ninyo.**
I will also ask someone to prepare your new room.

ARMAEL : **Salamat po at pinagbigyan n'yo ako.**
Thank you for giving way to my request.

Bokabularyo Vocabulary

Review/study the following words and expressions used in the dialogue:

ADJECTIVES/DESCRIPTIVE WORDS: **bakante** (vacant); **mainam** (good); **kakapit-kuwarto** (adjacent room)

VERBS: **paakyatin** (ask someone to come up); **ipapahanda/ipahahanda** (to ask someone to prepare something); **pumayag** (agreed); **pinagbigyan** (gave way to; literally, was given)

EXPRESSIONS: **kung ganoon ho…** (if that is so…); **doon na nga lamang** (then … just there);

INTERJECTIONS: **aba** (exclamation of surprise or wonder)

Mga Pangungusap Sentences

In this section, let us continue to review/practice causative and abilitative sentences. For causative sentences in the dialogue, focus on the infinitive and imperative forms using the affixes **pa-/ipa-**. We will review/study expressions you can use in giving arguments in the **Pagsasanay** section below.

In this first sentence, the verb is in the infinitive form with actor focus and the root word **akyat** is used with the affixes **pa-** and **-in**. Note the use of the modal **maaari** (can).

1. **Kailan ko ho ba maaaring paakyatin ang bellman para sa mga gamit ninyo?**
   When is it possible to ask the bellman to go up for your belongings?

Another sentence similar to this is:

2. **Maaari mong paakyatin mo ang bellman sa kuwarto para sa mga gamit ni Armael sa loob ng sampung minuto.**
   You can ask the bellman to to go up to the room for the belongings of Armael in ten minutes.

Now, you are, by now, familiar with causative sentences and just need more practice. If we were to say this sentence in the completed, incompleted and contemplative aspects, we can say:

3. **Pinaakyat mo ang bellman sa kuwarto para sa mga gamit ni Armael.**
   You asked the bellman to go up to the room for Armael's belongings.

4. **Pinaaakyat mo ang bellman sa kuwarto para sa mga gamit ni Armael.**
   You are asking the bellman to go up to the room for Armael's belongings.

5. **Paaakyatin mo ang bellman sa kuwarto para sa mga gamit ni Armael.**
   You will ask the bellman to go up to the room for Armael's belongings.

You also probably know that you can change the focus of the sentence to the causer of the action by using the affix **magpa-**:

6. **Ikaw ang nagpaakyat sa bellman sa kuwarto para sa mga gamit ni Armael.**
   You [were the one who] asked the bellman to go up to the room for Armael's belongings.

A sentence with a direction/location focus is possible, although in everyday life, one is likely to say this:

7. **Kuwarto ni Armael ang pinaakyatan mo sa bellman para sa mga gamit ni Armael.**
   [It was] Armael's room that you asked the bellman to go up to for Armael's belongings.

A similar sentence, with object focus, contemplated aspect is:

8. **Ipahahanda ko na rin ho ang bagong kuwarto ninyo.**
   I will also ask someone to prepare your new room.

Similarly, you can say:

9. **Magpahahanda ako ng bagong kuwarto ninyo.** (causer focus)

Now, let us review the abilitative sentence we find in the dialogue.

10. **Hindi ako makatulog dahil maingay ang mga bata sa kabilang kuwarto.**
    I cannot sleep because the children next door are loud.

Study the other sentences below and review affixes used for object, benefactive and locative focus.

11. **Nakapagreserba ako ng dalawang double room para sa pamilya ko.**
    I was able to reserve a double room for my family. (actor focus)

12. **Dalawang double room ang naireserba ko para sa pamilya ko.**
    Two double rooms is what I was able to reserve for my family. (object focus)

13. **Naireserba ko ng dalawang double room ang pamilya ko.**
    It was for my family that I was able to reserve two double rooms. (benefactive focus)

14. **Nailipat ako ng hotel clerk ng kuwarto sa ika-apat na palapag.**
    The hotel clerk was able to transfer me to a room on the fourth floor. (benefactive focus)

15. **Kuwarto sa ika-apat na palapag ang nalipatan ko.**
    A room on the fourth floor is where I was able to transfer to. (locative focus)

Pagsasanay: Mga Tanong at Sagot

Practice shifting focus in causative sentences. Please answer the questions below or provide the questions to the answers given. Some of the questions are from the dialogue and some can just be answered using your own experiences or an imagined situation.

1. TANONG : **Sino ang pinaakyat ng hotel clerk sa kuwarto ni Armael?**
   SAGOT : ______________________________.

2. TANONG : **Bakit nagpahanda ng bagong kuwarto ang hotel clerk?**
   SAGOT : ______________________________.

3. TANONG : **Bakit gustong magpalipat ng kuwarto si Armael?**
   SAGOT : ______________________________.

4. TANONG : **Kailan ka nakapagreserba ng kuwarto mo sa hotel?**
   SAGOT : ______________________________.

5. TANONG : **Anong oras mo gustong ipalinis ang kuwarto mo sa hotel?**
   SAGOT : ______________________________.

6. TANONG : ____?
   SAGOT : **Gustong magpalipat ni Armael sa ikasampung palapag.**

7. TANONG : ____?
   SAGOT : **Nailipat ng hotel clerk si Armael sa isang kuwarto sa ikasampung palapag.**

8. TANONG : ____?
   SAGOT : **Hindi makatulog si Armael dahil maingay ang mga bata.**

9. TANONG : ____?
   SAGOT : **Hindi ako nakapagreserba ng hotel dahil wala nang bakanteng kuwarto.**

10. TANONG : ____?
    SAGOT : **Suite na lang ang marereserba mo dahil puno na ang hotel.**

Pagsasanay: Mga Argumento Arguments

In the dialogue we just read, both Armael and the hotel clerk have arguments. First, please outline Armael's arguments as to why he should transfer to the better room for the same amount as his old room.

1. ____.
2. ____.

Now, please outline the hotel clerk's arguments as to why Armael should pay extra for the better room.

1. ____.
2. ____.

How was the argument resolved? What is going to happen?

1. ____.
2. ____.

Now study the following situations and create/write a dialogue. Classroom learners can work in pairs or small groups while individual learners can write down the dialogues. Use the words and phrases that you learned in the dialogue earlier. Here they are again, as well as other phrases that might be useful to you. Remember, that in Filipino culture, it is important to be polite when expressing a request or an opinion.

Kung puwede ho/kung maaaari ho	*If possible*
Hindi naman ho tama iyan.	*That is not right.*
Sa aking palagay	*In my opinion*
Ang gusto ko ho sana…	*What I would like is* (literally, what I would like that I hope….)
Ang suhestiyon/mungkahi ko ho…	*My suggestion is…*
Naniniwala ho ako na…	*I believe that…*
Paano ho natin malulutas ang problemang ito?	*How can we solve this problem?*
Ganoon na lang nga siguro…	*Perhaps that can just be the… (solution)*
Kakausapin ko ho si….	*I will talk to….*

SITUATION **1:** You booked your beach resort reservations online through a third party. When you get to the resort, you realize that the resort is far from the beach. You would like to get a reimbursement from the hotel so that you can transfer to a different resort.

SITUATION **2:** You are at the airport. Your flight was cancelled because of engine trouble. You need to stay another night in the island resort but you don't want to pay for your hotel room. The airline does not want to provide for hotel accommodations.

Situation 3: You just booked your hotel accommodations online. It was a non-refundable booking. Minutes later, you realized that you made a mistake and booked the wrong dates. You call the hotel to ask if your reservation can be changed.

Gramatika Grammar

Please continue your review/study of causative and abilitative sentences. These sentences are a bit challenging so several lessons focus on these sentences in this book. For this lesson/unit, we are reviewing and summarizing what we have learned about causative and abilitative sentences.

Causative Sentences

In past lessons, you have studied causative sentences with causer focus and actor focus.

In this lesson, you learned:

Salamat ho at pinagbigyan niyo ako. *Thank you for giving way to my request.* (literally, Thank you HONORIFIC and gave in you me.)

In the sentence above, **bigay** is used figuratively to mean "gave way to" or "gave in to someone." Let us study all kinds of causative sentences. First, take a look at two charts and sample sentences below for two verbs: **bigay** (give; not used figuratively) and **gawa** (make).

Bigay

Focus/affix	Inf/imp	Completed	Incompleted	Contemplated
Causer/**magpa**	magpabigay	nagpabigay	nagpapabigay	magpapabigay
Actor/**pa-in**	ipabigay	pinabigay	pinabibigay	ipabibigay
Object/**i** + **pa**	ipabigay	ipinabigay	ipinabibigay	ipabibigay
Receiver/Location/ Direction **pa** + **pag**	pabigyan	pinabigyan	pinabibigyan	pabibigyan
Instrument/**i** + **pa** + **pang**	ipambigay	ipinambigay	ipinambibigay	ipambibigay

Sample sentences (completed aspect):

Nagpabigay ako ng tiket para kay Maria kay Juan sa pamamagitan ng naipong mileage. *I gave a ticket to Maria through Juan through accumulated mileage.*
Si Juan ang pinabigay ko ng tiket kay Maria sa pamamagitan ng naipong mileage.
Tiket ang ipinabigay ko kay Maria kay Juan sa pamamagitan ng naipong mileage.
Pinabigyan ko ng tiket si Maria kay Juan sa pamamagitan ng naipong mileage.
Naipong mileage ang ipinambigay ko ng tiket kay Maria sa pamamagitan ni Juan.

Gawa (*Make*)

Focus/affix	Inf/imp	Completed	Incompleted	Contemplated
Causer/**magpa**	magpagawa	nagpagawa	nagpapagawa	magpapagawa
Actor/**pa-in**	ipagawa	pinagawa	pinagagawa	pagagawin
Object/**i** + **pa**	ipagawa	ipinagawa	ipinagagawa	ipagagawa
Location/ **pa** + **pag**	pagawan	pinagawan	pinagagawan	pagagawan
Instrument/**i** + **pa** + **pang**	ipanggawa	ipinanggawa	ipinapanggawa	ipapanggawa

Sample sentences (contemplated aspect):

Magpapagawa si Juan ng reserbasyon para sa nanay niya kay Maria sa pamamagitan ng iPad nito. *Juan will ask Maria to make reservations for his mother using her iPad.*
Si Maria ang pagagawin ni Juan ng reserbasyon para sa nanay niya sa pamamagitan ng iPad nito.
Reserbasyon para sa nanay niya ang ipagagawa ni Juan kay Maria sa pamamagitan ng iPad nito.
Ang nanay niya ang pinagawan ng reserbasyon ni Juan kay Maria sa pamamagitan ng iPad nito.
iPad ang ipinanggawa ni Maria ng reserbasyon ni Juan para sa nanay nito.

Abilitative Sentences

Now, let us use the same verbs above to make abilitative sentences.

Bigay

Focus/affix	Inf/imp	Completed	Incompleted	Contemplated
Actor focus/**naka-, nakapag**	makapagbigay	nakapagbigay	nakapagbibigay	makapagbibigay
Object focus/**na** or **na** + **i**	mabigay	nabigay	nabibigay	mabibigay
Benefactive or indirect object focus, **ma** + **i**	maibigay	naibigay	naibibigay	maibibigay

Focus/affix	Inf/imp	Completed	Incompleted	Contemplated
Locative or indirect object focus/**ma- an**	mabigyan	nabigyan	nabibigyan	mabibigyan
Instrumental/**mai** + **pa/pang**	maipambigay	naipambigay	naipapambigay	maipapambigay

Nakapagbigay ako ng tiket para kay Maria sa pamamagitan ng naipong mileage. *I gave a ticket to Maria through Juan redeemed through accumulated mileage.*
Tiket ang nabigay ko kay Maria sa pamamagitan ng naipong mileage.
Tiket ang naibigay ko kay Maria sa pamamagitan ng naipong mileage.
Nabigyan ko ng tiket si Maria sa pamamagitan ng naipong mileage.
Naipong mileage ang naipambigay ko ng tiket kay Maria.

Gawa

Focus/affix	Inf/imp	Completed	Incompleted	Contemplated
Actor focus/**naka-, nakapag**	makagawa	nakagawa	nakagagawa	makagagawa
Object focus/**na** or **na + i**	magawa	nagawa	nagagawa	magagawa
Benefactive or indirect object focus, **ma + i**	maigawa	naigawa	naigagawa	maigagawa
Locative or indirect object focus/**ma- an**	magawan	nagawan	nagagawan	magagawan
Instrumental/**mai + pa / pang**	maipanggawa	naipanggawa	naipanggagawa	maipanggagawa

Nakagawa si Maria ng reserbasyon para sa nanay ni Juan sa pamamagitan ng iPad niya. *Maria was able to make reservations for Juan's mother using her iPad.*
Nagawa ni Maria ang reserbasyon para sa nanay ni Juan sa pamamagitan ng iPad niya.
Naigawa ni Maria ng reserbasyon ang nanay ni Juan sa pamamagitan ng iPad niya.
Nagawan ni Maria ng reserbasyon ang nanay ni Juan sa pamamagitan ng iPad niya.
Naipanggagawa ni Maria ang iPad niya ng reserbasyon para sa nanay ni Juan.

What is the difference between the conjugations for **bigay** and for **gawa** that may have resulted in confusion? You might have noticed the following:

First, we used the affixes **na-an**, to form **nabigyan** when the focus was on Maria, the indirect object focus. We used both **nabigay** and **naibigay** when the focus was on the ticket. Why can we not use **naibigay** when Maria was the focus? Remember that when **bigay** is conjugated, it can change focus between the giver and receiver of the action. For example:

Binigay/Ibinigay ko... *I gave*....
Do not say: **Binigay ako...** (I was given.)—this is only true if you are a bride being "given away" at the altar during your wedding.

Following this train of thought, do not say:
Naibigay ni Maria ang nanay ni Juan.... (*This means that Maria gave away Juan's mother.*)

Thus, use the **na- an** affixes for similar words.

Second, we notice, however, that this is not true with the root word **gawa**. With **gawa**, we distinguish between the object (**reserbasyon**), and the beneficiary or location or indirect object of the action (the **nanay** or mother). You might get confused because native speakers will interchange the use of **naibigay** and **nabigyan**, or **naibibigay** and **nabibigyan**, and **maibibigay** and **mabibigyan**. Remember that both are fine; do not be disturbed by flexibility, as such is the nature of the language.

Moreover, some will say **nakakagawa**; others will say **nakagagawa**. Again, we are just careful about using the latter in written Filipino because editors need to be consistent and will follow editorial rules. In spoken Filipino, you can use whichever comes to your mind.

Mga Talang Pangkultura: Flexibility of Meaning

Talakayan: Hindi Pagkakaunawaan Misunderstandings

Reflecting on the culture notes, talk/write about your experiences. Classroom learners can form groups while individual learners can write about their experiences. Here are a few guide questions:

1. In visiting a friend or relative's house, or when a friend/relative has come to your house, have you had the experience of first refusing and then accepting food? Tell your group about it. **Sa pagbisita sa bahay ng kaibigan o kamag-anak, o sa pagbisita ng kaibigan o kamag-anak sa inyong bahay, may karanasan ba kayo tungkol sa una munang pagtanggi at pagkatapos ay pagtanggap ng pagkain? Ikuwento ito.**

2. In inviting friends or accepting invitations, have you experienced saying "yes" or "I will try" even if you or they have no intentions of going? Tell your group about it. **Sa pag-imbita sa kaibigan o sa pagtanggap sa imbitasyon, naranasan na ba ninyong magsabi ng "oo" o "susubukan ko" kahit na wala kayo o silang balak pumunta? Ikuwento ito.**

3. Does this flexibility of meaning bother you? Why or why not? **Nababagabag ba kayo sa pag-iiba-iba ng kahulugan? Bakit o bakit hindi?**

Pakikinig: Insidente sa Tubbataha Reef

The Tubbataha Reef Incident

Pagsasalin: Bukas na Liham ng Pagrereklamo

Open Letter of Complaint

Practice your translation skills by translating one or more paragraphs of the following open letter of complaint published by Professor Danilo Arao in his column *Konteksto* at *Pinoy Weekly*.[1] The rest of the letter is in the **Pagbabasa** section of this Lesson.

To prepare for this, review/study the following vocabulary words: **nakapagtataka** (surprising); **pagkakuha** (as soon as I received); **hiniling** (requested); **sapat** (enough); **kinatawan** (representative); **sa halip** (instead); **nangako** (promised).

For each of the paragraphs the first few words have been translated to help you along.

Bukas na liham sa mga opisyal ng Globe Telecom (Part 1)
Konteksto ni Danilo Araña Arao

Nakakuha ako ng dalawang *statement of account* (SOA) para sa Nobyembre at Disyembre 2012 mula sa inyong kompanya. May mga dapat daw akong bayaran. Nakapagtataka lang dahil noong 2009 ko pa hiniling ang permanenteng diskoneksiyon (*permanent disconnection*) ng aking Globe *mobile phone account*.

Pagkakuha ko pa lang ng unang SOA, agad-agad akong pumunta noong Disyembre sa isa ninyong branch para ipaliwanag ang konteksto ng aking sitwasyon. Ang sabi ng inyong *customer care representative*, nakapagtataka ngang nakakuha ako ng SOA dahil wala naman akong hiniling na *re-connection* ng aking linya. Dahil wala pa siyang sapat na impormasyon, nangako siyang tatawagan ako sa numerong ibinigay ko.

Makalipas ang isang buwan, wala akong nakuhang tawag mula sa inyong kinatawan. Sa halip ay nakuha ko ang ikalawang SOA. "Aba, ano ito? Bakit tumataas ang dapat ko raw bayaran?" Marami pa akong tanong na hindi sinagot ng nangakong tatawag sa akin!

[1] http://pinoyweekly.org/new/2013/01/bukas-na-liham-sa-mga-opisyal-ng-globe-telecom/. Posted 26 Jan 2013. Accessed 28 Jan 2013

I was able to get ....

____
____
____
____
____
____

After receiving the first SOA, I immediately went last December to one of your branches to explain the context of my situation.

____
____
____
____
____
____

After a month, I [still] have not received a call from your representative.

____
____
____
____
____
____

Pagbabasa Reading
Bukas na Liham ng Pagrereklamo Open Letter of Complaint

Here is the rest of Danilo Arao's letter. Review/study the following vocabulary words: **pansamantala** (temporary); **sinubukan** (tried); **pamantayan** (standards); **sinisingil** (being asked to pay); **pinakinabangan** (benefited from); **madla** (people; public); **walang pakundangan** (without any regard); **tandaan** (remember); **pakikitungo** (dealing; treatment).

Outline the arguments of the letter writer and answer the comprehension questions at the end of the passage.

Bukas na liham sa mga opisyal ng Globe Telecom (Part 2)
Konteksto ni Danilo Araña Arao

Nagdesisyon tuloy akong magpadala ng *email* noong Enero 2013 sa inyong kompanya para muling magtanong kung bakit sinisingil ako sa account na dapat ay tatlong taon nang wala. Hindi pa nakontento, nag-*post* pa ako sa *contact* form ng inyong *website* para masiguradong nakuha ang aking mensahe.

Muli, wala akong nakuhang sagot. Nagdesisyon akong bumalik sa inyong branch para magreklamo. Matapos ang aking mahabang paliwanag at paikot-ikot na debate sa inyong *customer care representative*, lumalabas sa datos ng inyong kompanya na ang nagkaroon lang daw ng permanenteng diskoneksiyon ay ang aking *main account* at ang *extension account* (para sa aking asawa) ay binigyan lang ng pansamantalang diskoneksiyon (*temporary disconnection*).

Sa loob-loob ko, paano kaya nangyari ito samantalang malinaw na ang aking hiniling ay permanenteng diskoneksiyon nang kausapin ko ang inyong *customer care representative* tatlong taon na ang nakaraan? At kahit na sabihing may pagkukulang ako sa pagpapaliwanag, hindi ba't nararapat lang na paalalahanan ako matapos ang ilang buwan ng diumanong pansamantalang diskoneksiyon kung interesado pa akong muling buhayin ito?

Pero sa halip na paalala, wala na akong narinig mula sa Globe sa napakahabang panahon. Sa katunayan, mula nang magkaroon ng diskoneksiyon sa aking *account* noong 2009 hanggang Nobyembre 2012, wala na akong nakuhang SOA. Tulad ng nabanggit ko, ang dalawang SOA ay bigla na lang dumating.

Ayon sa inyong empleyado, sinubukan daw akong kontakin noong Oktubre 2012 kung hihilingin ko ba ang reactivation ng aking Globe *account*. Nang tinanong ko kung anong petsa ng Oktubre nangyari ito at kung anong *contact number* ang ginamit, sinabi niyang wala siyang impormasyon. Basta ang alam lang daw niya ay sinubukan akong kausapin!

Kahit wala akong kahilingan para sa *reactivation*, malinaw na hinulaan ng Globe na gusto ko pang maging *customer* ninyo. Nang tinanong ko kung nasa kapangyarihan ninyo ito, ang sagot ng inyong empleyado ay oo: Nasa *terms of reference* diumano ang *unilateral* na desisyon ng Globe na muling buhayin ang account na may pansamantalang diskoneksiyon.

Sa pamantayan ng inyong kompanya, sapat na ang sinubukang kontakin ako diumano noong Oktubre 2012 at, nang hindi raw ako nakausap, nagdesisyon kayong muling buhayin ang *account* ko. Dahil sa inyong desisyon, sinisingil ninyo ako ngayon para sa ilang buwang *monthly recurring fee* (MRF) kahit na malinaw na hindi ko naman pinakinabangan ang mga ito!

Napakasaya, hindi ba? Para ipamukha sa inyo ang aking pagkadismaya, huwag kayong mag-alala't binayaran ko na nang buo ang anumang sinisingil ninyo (bukod pa sa malinaw na utos ko sa inyong *customer care representative* na bigyan ang aking Globe account ng ABSOLUTO, GARANTISADO, SIGURADO AT PERMANENTENG DISKONEKSIYON). Para malaman ninyo ang aking nadarama, kailangan naman ninyong mag-alala dahil malalaman din ito ng buong madla.

Hindi sapat, para sa akin, ang simpleng paliwanag na ang isang *temporarily disconnected account* ay basta-basta bubuhayin kung kailan naisin ng inyong kompanya (kahit na walang paalam sa customer), at walang-pakundangang sisingilin ang kawawang kliyente para sa serbisyong hindi na niya ginagamit.

Oo, binayaran ko na lang kayo kahit na alam kong ako ang nasa tama. Hindi ko na pahahabain pa ang aking pakikipagkatwiran sa inyong kompanyang bukod sa hindi marunong makinig sa katwiran ay ayaw pang sumagot sa *online inquiry* (at lalong mahirap makontak ang *landline*, batay na rin sa litanya ng marami ninyong kasalukuyan at dating kliyente). Kung ang aking binayaran ay nangangahulugang hindi na ako magpapabalik-balik sa inyong *branch* para ulit-ulitin ang aking kaso, mababaw ko nang tagumpay ito (kahit na alam kong kayo pa rin ang nanalo dahil nakuha ninyo ang pera ko).

Tunay na mahirap makipagdebate sa isang higanteng tulad ng Globe kahit na ang ebidensiya at lohika ay wala sa panig ninyo. Siguradong tumaba na naman ang inyong bulsa dahil pinagkakitaan ninyo ako.

Pero tandaan ninyong sinulat ko naman ang bukas na liham na ito hindi para sa inyo, kundi para sa iba pang mamamayang naghahanap ng mahusay na serbisyo at makataong pakikitungo. Malinaw na wala ang mga ito sa kompanya ninyo!

1. What were the arguments of the letter writer?
2. What were the arguments of the company?
3. Why did the writer say towards the end that he will not elaborate any longer?
4. For whom did the writer write the letter?

Pagsusulat Writing
Pagbibigay ng Opinyon Giving an Opinion

Write one of the following:

1. A review of a recent trip (airline, hotel, resort);
2. A letter of complaint;
3. Your own opinions on the Tubbataha Reef incident.

Paglalagom Summing Up

In this lesson, you have:

- Studied words and phrases so that you can express yourself if you want to complain and give arguments;
- Reviewed and expanded your knowledge about causative and abilitative sentences;
- Listened to and read about opinions.

Aralin
Lesson
19

Anong Tingin Mo sa...?
What Do You Think of...?

In this lesson, we are learning how to give opinions on films, literary texts, music, dance, and other art forms.

 Diyalogo: Ang Ganda ng Pelikula!

KATIE : **Nagustuhan mo ba ang pelikula?**
Did you like the film?

KATHLEEN : **Oo, nagandahan ako. Ikaw?**
Yes, I find it good. You?

KATIE : **Nabagalan ako sa simula. Aling bahagi ang nagustuhan mo?**
I find the beginning slow. What part did you like?

KATHLEEN : **Natawa ako sa maraming bahagi. Nakakatawa ang iskrip.**
I laughed in many parts. The script was funny.

KATIE : **Ang husay rin ang pagkakaganap ng bida at kontrabida.**
The acting of the protagonist and antagonist was funny too.

KATHLEEN : **Pero napaiyak ako sa pagtatapos.**
But I was made to cry [=cried] at the end.

KATIE : **Ako rin. Hindi ko masyadong nagustuhan ang pagtatapos. Masyadong malungkot.**
Me too. I did not like the ending so much. It was too sad.

KATHLEEN : **Gusto mo bang manood uli ng pelikula sa susunod na linggo?**
Do you want to watch a movie again next week?

KATIE : **Aba, siyempre. Ang balita ko, maganda raw iyong idinirehe ni Joel Lamangan.**
Of course. I heard that the one Joel Lamangan directed was good.

KATHLEEN : **Tungkol saan ang pelikula?**
What is the movie about?

KATIE : **Tungkol sa karapatang pantao. Kuwento ng mga estudyanteng dinukot ng militar.**
It is about human rights. They are stories of students who were kidnapped by the military.

KATHLEEN : **Saan palabas?**
Where will it be shown?

KATIE : **Sa Mabuhay Cinema.**
At Mabuhay Cinema.

Bokabularyo Vocabulary

Review/study the following words:

WRITERS AND ARTISTS: manunulat/awtor (writer); **mandudula** (playwright); **kuwentista** (fictionist); **makata** (poet); **direktor** (director); **sinematograpo** (cinematographer); **artista** (actor); **pintor** (painter); **iskultor** (sculptor); **musikero** (musician); **kompositor** (composer); **mang-aawit** (singer); **mananayaw** (dancer); **koreograpo** (choreographer); **taga-disenyo ng ilaw** (lighting designer); **taga-disenyo ng kasuotan** (costume designer); **taga-disenyo ng entablado** (stage designer); **taga-disenyo ng produksiyon** (production designer)

WORDS THAT RELATE TO FORMS, GENRES, TYPES, AND COMPONENTS OF ARTISTIC WORK: pelikula/sine (film); **programa sa telebisyon** (television program); **melodrama** (melodrama); **istorya/naratibo** (story/narrative); **aksiyon** (action); **komedi** (comedy); **realistiko** (realistic); **ekspresyonistiko** (expressionistic); **katutubo** (indigenous);

tradisyonal (traditional); **makabago/moderno** (modern); **eksperimental** (experimental); **tema** (theme); **paksa** (topic); **maiksing pelikula** (short film); **bida** (hero/heroine/protagonist); **kontrabida** (antagonist); **mga katulong na aktor** (supporting actors); **tagapagsalaysay** (narrator); **pangunahing tauhan** (main character); **punto de bista** (point of view); **lunan/tagpuan** (setting); **panahon** (time/period); **larawan** (painting/photographs); **dibuho** (drawing); **iskultura** (sculpture); **komposisyon** (composition); **koreograpiya** (choreography); **galaw** (movement)

ADJECTIVES THAT YOU CAN USE IN GIVING COMMENTS ABOUT A FILM, PLAY, SONG, DANCE, OR ARTWORK: **maganda** (good/beautiful); **napakaganda** (very good/very beautiful); **mabagal** (slow); **mabilis** (fast); **pangit** (not good); **mahusay** (well-made); **interesante** (interesting); **nakababagot/nakakabagot** (boring); **nakatatawa/nakakatawa** (makes one laugh); **nakagagalit/nakakagalit** (makes one angry); **nakalilibang/nakakalibang** (makes one amused); **nakaaantok/nakakaantok** (makes one sleepy)

NOUNS: **pagganap** (acting); **pagkakaganap/pagkakaarte** (the way someone acted out a role); **pagsayaw** (dancing); **pagkakasayaw** (the way someone danced); **pagkanta** (singing); **pagkakakanta** (the way someone sang a song); **buod** (summary); **pagkakaguhit** (the way something was drawn); **pagkakapinta** (the way something was painted); **pagakahubog** (the way something was sculpted); **balangkas** (outline); **suliranin** (problems)

PHRASES that you can use in giving comments:

nakakaantig ng damdamin	*touches one's feelings*
nakakabuhay ng loob	*makes one invigorated*
puno ng aksiyon	*full of action*
wala sa tono	*out of tune*
Ang ganda ng pagkakadirehe ng …	*The direction was good...*
Ang ganda ng pagkakasulat …	*The writing was good...*
Mabilis ang takbo ng pelikula …	*The pacing of the film was fast...*
Napaiyak ako sa libro …	*The book made me cry...*
Nakakaiyak ang libro ...	*The book makes one cry...*
Gusto ko ang bahaging …	*I like the part where...*
Gusto ko ang simula ...	*I like the beginning...*
Gusto ko ang pagtatapos …	*I like the ending...*
Hindi ko gusto … /Ayaw ko …	*I don't like...*
Tinalakay ng libro ang ...	*The book discussed...*

Mga Pangungusap Sentences

Study the following sentences about possible reactions to a film/play/song/dance/show:

1. **Napaiyak ako dahil sa pelikula.**
   I was made to cry [=cried] because of the film.
2. **Natawa ako sa maraming eksena ng dula.**
   I laughed at many scenes of the play.
3. **Natuwa ako dahil napakaganda ng pagkakasayaw niya ng tinikling.**
   I was happy because she danced the tinikling *so well.*

Now, here are some sentences you can use when talking about the summary or outline of a film/play/song/dance/show:

4. **Mahahanap mo ang buod ng pelikula sa website na ito.**
   You can find the summary of the film on this website.
5. **Ibinabalangkas ng pelikula ang mga suliranin ng lipunan.**
   The film outlines the problems of society.
6. **Isinisiwalat ng libro ang mga katiwalian ng lipunang Filipino.**
   The book reveals corruption in Philippine society.

Here are some questions you can use when eliciting opinion:

7. **Ano ang nagustuhan mo sa dula?**
   What did you like in the play?
8. **Ano ang naging pakiramdam mo nang marinig mo ang kanta/awit?**
   What did you feel when you heard the song?
9. **Sa aling bahagi ng pelikula ka natawa?**
   In which part of the play did you laugh?
   [=Which part of the play made you laugh?])

Finally, here are some sentences you can use when giving comments.

10. **Nagustuhan ko ang larawan dahil napakahusay ng pagkakapinta.**
    I liked the painting because it was painted very well.
11. **Nabagalan ako sa simula ng pelikula.**
    I found the beginning of the film slow.
12. **Nagandahan ako sa pagtatapos ng libro.**
    I found the ending of the book beautiful.
13. **Gusto ko ang mga bahaging puno ng aksiyon.**
    I liked the parts that were filled with action [=action-packed].

Pagsasanay

Practice the vocabulary words, phrases and sentences you have learned by asking and answering questions. Classroom learners can form pairs while individual learners can write down their answers.

1. TANONG : **Bakit ka napaiyak?**
   SAGOT : ______________________________.

2. TANONG : **Saan ka nabagalan, sa simula, o sa pagtatapos ng pelikula?**
   SAGOT : ______________________________.

3. TANONG : **Aling palabas sa telebisyon ang nagugustuhan mo?**
   SAGOT : ______________________________.

4. TANONG : **Saan ko mahahanap ang buod ng librong Noli me tangere *ni Jose Rizal*?**
   SAGOT : ______________________________.

5. TANONG : **Bakit mo gusto ang TV show na ______________?**
   SAGOT : ______________________________.

6. TANONG : ______________________________?
   SAGOT : **Tungkol sa mga bata ang kanta.**

7. TANONG : ______________________________?
   SAGOT : **Ang mang-aawit na nakasuot ng asul ang wala sa tono.**

8. TANONG : ______________________________?
   SAGOT : **Kuwento nina Romeo and Juliet ang ibinabalangkas ng sayaw.**

9. TANONG : ______________________________?
   SAGOT : **Nagandahan ako sa simula ng konsiyerto.**

10. TANONG : ______________________________?
    SAGOT : **Nakakabuhay ng loob ang pagkakaawit ni Monique ng kanta.**

Pagsasanay

Create/Write dialogues for the following situations. Classroom learners can work in pairs or groups. Use the words, phrases, and sentences you learned.

SITUATION 1: You and your friend had just watched an action film. You liked the film but your friend did not agree with you. He/she did not like the leads and supporting actors of the film, and found the movie too melodramatic. You liked the story and the film made you cry.

____

____

____

____

____

____

____

Situation 2: You and your cousin had just finished reading the same book. You found the book boring but your cousin found it very interesting. He/she liked the way it was written as well as the ending. You only liked the part about the main character's trip to Alaska.

____

____

____

____

____

____

____

Situation 3: You and your classmate went to see a musical play. You liked the modern choreography and your classmate liked the use of traditional instruments. The dancers were good but one singer was out of tune in one song.

____

____

____

____

____

____

____

Gramatika Grammar

The affixes "na- an"

With the affixes **na-an**, the focus is on two things: "ability," and focusing on the location of the action. Do not be confused, however, this does not mean location as in "place" but where the action is directed.

You have studied this in earlier lessons. For example, look at the verb **bili**.

Bumili ako ng libro para kay Juan. *I bought a book for Juan.* (actor focus)
Libro ang binili ko para kay Juan. (object focus)
Ibinili ko ng libro si Juan. (location focus)
Nakabili ako ng libro para kay Juan. *I was able to buy a book for Juan.* (actor focus)
Libro ang nabili ko para kay Juan. (location focus)
Nabilhan ko ng libro si Juan. (location focus)

You can use **na-an** for your reactions to films, books, theater and other art and culture forms. For example:

Nagustuhan ko ang pelikula.
Nasiyahan ako sa libro.
Nasarapan ako sa luto ni Chef Josh.
Nabagalan ako sa takbo ng programa.

Mga Talang Pangkultura Muling Pagsusuri sa mga Pinahalagahan ng mga Filipino Rethinking Filipino Values

Talakayan: Modes of Social interaction

Discuss the modes of interaction as identified by Enriquez and Santiago. You can choose one or two of the guide questions below. Classroom learners can form groups while individual learners can write down their thoughts.

1. Which of these Filipino words/phrases have you heard and in what context—**walanghiya** (shameless); **nakakahiya** (shameful); **walang utang na loob** (no debt of gratitude), and **makisama ka naman** (get along with)? **Alin sa mga salita/parirala na ito ang narinig niyo na at sa anong konteksto—walanghiya; nakakahiya; walang utang na loob; at makisama ka naman?**

2. What do you think of Professor San Juan's comment that these so-called "values" are problematic because they essentialize Filipinos? **Ano ang tingin mo sa komento ni Propesor San Juan tungkol sa mga pagpapahalagang ito na problematiko raw dahil sinasabing ang mga ito lamang ang nagbibigay-identidad sa mga Filipino?**

Pakikinig: Art, Art ka Diyan by Lourd de Veyra
So You're Talking about Art

Talakayan: Sining at Lipunan Art and Society

In the Philippines in the 1940s, writers Salvador P. Lopez and Jose Garcia Villa debated on literature and society. Lopez, in his essay "Literature and Society," argued that art must have substance while Villa believed in "art for art's sake."

Classroom learners can form groups to discuss one the following questions while individual learners can write down their opinions.

1. Do you agree with Lopez or with Villa? Why? **Sumasang-ayon ka ba kay Lopez o kay Villa? Bakit?**
2. What examples can you give to support your point of view? **Anong mga halimbawa ang maibibigay mo para suportahan ang iyong punto de bista?**

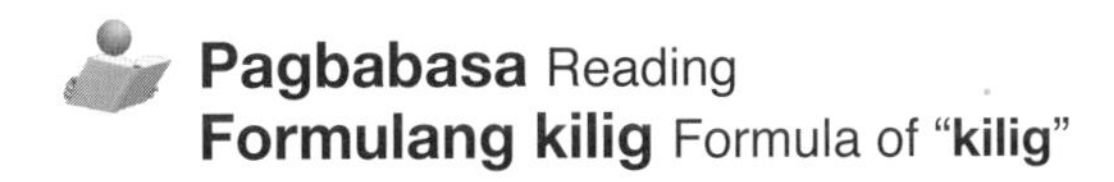

Pagbabasa Reading
Formulang kilig Formula of "kilig"

Read the following film review from scholar Rolando B. Tolentino published in *Pinoy Weekly* posted on December 4, 2011. Before reading, review/study the following vocabulary words: **pagtambalin** (pair up); **napatunayan** (was proven); **matagumpay** (successful); **pipigilin** (will stop); **magkakatuluyan** (will be together); **mamilipit** (to squirm; literally, to twist); **kalahok** (participant); **sa katunayan** (in fact); **pagpapaubaya** (relinquishing); **pakiwari** (opinion); **kalakaran** (usual ways); **pag-ambag** (contribution).

Please answer the comprehension questions that follow the passage.

Formulang kilig
ni Rolando B. Tolentino
Review: *Won't Last a Day Without You* (Raz dela Torre, direktor, 2011)

Malaking negosyo ang produksyon ng kilig. Pagtambalin ang matagumpay na mga loveteam (Gerald Anderson at Kim Chu, Sarah Geronimo at John Lloyd Cruz), at kung di na matagumpay, i-mash-up (Gerald at Sarah). Napatunayan na matagumpay ang Gerald-Sarah team-up dahil sa matagumpay na unang pagtatambal, Catch me... I'm in Love (Mae Cruz, 2011 din!).

Ilagay ang team-up sa interesanteng sitwasyong makaka-relate ang kabataan: si DJ Heidee (Sarah) ay pinayuhan sa kanyang show si Melissa (Meagan Young) na makipagbreak-up sa kanyang playboy na boyfriend, si Andrew (Gerald). Nang magbalak si Andrew na i-report si DJ Heidee at ang istasyon sa nakakataas na awtoridad, pumayag ang babae na tulungan si Andrew na i-win-over muli si Melissa. Sa proseso, mai-inlove ang dalawa pero pipigilin ni DJ Heidee dahil nga ayaw niya muling maging inappropriate. Siempre, alam na ng lahat ang ending, kung sino ang magkakatuluyan.

Mahirap bigyan-definisyon ang kilig, walang exaktong kahulugan sa ingles. Ang referensya lamang ay sa karanasan ukol sa pag-ibig: blush kapag nandiyan ang crush, masayang mamilipit kapag nasa awkward situation na kalahok ang sinisinta, ang rush kapag natutupad ang nais matupad sa ngalan ng pag-ibig. Sa katunayan, may Facebook account ang kilig, "the best of super kilig quotes."

Nagtatagumpay ang pelikula dahil may inaasahan sa manonood, ang tinatawag na "suspension of disbelief" o ang pagpapaubaya sa operasyon ng pelikula (naratibo, special effects, acting at maging ang mismong panonood) na ito ay "tunay" na realidad. Hindi ka manonood na bwinibwiset ang sarili: iisiping may harness lang naman si Superman o Darna kaya ito nakakalipad, o sa bugbugan sa action hero na hindi naman mamamatay ang bida.

Pero sa formula films, doble ang suspension of disbelief: na dahil pelikula ito, totoo at lehitimong karanasan ito; at na ang kakatwang kombinasyong sangkap sa formula film ay natural at organiko naman. Ang nauna ay nagtatagumpay dahil nagbayad tayo ng P180 para sa tiket, kaya paniniwalain ng manonood ang kanilang sarili sa posibilidad at reafirmasyon ng gayong formula.

Ang huli ay pagsang-ayon din dahil sa prior knowledge building na ginawa na ng entertainment corporation sa atin. Binuild-up sila bilang magka-loveteam, pina-duet sa variety shows, ginawang covers ng glossy magazines nila, ginawan ng MTV ang theme song ng pelikula.

Sa Facebook account, narito ang ilang wall posts:

Mula kay Advincula: "It doesn't matter if the guy is perfect or the girl is perfect, as long as they are perfect for each other."

Mula sa mismong site owner: "Love is a symbol of eternity. It wipes out all sense of time, destroying all memory of a beginning and all fear of an end.

"Wala naman talagang PANAKIP-BUTAS eh, nagkataon lang na NANDOON ka, noong panahong NAWALAN siya."

"Hanapin mo yung taong tanggap ka, hindi yung taong pinipilit mong tanggapin ka."

Ang mga post ay cliché naman talaga. Nagtatagumpay lang sila dahil pinili ng mambabasa, at ka-FB na maniwala sa mode ng kilig bilang tampok na pakiwari. Hindi ka naman magfre-friend dito kung hindi naniniwala sa premis at magpapa-KJ dito. Gayundin sa pelikula at konsumerismo, hindi ka papaloob dito kung hindi ka naniniwala sa premis at rules of the game nito.

Matagumpay ang pelikulang dulot ay kilig dahil kumita ito ng P20 milyon sa unang araw na pagpapalabas nito. Kahit pa mas telenovella ang dating–hindi cinematiko ang saklaw ng mas kalkuladong pagbibitaw ng linya sa mis en scene, halimbawa—pero kinilig ang kasama ko, pati ang sangkatauhang nanood ng pelikula.

Sa sabayang paglabas ng sinehan, natanaw ko ang nakasabayan ko sa dilim na manonood, mga ordinaryong mamamayang gumasta para magpakaligaya. At nalungkot ako. Sa buhay sa kapitalismo, walang nasa labas ng sistema. May kapasidad ang sistema na ipaloob tayo sa kalakaran nito. Sa sine, pinili nating pumaloob. Highway robbery o kusang pagaambag sa ngalan ng kilig na pagdanas ng buhay sa kapitalismo?

1. What was the film *Won't Last a Day Without You* about?
2. Who were the stars of this film?
3. Please explain the word **kilig**.
4. According to Rolando Tolentino, how are love teams made popular?
5. What are the conventions of **kilig** formula films?
6. Why do **kilig** formula films succeed in drawing crowds, as proven by the film discussed?
7. How did Tolentino relate the film to capitalism?

Pagsusulat Writing
Rebyu Review

Practice the vocabulary words and reasoning skills you have learned in this lesson by writing a short review of a film, a television show or a novel.

Here are a few suggestions on how to go about your review depending on the text you choose:

1. You may want to talk about conventions, styles or formulas;
2. You may contextualize the text in its particular time period or setting;
3. You may want use devices such as quotations, humor, or irony;
4. You may want to do an intertextual reading, comparing the text to another film, television show or novel.

Paglalagom Summing Up

In this lesson, you have:

- Learned words and phrases you can use to express your opinion about a book, a film or an artwork;
- Reviewed affixes related to ability and location focus;
- Created/dialogues and written a short review.

For the remaining pages of this book (pages 289 to 320: Lesson 20, Grammar Index, and Glossary) please refer to the online audio recordings.

To Download or Stream Audio Recordings:

1. You must have an internet connection.
2. Type the URL below into your web browser.

https://www.tuttlepublishing.com/intermediate-tagalog-audio-and-pdfs

For support email us at info@tuttlepublishing.com.